A LONGMAN TOPICS READER

The Changing World of Work

MARJORIE FORD
Stanford University

PEARSON
Longman

New York   San Francisco   Boston
London   Toronto   Sydney   Tokyo   Singapore   Madrid
Mexico City   Munich   Paris   Cape Town   Hong Kong   Montreal

Senior Acquisitions Editor: Lynn M. Huddon
Senior Marketing Manager: Alexandra Rivas-Smith
Production Manager: Eric Jorgensen
Project Coordination, Text Design, and Electronic Page Makeup:
    GGS Book Services, Atlantic Highlands
Cover Designer-Manager: Wendy Ann Fredericks
Cover Photo: Erik Buraas—Photonica
Manufacturing Manager: Mary Fischer
Printer and Binder: R. R. Donnelley & Sons
Cover Printer: Coral Graphic Services

For permission to use copyrighted material, grateful acknowledgment
is made to the copyright holders on page 232, which is hereby made
part of this copyright page.

Library of Congress Cataloging-in-Publication Data
Ford, Majorie.
    The changing world of work / Marjorie Ford.
        p. cm. — (A Longman topics reader)
    ISBN 0-321-27332-X
    1. College students—Employment—United States. 2. College
students—Vocational guidance—United States. 3. Work—United
States. I. Title. II. Series: Longman topics.
HD6276.52.U5F67 2005
331.1'0973—dc22   2005043590

Visit us at http://www.ablongman.com

ISBN 0-321-27332-X

12345678910—DOH—08 07 06 05

CONTENTS

CHAPTER 4   The Working Poor   140

CHAPTER 5   Working for Change   195

RHETORICAL CONTENTS

v

Examples and Illustration

Metaphor/Analogy: Personal Narrative and Illustration

Process Writing

Refutation

Solutions Argument

Support Using Facts and Statistics

PREFACE

The Changing World of Work is a short anthology of readings designed to help college writing students think critically about how their education and life experiences are preparing them for their future life as workers. The Changing World of Work makes the assumption that we as citizens need to examine and better understand the changing nature of work in modern society. The selections chosen here will help students reflect on the historical principles that shaped the American dream and its expectations of what work meant from the time our country was born through the Industrial Revolution up to the modern age of computers. The selections, in various forms of writing, focus on the economic, political, social, and technological issues that are changing the role of work in the life of each individual. I hope that the readings will open a dialogue about how students and adults can take an active part in preparing to make their working lives more meaningful and encourage them to make positive contributions to society at large. Although some of the readings discuss the unjust, unhealthy, and sometimes brutal realities of life in today's workplace, other readings point to paths that will improve the lives of the everyday worker as well as the decisions of individuals who have turned in their career choices toward an allegiance to a larger sense of community and national responsibility, trying to create better jobs, social services, and educational reform.

The Changing World of Work is divided into five chapters, each examining a significant aspect of work today:

- Chapter 1, Valuing Work
- Chapter 2, Work and Family Life
- Chapter 3, Working with Technology
- Chapter 4, The Working Poor
- Chapter 5, Working for Change

Each chapter features essays of varying lengths and reading levels and discussion questions as well as writing assignments designed to help students read and write more perceptively in response to the selections and to think more critically about their roles as workers and citizens.

Special features of *The Changing World of Work* include the following:

- Twenty-eight essays, many of them written quite recently, each of which emphasizes a different aspect of the chapter's theme and reflects on the larger questions about the meaning of work in America today
- Selections chosen to reflect a balance of political, gender, and cultural perspectives, as well as literary styles and reading levels
- Five chapters, each of which explores a different question or issue related to the modern-day work world
- Chapter introductions that explore the historical issues surrounding the chapter topic and then discuss how such issues are being redefined in recent times
- Author biographies for each selection
- A "Questions for Discussion" section at the end of each selection, designed to facilitate close reading and to encourage students to take critical positions on the essay and its issues
- An "Ideas for Writing" section at the end of each selection that encourages argument and analysis, as well as asking students to apply the concerns of the writers excerpted here to their own lives and communities
- An "Extending the Theme" section at the end of each chapter, calling for either a synthesis of several different issues or further work involving Internet, library, or field research or participation in citizen organizations devoted to workplace revitalization, education, and social or political change

ACKNOWLEDGMENTS

First, I would like to thank my editor Lynn Huddon for her guidance throughout the project as we worked to define the theme for the text, to respond intelligently to the reviewers' insights, and to make the book relevant to today's college students. Special thanks are owed to Esther Hollander, Lynn Huddon's assistant, who was always ready to help us with the materials that we needed. Finally, I thank our reviewers for their insights and suggestions: Cheryl Cardoza, Truckee Meadows Community College; David Curtis, Belmont University; Paula Eschliman, Richland College; Nancy M. Grace, The College of Wooster; Anita Akuee Johnson, Whatcom Community College; Lucretia S. Pollard, Ohio State University; and Lucille M. Schultz, University of Cincinnati.

MARJORIE FORD

CHAPTER 1

Valuing Work

What value do you place on working? Have you ever had a job that meant more to you than simply learning a skill or receiving a paycheck? What value and meaning do you hope to find in your career or other future working experiences? The answers to these questions can help you identify what you want from your life and what you wish to achieve. For most people, the motivation to work begins with the desire to fulfill economic needs: to earn money for food, clothing, transportation, housing, and health care. One thing that has changed in recent years is the broad range of job opportunities available in our complex, technologically oriented, rapidly changing society. This chapter presents different perspectives on why people work and the values that guide their choices. We hope reading the selections that follow will inspire you to think about how values motivate people to make work-related choices.

As we assembled the readings for this chapter and wrote the questions that follow each selection, we wanted to mirror some of the diverse reasons why people decide to value a particular kind of work. We begin by examining one of the most common types of labor, factory work, where value is placed on the sense of solidarity and mutual concern among workers that is part of the ethos of the union movement. In our first selection, the poem "What Work Is," former steel-mill laborer Philip Levine describes waiting for work in the rain, something that many factory employees endure on a regular basis. Levine's narrator values these men for their patience and their brotherhood: "[t]he love flooding you for your brother." He emphasizes that working with others can bring a sense of companionship and empathy that are at the heart of being human. Learning to love your "brother" has always been a value fundamental to the motivation to work and to the creation of a good life.

Creating community through caring for others is a basic value common to many types of work. Knowing how the values of our country have evolved since the founding fathers came to this continent to establish a life that allowed individuals freedom and equality provides a context for understanding how people make value choices about work. The selection "Value-Free" by John B. Judis develops a complex and thought-provoking analysis of how changes in people's concepts of God, industrialism, technology, and consumerism have shaped American culture. Although our modern culture may seem on the surface to be "value-free," Judis argues against this claim and for the idea that people's work choices may indeed be based on new values that are crucial to the individual's self-respect and identity. Reading this selection will help you to understand the changing relationships between work and values. We hope that it will also encourage you to think about why you and the people around you have chosen the work they do.

As Judis emphasizes, work is closely connected to values based on both lifestyle and the idea of leading a religious life. However, some thinkers carry these ideas further, seeking work attitudes and settings that can enhance their sense of the spiritual, of the fundamental meaning and purpose in life. The Dali Lama, one of today's most important spiritual leaders, shares his views on work in an interview with psychiatrist Howard C. Cutler in our next selection entitled "Happiness at Work: Job, Career, and Calling." The Dali Lama equates spiritual happiness at work with individuals' authentic interest in their life work's mission or purpose. While he values motivation, the Dali Lama believes that jealousy, the desire to gain respect or recognition, or the need to accumulate wealth and material goods cannot lead to a spiritual or happy work life. He considers it necessary to have, in the act of helping other people, a higher purpose or meaning in one's work.

Many writers and leaders share a similar belief, valuing meaningful work that is of service to one's community. In "Work Makes Life Sweet," bell hooks, an acclaimed African-American writer, emphasizes the importance of her ancestors' deep sense of the importance of working for, and with others, in order to survive and to preserve their own dignity and sense of community. Hooks points out that although black people before World War II were not afforded as many privileges as African Americans today, working for one another made their lives "sweet." Hooks believes that black women today need to understand what her elders knew as "right livelihood." She warns that working for status and money alone will undermine an individual's ability to achieve success or happiness. Both the Dali Lama and bell hooks value a higher purpose for working as the way to fulfillment in life.

What the Dali Lama refers to as "a calling" and what bell hooks defines as "a mission" in one's life work can only be discovered through creative visualization of the world around us as well as an inner energy and devotion to finding work that supports one's authentic values. Creativity in the workplace is the subject of the next selection, "The Creative Class" from *The Rise of the Creative Class*, by Richard Florida, a well-known economic advisor, writer, and professor of economics. In this essay he discusses a "creative class" that is emerging in our complex technological world. He sees the growth of this creative class as an acknowledgment of the workplace's need for people who can think and explore existing realities deeply and playfully in order to develop new products and imaginative approaches to critical issues. Play, individuality, flexibility, and a willingness to take risks are characteristics of the businesspeople in this new class.

Passion, creativity, and the desire to help others are all positive values that can lead us to find fulfillment in our work. The final chapter selection. "Second-Grade Teacher" by Katy Bracken, is an inspiring personal account of how one young person found work that she valued deeply. Bracken had to struggle to discover rewarding work as a teacher after realizing that she could not make dancing her lifetime calling. She desires and finds a job through which she can share her creativity and caring. While her narrative is a simple one, her transformation from dancer to teacher took determination and courage. Her values helped her to find the "right livelihood."

We believe that this set of readings will help you to think critically about the different values that people place on work and how our socioeconomic system changes as new values emerge in the workplace. These readings can encourage and support you in your efforts to be creative, individualistic, and flexible as you come to understand the values that you wish to pursue through your life's work.

What Work Is
PHILIP LEVINE

Philip Levine (b. 1928) was born in Detroit to Russian Jewish im-
migrant parents. He later attended Wayne State University and the
University of Iowa. Levine's poetic voice was shaped in the 1950s
when he worked in the automobile plants of Detroit. There he de-
cided "to find a voice for the voiceless, the working men and women
of America's industrial cities." Levine taught at California State
University at Fresno until his retirement. He has received many
awards for his poetry, including the National Book Critics Circle
Award, the American Book Award, the National Book Award for
What Work Is (1991), and the Pulitzer Prize for The Simple Truth
(1994). Two of his most recent works include Unselected Poems
(1997) and The Mercy (1999). In the poem that follows, Levine
writes about how a factory laborer defines the meaning of work
through a sense of solidarity with his fellow workers.

---------------- ✦ ----------------

We stand in the rain in a long line
waiting at Ford Highland Park. For work.
You know what work is — if you're
old enough to read this you know what
work is, although you may not do it.   5
Forget you. This is about waiting,
shifting from one foot to another.
Feeling the light rain falling like mist
into your hair, blurring your vision
until you think you see your own brother   10
ahead of you maybe ten places.
You rub your glasses with your fingers,
and of course it's someone else's brother,
narrower across the shoulders than
yours but with the same sad slouch, the grip   15
that does not hide the stubbornness,
the sad refusal to give in to
rain, to the hours wasted waiting,
to the knowledge that somewhere ahead
a man is waiting who will say, "No,   20

we're not hiring today," for any
reason he wants. You love your brother,
the love flooding you for your brother,
who's not beside you or behind or
ahead because he's home trying to   25
sleep off a miserable night shift
at Cadillac so he can get up
before noon to study his German.
Works eight hours a night so he can sing
Wagner, the opera you hate most,   30
the worst music ever invented.
How long has it been since you told him
you loved him, held his wide shoulders,
opened your eyes wide and said those words,
and maybe kissed his cheek? You've never   35
done something so simple, so obvious,
not because you're too young or too dumb,
not because you're jealous or even mean
or incapable of crying in
the presence of another man, no,   40
just because you don't know what work is.

Questions for Discussion

1. What was your first response to the original question about work? Does the
   poem provide an answer for the issue of work implied by its title? Why does
   the poem's speaker, despite his initial simple response ("you know what work
   is"), continue to complicate the meaning of work as the poem moves along?
2. Why do you think the speaker makes the dismissive comment, "forget you"
   (line 6)? In what sense is forgetting oneself or being forgotten an aspect of
   work?
3. The speaker introduces a character, his "own brother," yet has him disappear
   from the workplace. What is the emotional relationship between the speaker
   and the brother? Why is the speaker critical of his brother's intellectual
   endeavors?
4. Why has the speaker never "kissed his [brother's] cheek"? Is there a relationship between this absence of familiar affection and the narrator's admitted
   ignorance in the poem's final line of "what work is"? What broader, deeper
   meaning has the word "work" acquired by the conclusion of the poem?

Ideas for Writing

1. Making reference to some of the critical comments on the meaning of work implied in Levine's poem, write an extended definition of work based on your own reading and work experiences.
2. Write an essay analyzing the comment that the poem makes about the alienating effects of industrial labor. How does Levine's idea of work differ from a traditional Marxist analysis of workers' feelings of disempowerment and wage-slavery?

Value-Free

JOHN B. JUDIS

John B. Judis attended the University of California at Berkeley, earning his B.A. in 1963 and his M.A. in 1965. While at Berkeley, Judis taught in the philosophy department, became a member of Students for a Democratic Society, and in 1969 was the founding editor of the Socialist Revolution *publication. With his roots established in politics and journalism, Judis went on to write magazine articles for publications such as* The American Prospect, The New York Times Magazine. The Washington Post, *and* Mother Jones. *He has also written books related to the nature of democracy, economics, and work, including* The Paradox of American Democracy: Elites, Special Interests, and the Betrayal of the Public Trust *(2001) and* The Emerging Democratic Majority *(2004). Currently, he is a senior editor for* The New Republic *where the following article. "Value-Free" (1999), originally appeared. In this article Judis examines the way historical events and social change have shaped the kind of values Americans look for in their work.*

---------------- ✦ ----------------

Hardly a day goes by when we don't hear a politician, preacher, or pundit bemoaning the decline in the nation's morals. But it is not just Gary Bauer decrying the "virtue deficit." The *San Antonio Express-News* editorialized earlier this year: "The 1980s were known as the decade of self-indulgence and trickle-down economics. The 1990s will be known as the decade of moral decline."A *Washington Post* survey last August found that 78 percent of Americans believe that the "morals of young Americans have declined."

America has had its prophets of moral doom since the Pilgrims landed. But, interestingly, the current culture war is not about how extensively Americans are violating accepted moral standards but about what those standards should be. It's not whether teenagers are having sex but whether they think it is wrong to do so.

Morality is, of course, an elusive and difficult subject, but at the center of contemporary concerns about moral decline is a familiar complex of issues about work, leisure, sex, love, family, the role of women, the place of religion, and the importance of self-denial. Should the goal of life be to achieve happiness or to please God? Should the goal of work be to make as much money as possible or to improve the situation of one's fellow humans? Should divorce be discouraged? Should abortion be permitted? Should homosexuality be tolerated? Is morality based upon religion? These debates herald a time of national moral and religious transition.

America's moral flux can be explained, at least in part, by everything from the introduction of birth control pills to the rise in life expectancy. But the fundamental explanation has to do with the relationship—noted by both Karl Marx and Max Weber—between the moral imperatives economic life generates and our broader moral and religious beliefs. As this basic relationship has changed during the twentieth century, it has undermined traditional morality and religion, contributing to the moral uncertainty in which we now find ourselves. And the change hinges on the meaning of saving and self-denial.

From the 1850s through the early decades of the twentieth   5
century, the United States experienced an industrial revolution. During this period of capital accumulation, businessmen didn't consume their profits; they saved them and invested them in new plants, machinery, and raw materials in order to produce more goods at a lower cost. The accumulation of capital depended on saving. In an 1889 textbook, Francis Walker, the president of MIT, wrote: "At every step of its progress capital follows one law. It arises solely out of saving. It stands always for self-denial and abstinence." And what applied to the businessmen's income also applied to workers' wages. If businessmen paid their workers more than a subsistence wage, businesses would not have sufficient profit to invest and expand production. Workers accepted this, and, in this sense, their self-denial was also essential to industrialization.

This system of production was seen to be normal and necessary, according to certain religious and moral precepts that were rooted in the dissenting Protestant denominations that dominated the Northern colonies. For these Protestant groups, the goal of life was salvation in the afterlife. Success in work was an indication that a person would be saved. The aim of work was not to accumulate riches per se but to contribute to God's glory. This meant accumulating, rather than spending, what one earned and expanding its value. Work itself was a means of purifying the self against the sinful pleasures of the body. Indulgence in bodily pleasures—from sex outside of procreation to social dancing— was a sin. Idleness was a temptation to sin. As John Wesley, the founder of Methodism, put it. "We must exhort all Christians to gain all they can and to save all they can."

These tenets became central to Americans' work ethic. In 1701, Cotton Mather enjoined his parishioners. "Away to your business, lay out your strength in it, put forth your skill in it." One hundred and fifty years later, Henry Ward Beecher warned that "the indolent mind is not empty, but full of vermin." Secular as well as religious thinkers invoked the connection between economics and morals. William Graham Sumner, the foremost American disciple of Herbert Spencer, wrote in 1885: "The only two things which really tell on the welfare of man on earth are hard work and self-denial (in technical language, labor and capital), and these tell most when they are brought to bear directly upon the effort to earn an honest living, to accumulate capital, and to bring up a family of children to be industrious and self-denying in their turn."

In the first half of the twentieth century, the system of production that this Protestant work ethic sustained was utterly transformed. From 1900 to 1930, industrial productivity rose about twice as fast as it did from 1870 to 1900, largely because of the introduction of scientific management and the replacement of steam power by electricity. By the 1920s, as historian Martin Sklar has documented, it had become possible to increase output while decreasing the total number of workers engaged in goods production. During the '20s, overall manufacturing output increased 64 percent, but the number of manufacturing workers dropped by 300,000. This changed the role of saving.

Why? The industrial revolution depended upon the fact that both consumer goods workers and their employers would lay aside a certain portion of those goods (in the form of wages and profits, respectively) to be consumed by new workers hired to produce machines and other capital goods. In the '20s, however, it became possible to expand the production of consumer goods without increasing the number of workers engaged in goods production. In fact, the number of capital goods workers actually fell during the '20s, from 3.3 million to 2.9 million. This meant that goods producers no longer had to lay aside an additional part of their income for new workers. They no longer had to save as much as they had saved before.

By way of analogy, imagine an office in 1985 that produced   10
greeting cards on a mini-computer that cost $50,000 and required several trained technicians to operate. Seven years later, the company could have taken a small percentage of the money it had put away to replace that machine and bought a new computer for $5,000 that would produce more cards with much less expensive labor. There would be no new net investment, merely the replacement of an older machine with a new one. If you imagine such a process taking place in the economy as a whole, you can get some idea of how the American economy changed in the '20s.

A similar paradox affected workers' self-denial. In the nineteenth century, wages had to be kept down to provide profits to invest in the newly growing capital goods industries. The growth of these industries required new workers who created new demand for consumer goods, which caused the consumer goods industries to make new investments, reigniting the process of accumulation. But, in the '20s, the process broke down because, again, the capital goods sector stopped growing. When new workers weren't hired, new demand for consumer goods dwindled. Consumer goods industries became so productive that they reduced the demand for their own goods every time they expanded production.

This created a crisis of overproduction that contributed to the depth and persistence of the Depression in the 1930s. Rising productivity led to an accumulation of profits that, in the absence of new investment outlets, found its way into the overvalued stock market. Workers' self denial resulted not in new investment but in a lack of effective demand for the goods they produced. It was what Keynes called the "fallacy of saving."

In the early '30s, many Americans feared that capitalism had become obsolete and that there was no way to overcome the threat of overproduction that the new productivity had created. They were wrong: American capitalism recovered and flourished for the next 60 years by creating new outlets for investment and new demand for the goods that were produced. But these measures also undermined the foundations of the older Protestant work ethic.

The government subsidized both consumer demand and the demand for capital goods through welfare programs, public works, guaranteed loans for housing, highway construction, and military spending. Businesses acceded to wage increases and used various forms of easy consumer credit to encourage spending. Advertising also exploded, especially after the introduction of television. But, more important, businesses vastly expanded into realms that had been either unexplored or previously reserved for upper-class luxuries. They now sold fun and leisure and mental and physical health to the working class; they marketed not merely edible food but gourmet delights and prepackaged and frozen food. They sold fashion and not merely clothes.

15   They sold these new goods and services through advertising, but the advertising itself had to create new needs and a new conception of what Americans should want to have and want to be. Advertising, along with popular entertainment, promoted the idea of a new American quite unlike the older American of the Protestant work ethic. For this new American, the goal of life was not salvation in the afterlife but happiness now. The goal of work was a comfortable and pleasurable life for yourself and for your family. Physical pleasure, through sex, sports, social activity, entertainment, and eating was an integral part of happiness. Leisure was a reward for having worked, and the enjoyment of leisure was an important part of happiness.

The older life had been based on saving and self-denial; the new one was based on spending and self-fulfillment—the "good life." In the '60s, Americans began to look for the right "lifestyle." The older American had inherited his identity; the new American chose his identity, constructed his appearance (through diet, fashion, and cosmetics), created a personality (through education and even psychotherapy), and selected a career. One achieved happiness by choosing the right lifestyle.

This obsession with lifestyle has been reflected in the books Americans have read. For the past three decades, the nonfiction best-seller lists have been dominated by books explaining how to achieve happiness through adopting a certain lifestyle—from Thomas A. Harris's *I'm OK, You're OK* to Nancy Friday's *My Mother, My Self* down to Stephen Covey's *The Seven Habits of Highly Effective People* to Suze Orman's current best seller, *The Courage to Be Rich*.

Orman, who has become a superstar on public television, tells her own story of achieving the good life. After working for seven years as a waitress after college, she decided to get a job as a stockbroker. "I remember how proud my mom was when, years later, I was able to buy my first luxury car," she writes. She then decided to start her own financial group, but after only a year, someone stole all her client records. She then deeply into debt. She then describes a Bunyanesque "turning point" in her life. Sitting in a Denny's restaurant, she "looked closely at the woman waiting on me, and it dawned that she surely had more money than I did.

I might have looked richer, wearing my designer clothes and with my fancy car parked outside. But I knew that the only wealth that I had at this point was a negative, drawn in red ink. Looking again, I could see clearly that this waitress was also happier than I was, and more honest. I was the poor one, inside and out. Where would I find the courage I needed, the courage to change?"

In the standard Christian tale, the rich man realizes that the beggar is more virtuous and will be rewarded in the afterlife. But, in Orman's morality tale, both virtue and the promise of eternal life have disappeared. What Orman realizes is that her wealth is superficial because her business is in arrears and that the waitress actually has more money than she does and is therefore happier. Orman's "fancy car" couldn't bring her happiness because the bank still owned it. Seized with this insight into her true condition, she rebuilds her business—a business that consists of telling people how to manage their Roth IRAs—and regains the "courage to be rich."

The new capitalism has transformed religion itself into prima- 20 rily a social and therapeutic activity. Shorn of its promise of otherworldly salvation, religion has become a lifestyle strategy—from Norman Vincent Peale's 1952 best-seller. *The Power of Positive Thinking*, to televangelist Robert H. Schuller's best-selling 1988 guide to make it, *Success Is Never Ending, Failure Is Never Final*. Last year, the host of a sports talk show was questioning a Dallas Cowboys representative about whether star player Deion Sanders's newfound commitment to religion was simply another "fad" that he was embracing. The rep became indignant at this slight to Sanders. "Being a Christian," he explained to the incredulous host, "has become Deion's lifestyle."

The "culture war" of the past decades has pitted descendants of the movements of the 60s against conservative Republicans and members of the religious right. It has had all the trappings of the final battle between good and evil on Armageddon, but it is really being fought on the much more prosaic terrain of modern capitalism. The two sides have much in common. They share not only a goal of worldly success but also a rejection of the purely individual strategy for salvation favored by Orman or Covey. They stand for visions of the good society and not simply the good life.

The counterculture of the '60s was part of the new capitalism but was also a reaction to the form it had taken after World War II. It fused cultural experimentation with politics: the search for the good life with the crusade for a good society. It featured communes, widespread use of drugs, and sexual liberation, but it also gave rise to the feminist, environmental and consumer movements.

The feminist movement was an attempt to secure not merely economic equality but equal opportunity to define one's existence; the environmental and consumer movements aimed to include safe cars and healthy food and clean air and water in the definition of the good life.

The religious right was descended from the Fundamentalists and Pentecostals of the early twentieth century who counseled Christians to save themselves before the world's end. These early Fundamentalists represented the last stand of the old Protestantism. Today's religious activists of the Christian Coalition have become worldly in their aims. They seek not to save their own souls but to reform present-day America. And they have expanded their own purview from restoring prayer in public school to cutting capital gains taxes.

Though not a fundamentalist Christian himself, William Bennett illustrates the trend. Bennett (like Orman) embraces the older virtues for newer ends. In *The Sprit of America* for instance, he touts frugality as a virtue, but not for the same reasons that Wesley did. "In our modern age of easy credit and consumer debt, of great affluence and great decadence," he writes, "it is important to recall that industry and frugality are the sources not only of material success but of good and satisfactory living as well."

25   If you look at this culture war not from the perspective of the moment but from the sweep of two centuries, it looks like a family quarrel. One could imagine the adherents of the counterculture and the religious right as passengers in a spaceship furiously debating which direction it should go, when, unbeknownst to them, it is primarily being directed from below by remote control. Its overall direction is already mapped out. The best that the critics can do is steer it to the right or the left.

So, does the replacement of the older Protestant *work ethic* represent a decline in morality, as some conservatives insist? I would suggest that it is far preferable to worry about how to achieve happiness on earth than to tolerate unhappiness and even misery in the pursuit of an imagined afterlife. It is also a decided advance that the average citizen can now take advantage of activities and opportunities once reserved for a wealthy few—like travel, education, psychotherapy, athletics, and preventive medicine. Most Americans can now enjoy the aesthetic dimension of fine clothes and food. And they can participate in sexual activities that were formerly performed secretly under a burden of crippling guilt.

Within this given framework, one can still find ample room for questioning whether certain kinds of behavior represent, if not a decline in morality, a departure from it. These include not simply obvious examples of criminal behavior but also the egregious pursuit of luxury that Robert Frank documents in his new book, *Luxury Fever*—from face-lifts to castles in the Hamptons—and the rabid intolerance of social differences (yes, lifestyles!) that is fueled by Bauer, Pat Buchanan, and others who claim the mantle of God. One can also find justification for encouraging social rather than purely individual solutions to the achievement of the good life—an objective that liberal and Christian right movements share but that they seek to achieve in very different ways. What is at stake is not the decline of morality but its redefinition—a process in which all Americans, from born-again to New Age to agnostic, are already participating.

Questions for Discussion

1. What is Judis's thesis? How and why does he place economics and religion at the center of his argument?
2. How does Judis define the Protestant ethic that gave identity to Americans and their work values from colonial times until the end of the 19th century?
3. How did industrialism, recovery from the Great Depression, new realms for business, advertising, and the mass media transform the Protestant work ethic into what Judis calls "the new capitalism"? How does he compare and contrast the new capitalism and the Protestant work ethic? Why does he think that the new capitalism can promote positive values? What do his opponents think?
4. What facts and rhetorical strategies does Judis use to add credibility to his argument?

Ideas for Writing

1. Do you agree with Judis that the new capitalism can promote positive values and cannot be blamed for "the decline of morality" that so many citizens see in American culture? Write an argument in support of his theory or one that argues against it. If you believe that there is a "decline of morality" in American culture, discuss the changes that you think need to be made.
2. The relationship between economics and spirituality has changed over the past century. Write an analysis and interpretation of what you understand the relationship between economics and spiritual values to be in America today.

Happiness at Work:
Job, Career, and Calling
DALAI LAMA AND HOWARD C. CUTLER

The Dalai Lama (b. 1935) and Howard C. Cutler, M.D., coauthored both The Art of Happiness: A Handbook for Living *(1998) and* The Art of Happiness at Work *(2003). The Dalai Lama is the political and spiritual leader of the Tibetan people and a world-renowned teacher of spiritual ways of living. He has received the Wallenberg Award (conferred by the U.S. Congressional Human Rights Foundation) and the Albert Schweitzer Award; in 1989 he received the Nobel Peace Prize for his efforts to find a peaceful solution to the Tibetan struggle for liberty. Cutler is a psychiatrist who received his medical degree from the College of Medicine at the University of Arizona and is a diplomat of the American Board of Psychiatry and Neurology. In the essay that follows, excerpted from* The Art of Happiness at Work, *Cutler questions the Dalai Lama about how to find happiness in work, which occupies such a large part of our waking lives.*

———————— ✦ ————————

In exploring the three primary orientations toward work—job, career, and calling—we had spoken at length about the first category in our discussion about money as one's primary motivation for working. But the Dalai Lama was right in pointing out that a career orientation with the primary emphasis on promotion, job titles, and designations can potentially be equally a source of misery. Diane serves as an example of the potentially destructive consequences of career orientation associated with an excessive preoccupation with higher status and greater wealth.

Diane is a lawyer, a very talented prosecutor. Despite being an eloquent speaker, capable of swaying a tough jury with brilliant arguments and impassioned pleas, when asked why she became a lawyer she is suddenly at a complete loss for words. Perhaps this is because she has always been torn between two opposing views of her work: on one hand seeing her profession as a vehicle to wealth, status, and others' validation of her intelligence, and on the other hand seeing it as a means to protect people from criminals, from the predators who destroy lives and undermine society. Unfortunately, her "one hand" gradually became stronger than "the other" as her driving personal ambition overpowered her sincere desire to be of service to others.

She had started out in the attorney general's office with a very promising career. She won case after case, rising up the ladder very quickly. But by her late thirties she couldn't resist the lure of the money being made by colleagues in large corporate firms, or in personal injury law. By the time she went into the private sector, however, she was facing a glass ceiling and age discrimination— she was too old to be a junior associate, and she had been in criminal law too long to make a lateral move. She became a solo practitioner but was never able to make the money or achieve the renown she so longed for.

Of course, that didn't extinguish her craving for wealth and recognition. In fact, it grew stronger over the years, fueled by her habit of pouring over alumni bulletins, professional journals, and local newspapers, furiously scanning the pages for reports of the latest achievements of her colleagues. Consumed by competitiveness and jealousy, each award or honor given to another attorney, each promotion to partner, each large jury award in a personal injury suit (of course calculating to the penny the 30 percent fee received by her colleague), was like a blow to her. The cumulative effect resulted in years of misery, and a growing bitterness which eventually eroded her relationships with friends and family.

Diane's steadfast refusal to let go of her endless quest for riches and fame in the private sector is particularly sad in view of her tremendous talent and abilities as a prosecutor. It has led her to continually turn down offers from the attorney general's office to return in a higher-ranking position and with much more visibility. Plagued by the accomplishments of her colleagues in the private sector, determined to match and surpass their success, she is virtually assured a life of continued unhappiness. 5

Commenting on Diane's chronic dissatisfaction, a former associate in the attorney general's office observed, "It's so sad, and so frustrating! Diane really has what it takes to be a great prosecutor, to really make a difference. And there are so many lawyers I know who would love to have her talent. I don't know, it's like she could never relax and enjoy her success, she always wanted something different. But the thing is, she's such an amazing prosecutor that listening to her complain about not getting what she wants in her private practice kind of reminds me of a beauty queen worrying over and whining about one pimple to a friend who has terminal acne."

Do you have any thoughts about how an ordinary person can change how he or she views work or attitudes toward work? In other words, how can we change our attitude from either the job or career approach to the calling approach? Are there any ways that you can suggest?"

The Dalai Lama thought awhile. "I'm not sure. But for example, let us imagine a farmer: when he does his work, how could he see it as a calling? Perhaps he could try to see the higher purpose to his work and then reflect on it. Maybe think about his taking care of nature, cultivating life. Or, in the case of a factory worker, he or she could think about the ultimate benefit of the particular machine they are making. I don't know. I think for some it might be difficult, but they can try to look for purpose.

"Now, I would think that certain professions, like social workers, teachers, health workers, would see their work as a calling."

10   "You know, interestingly enough," I pointed out, "you would think that our view of our work depends on the nature of the job. In some jobs—for example, some kinds of unskilled labor, or what are considered menial jobs—you would think that people would see their job just as a means to earn money, while a social worker or a nurse or a doctor would see it more as a calling. But it is not the case that there is a division based on the job. In fact, the very same study that identified the three primary categories of how we view work found that there was the same division, no matter what the particular field or job. They studied a group of college administrators all with the same job, same level of education, same setting, and so on, and they found that a third saw their work as a job, a third as a career, and a third as a calling. So, even among nurses, physicians, or social workers, some just see it as a job, some see it as a career, focusing on more promotions or advancement, and some people see it as a calling. It seems to be based more on the psychology of the person and their view of their work, rather than the nature of the work itself."

"Yes, I can see how that may be true," said the Dalai Lama. "For example, the Buddhist monk students are supposed to study for a higher purpose—for liberation—but some may not carry that motivation. But that may be due to environment. Maybe they have no one who gives them good advice, helps them to see the wider view and the ultimate purpose. So if the social worker is properly trained and guided, and care and attention is paid to cultivating the proper motivation right from the beginning, then they might be better able to see their work as a calling."

"Well obviously, if one is in a job like social work or other helping professions, there's at least a good potential there for that to be a 'calling' because they're directly helping other people, making society better. Now I'm just throwing around some ideas here, trying to clarify things, but I'm just wondering what your thoughts are about the achievement of excellence as the higher motivation or purpose of one's work—not necessarily helping society or helping others or a higher purpose in that sense, but a different kind of higher purpose: one is working because one wants to really achieve excellence in whatever activity they are doing. Such people want to develop their own personal potential to its highest degree through their work. So there the focus would be on gaining deep satisfaction purely from just doing a good job Would you consider that to be a 'higher purpose' and put it in the category of a 'calling'?"

"I think probably that could also be categorized as 'calling,'" the Dalai Lama replied, but with a tentative inflection in his voice. "Now, generally speaking, personally I think it is best if the higher purpose or meaning in one's work involves being of some help to other people. But there are many different kinds of people, differing viewpoints, interests, and dispositions. So, I think it is definitely possible that for some people, the higher purpose may simply be striving for excellence in their work, and doing that with a sense of creativity. Here, the focus may be on the creative process, and the high quality of the work itself. And I think that could transform the view from a mere job or a career to a calling. But again, here one has to have the proper motivation—not carrying on one's work out of strong competition or a sense of jealousy. That's important.

"So, for example, I think in the past, and even now, there have been many scientists who are driven to carry out experiments just out of scientific curiosity and their strong interest in their particular field, just to see what they could find out. And I think these people could see their work as a calling. And as it turns out, often these scientists have made new discoveries, things which ultimately benefit others, even if that was not their original intention."

"I think that's a good example," I noted.

"Of course, there's a danger in that sometimes," he cautioned. "For example, there have been scientists engaged in research to produce new weapons of mass destruction. Particularly you Americans!" He laughed. "And I think they perhaps also saw their work as a calling, to come up with things to destroy the enemy, and perhaps in their mind to protect their own people. But then you have some leaders, like Hitler, who would use their discoveries in the wrong way."

I continued, "Well, as I mentioned, there are certain professions where potentially it may be easier to approach work with the 'calling' attitude. Fields like social work, medicine, religious teachers or high-school teachers. That type of thing. But we've mentioned the

15

idea that there are millions of people who don't have the opportunity or interest to be great scientists or social workers, teachers or health care workers. Jobs where it is not as obvious how they have a higher purpose to benefit others, where it might be harder to view their work as a calling. For example, there are many jobs that are perceived as only interested in making money—bankers, stockbrokers, and so on—or interested in advancement, status, or power—corporate executives, lawyers, or other kinds of professions."

"Yes, that's true," the Dalai Lama replied, "but as I mentioned, there are many different people in the world, and so there may be many different approaches to discovering a higher purpose and meaning to one's work, which then leads to viewing one's job as this 'calling' that you are talking about. And then this would increase their work satisfaction. So, for example, a person may have a boring job, but that person may be supporting his or her family, children, or elderly parents. Then helping and supporting one's family could be that person's higher purpose, and when they get bored or dissatisfied with their work, they can deliberately reflect on providing for the happiness and comfort of their family, visualize each family member and how this work is providing food and shelter for that individual, and then I think this can give the worker more strength. So, then whether they like the work or not, there is still a purpose. But I think we have already mentioned that if you look at the work just for your own salary, no other purpose, then I think it becomes boring, you want other work."

"But of course there are still millions of single people who don't have a family to take care of," I pointed out. "Do you think there's a way of cultivating a higher motivation that they can remind themselves of in the work setting?"

20   "This is no problem," said the Dalai Lama without hesitation. "There are still many lines of reasoning a person can use to discover this higher purpose, the wider benefit of their work."

"Can you give some examples?"

The Dalai Lama pointed at the tape recorder on the coffee table in front of us.

"Now, look at this machine. I think at least a few thousand people had their hand in the making of this. And each one made a contribution, so we can now use this as part of making our book that might be of some help to other people. In the same way, there are many thousands of people who provide the food we eat, the clothes we wear. An individual worker on an assembly line somewhere may not directly see the benefit of his or her hard labor, but through a little analysis they can realize the indirect benefits to others and be proud of what they do, and have a sense of accomplishment. Workers all over the world are bringing happiness to others, even though they may not see this. I think that often if one works for a large company, on the surface it may appear that one's job is insignificant, that an individual worker doesn't have much impact directly on the big company. But if we investigate deeper, we may realize that our jobs can have indirect effects on people we may never even meet. I think that in a small way, perhaps through our work, we can make some contribution to others.

"Now, others, for instance, may be working for the government in some way, and thus see working for their country as the higher purpose. For example, in the 1950s there were many Chinese, including soldiers, who genuinely felt that they were working for the benefit of others, at least for the benefit of the Party, and that meant the benefit of the people. So they had a strong conviction of their purpose, and even sacrificed their lives. And they didn't care about personal gains. Similarly, in the monastic world there are many individual monks who choose to live in seclusion as hermits in the mountains, under basic conditions and great hardships. They have the option to remain in the monastery and have a life of greater comfort and ease. But because they have a much higher purpose in their mind, because their goal is to achieve liberation so that they can better be of service to all beings, they are willing to confront the immediate hardships. I think these people enjoy a certain mental satisfaction from their work."

The Dalai Lama sipped his tea as he reflected. "There is always a way to find a higher purpose to one's work. Of course, there may be some individuals who may not need to work because of their special financial circumstances. Under such circumstances, they can enjoy their freedom and enjoy the privilege they have, and that's one thing. But among those who need to work to make a living, then it is important for these individuals to recognize that, first of all, they are part of a society. They are members of the human society that they are living in. And also, they should recognize that by actively participating in this workforce, in some way they are acting out their role as a good citizen in their society, a productive member of society. And in this way, they can realize that indirectly they are making a contribution to the entire society. So if they think along these lines, then they can see some purpose in what they are doing that is beyond just providing a means of livelihood for themselves. That alone can be enough to give them a sense of purpose, a sense of calling. And this idea can be reinforced if they simply ask themselves, *What is the other alternative?* Just hanging around. Then there is the danger of drifting into some unhealthy habits, such as resorting to drugs, being part of a gang, or acting as a destructive member of society. So, there, not only are you not contributing to the society that you live in, but in fact you are undermining the very stability of the society that you are part of. If any worker thinks along those lines, they will see a higher purpose to their work."

The Dalai Lama paused again and laughed. "I'm thinking that there may be a bit of irony here. We're discussing these things that may end up in a book, and it may seem that I'm making these suggestions to the American citizens, but whether the Tibetans, my own community, pay attention to these things is open to question. They don't always listen to me!"

"Well, maybe we can get our book translated into Tibetan," I kidded him.

Questions for Discussion

1. According to this article, what are the "three primary orientations toward work"? What makes one profession a "calling"? Why can one profession be a "calling" to one person and merely a "job" to another?

2. According to the Dalai Lama, which approach toward work causes the most human suffering and why? What is the goal of this type of work? Why does this point of view toward work cause so much unhappiness?

3. Which category of work brings a person the most happiness and satisfaction? What would you say is the key to finding happiness in work? Do you agree with the Dalai Lama's conclusion about work? Why or why not? Explain.

4. According to this essay, what are some "lines of reasoning" that one can develop in order to change one's view of work from a negative one into a positive one? Can you think of any other approaches that will make work more enjoyable and meaningful?

Ideas for Writing

1. The Dalai Lama says that there could be "many different approaches to discovering a higher purpose and meaning to one's work." Write an essay exploring the Dalai Lama's approach to finding meaning in work. Discuss why you believe in his approach, or suggest another approach to work that makes more sense to you.

2. Write an essay discussing the three categories of work described in this interview. Choose a profession or job you have had; then describe how it could be placed in any of the three categories and if it might ever become a "calling."

Work Makes Life Sweet

BELL HOOKS

Born in Hopkinsville, Kentucky (in 1952), bell hooks changed her name to honor her grandmother and to establish a persona separate from Gloria Watkins, her birth name. She earned her B.A. in 1973 at Stanford and her Ph.D. at the University of Santa Cruz in 1983. Hooks taught English and African-American Literature at Oberlin College, and is currently a professor of English at the City University of New York. She is deeply engaged with issues of identity, culture, gender, racism, and social change, and is one of the most widely read African-American writers of our time. Her recent works include Remembered Rapture: The Writer at Work *(1999),* Where We Stand: Class Matters *(2000), and* Communion: The Female Search for Love *(2002). The selection below is excerpted from* Sisters of Yam: Black Women and Self-Recovery *(1993). In it she examines the changing attitudes of black women toward work and the rewards of the work ethic in traditional African-America families.*

---------------- ✦ ----------------

"Work makes life sweet!" I often heard this phrase growing up, mainly from old black folks who did not have jobs in the traditional sense of the word. They were usually self-employed, living off the land, selling fishing worms, picking up an odd job here and there. They were people who had a passion for work. They took pride in a job done well. My Aunt Margaret took in ironing. Folks brought her clothes from miles around because she was such an expert. That was in the days when using starch was common and she knew how to do an excellent job. Watching her iron with skill and grace was like watching a ballerina dance. Like all the other black girls raised in the fifties that I knew, it was clear to me that I would be a working woman. Even though our mother stayed home, raising her seven children, we saw her constantly at work, washing, ironing, cleaning, and cooking (she is an incredible cook). And she never allowed her six girls to imagine we would not be working women. No, she let us know that we would work and be proud to work.

The vast majority of black women in the United States know in girlhood that we will be workers. Despite sexist and racist stereotypes about black women living off welfare, most black women who receive welfare have been in the workforce. In *Hard*

Times Cotton Mill Girls,[1] one can read about black women who went to work in the cotton mills, usually leaving farm labor or domestic service. Katie Geneva Cannon[2] remembers: "It was always assumed that we would work. Work was a given in life, almost like breathing and sleeping. I'm always surprised when I hear people talking about somebody taking care of them, because we always knew that we were going to work." Like older generations of southern black women, we were taught not only that we would be workers, but that there was no "shame" in doing any honest job. The black women around us who worked as maids, who stripped tobacco when it was the season, were accorded dignity and respect. We learned in our black churches and in our schools that it "was not what you did, but how you did it" that mattered.

A philosophy of work that emphasizes commitment to any task was useful to black people living in a racist society that for so many years made only certain jobs (usually service work or other labor deemed "undesirable") available to us. Just as many Buddhist traditions teach that any task becomes sacred when we do it mindfully and with care, southern black work traditions taught us the importance of working with integrity irrespective of the task. Yet these attitudes towards work did not blind anyone to the reality that racism made it difficult to work for white people. It took "gumption" to work with integrity in settings where white folks were disrespectful and downright hateful. And it was obvious to me as a child that the black people who were saying "work makes life sweet" were the folks who did not work for whites, who did what they wanted to do. For example, those who sold fishing worms were usually folks who loved to fish. Clearly there was a meaningful connection between positive thinking about work and those who did the work that they had chosen.

Most of us did not enter the workforce thinking of work in terms of finding a "calling" or a vocation. Instead, we thought of work as a way to make money. Many of us started our work lives early and we worked to acquire money to buy necessities. Some of us worked to buy school books or needed or desired clothing. Despite the emphasis on "right livelihood" that was present in our life growing up, my sisters and I were more inclined to think of work in relation to doing what you needed to do to get money to buy what you wanted. In general, we have had unsatisfying work lives. Ironically, Mama entered the paid workforce very late, after we were all raised, working for the school system and at times in domestic service, yet there are ways in which she has found work outside the home more rewarding than any of her children. The black women I talked with about work tended to see jobs primarily as a means to an end, as a way to make money to provide for material needs. Since so many working black women often have dependents, whether children or other relatives, they enter the workforce with the realistic conviction that they need to make money for survival purposes. This attitude coupled with the reality of a job market that remains deeply shaped by racism and sexism means that as black women we often end up working jobs that we do not like. Many of us feel that we do not have a lot of options. Of the women I interviewed, the ones who saw themselves as having options tended to have the highest levels of education. Yet nearly all the black women I spoke with agreed that they would always choose to work, even if they did not need to. It was only a very few young black females, teenagers and folks in their early twenties, who talked with me about fantasy lives where they would be taken care of by someone else.

Speaking with young black women who rely on welfare bene-   5 fits to survive economically, I found that overall they wanted to work. However, they are acutely aware of the difference between a job and a fulfilling vocation. Most of them felt that it would not be a sign of progress for them to "get off welfare" and work low-paying jobs, in situations that could be stressful or dehumanizing. Individuals receiving welfare who are trying to develop skills, to attend school or college, often find that they are treated with much greater hostility by social-service workers than if they were just sitting at home watching television. One woman seeking assistance was told by an angry white woman worker, "welfare is not going to pay for you to get your B.A." This young woman had been making many personal sacrifices to try and develop skills and educational resources that would enable her to be gainfully employed and she was constantly disappointed by the level of resentment toward her whenever she needed to deal with social services.

Through the years, in my own working life, I have noticed that many black women do not like or enjoy their work. The vast majority of women I talked to . . . agreed that they were not satisfied with their working lives even though they see themselves as performing well on the job. That is why I talk so much about work-related stress in [*Remembered Rapture*]. It is practically impossible to maintain a spirit of emotional well-being if one is daily doing work that is unsatisfying, that causes intense stress, and that gives little satisfaction. Again and again, I found that many black women I interviewed had far superior skills than the jobs they were performing called for but were held back because of their "lack of education," or in some cases, "necessary experience." This routinely prevented them from moving upward. While they performed their jobs well, they felt added tension generated in the work environment by supervisors who often saw them as "too uppity" or by their own struggle to maintain interest in their assigned tasks. One white-woman administrator shared that the clearly overly skilled black woman who works as an administrative assistant in her office was resented by white male "bosses" who felt that she did not have the proper attitude of a "subordinate." When I spoke to this woman she acknowledged not liking her job, stating that her lack of education and the urgent need to raise children and send them to college had prevented her from working towards a chosen career. She holds to the dream that she will return to school and someday gain the necessary education that will give her access to the career she desires and deserves. Work is so often a source of pain and frustration.

Learning how to think about work and our job choices from the standpoint of "right livelihood" enhances black female well-being. Our self-recovery is fundamentally linked to experiencing that quality of "work that makes life sweet." In one of my favorite self-help books, Marsha Sinetar's *Do What You Love, the Money Will Follow*, the author defines right livelihood as a concept initially coming from the teachings of Buddha which emphasized "work consciously chosen, done with full awareness and care, and leading to enlightenment." This is an attitude toward work that our society does not promote, and it especially does not encourage black females to think of work in this way. As Sinetar notes:

> Right Livelihood, in both its ancient and its contemporary sense, embodies self-expression, commitment, mindfulness, and conscious choice. Finding and doing work of this sort is predicated upon high self-esteem and self-trust, since only those who like themselves, who subjectively feel they are trustworthy and deserving dare to choose on behalf of what is right and true for them. When the powerful quality of conscious choice is present in our work, we can be enormously productive. When we consciously choose to do work we enjoy, not only can we get things done, we can get them done well and be intrinsically rewarded for our effort.

Black women need to learn about "right livelihood." Even though I had been raised in a world where elderly black people had this wisdom, I was more socialized by the get-ahead generation that felt how much money you were making was more important than what you did to make that money. We have difficult choices ahead. As black females collectively develop greater self-esteem, a greater sense of entitlement, we will learn from one another's example how to practice right livelihood. Of the black women I interviewed the individuals who enjoyed their work the most felt they were realizing a particular vocation or calling. C.J. (now almost forty) recalls that generations of her family were college-educated. She was taught to choose work that would be linked with the political desire to enhance the overall well-being of black people. C.J. says, "I went to college with a mission and a passion to have my work be about African-Americans. The spirit of mission came to me from my family, who taught us that you don't just work to get money, you work to create meaning for yourself and other people." With this philosophy as a guiding standpoint, she has always had a satisfying work life.

When one of my sisters, a welfare recipient, decided to return to college, I encouraged her to try and recall her childhood vocational dreams and to allow herself adult dreams, so that she would not be pushed into preparing for a job that holds no interest for her. Many of us must work hard to unlearn the socialization that teaches us that we should just be lucky to get any old job. We can begin to think about our work lives in terms of vocation and calling. One black woman I interviewed, who has worked as a housewife for many years, began to experience agoraphobia. Struggling to regain her emotional well-being, she saw a therapist, against the will of her family. In this therapeutic setting, she received affirmation for her desire to finish her undergraduate degree and continue in a graduate program. She found that finishing a master's and becoming a college teacher gave her enormous satisfaction. Yet this achievement was not fully appreciated by her husband. A worker in a factory, whose job is long and tedious, he was jealous of her newfound excitement about work. Since her work brings her in touch with the public, it yields rewards unlike any he can hope to receive from his job. Although she has encouraged him to go back to school (one of his unfulfilled goals), he is reluctant. Despite these relational tensions, she has found that "loving" her work has helped her attend to and transform previous feelings of low self-esteem.

A few of the black women I interviewed claimed to be doing work they liked but complained bitterly about their jobs, particularly where they must make decisions that affect the work lives of other people. One woman had been involved in a decision-making process that required her to take a stance that would leave another person jobless. Though many of her peers were proud of the way she handled this difficult decision, her response was to feel "victimized." Indeed, she kept referring to herself as "battered." This response troubled me for it seemed to bespeak a

10

contradiction many women experience in positions of power. Though we may like the status of a power position and wielding power, we may still want to see ourselves as "victims" in the process, especially if we must act in ways that "good girls, dutiful daughters" have been taught are "bad."

I suggested to the women I interviewed that they had chosen particular careers that involved "playing hard ball" yet they seemed to be undermining the value of their choices and the excellence of their work by complaining that they had to get their hands dirty and suffer some bruises. I shared with them my sense that if you choose to play hardball then you should be prepared for the bruises and not be devastated when they occur. In some ways it seemed to me these black women wanted to be "equals" in a man's world while they simultaneously wanted to be treated like fragile "ladies." Had they been able to assume full responsibility for their career choices, they would have enjoyed their work more and been able to reward themselves for jobs well done. In some cases it seemed that the individuals were addicted to being martyrs. They wanted to control everything, to be the person "in power" but also resented the position. These individuals . . . seemed not to know when to set boundaries or that work duties could be shared. They frequently over-extended themselves. When we over-extend ourselves in work settings, pushing ourselves to the breaking point, we rarely feel positive about tasks even if we are performing them well.

Since many people rely on powerful black women in jobs (unwittingly turning us into "mammies" who will bear all the burdens—and there are certainly those among us who take pride in this role), we can easily become tragically over-extended. I noticed that a number of us (myself included) talk about starting off in careers that we really "loved" but over-working to the point of "burn-out" so that the pleasure we initially found dissipated. I remember finding a self-help book that listed twelve symptoms of "burn-out," encouraging readers to go down the list and check those that described their experience. At the end, it said, "If you checked three or more of these boxes, chances are you are probably suffering from burn-out." I found I had checked all twelve! That let me know it was time for a change. Yet changing was not easy. When you do something and you do it well, it is hard to take a break, or to confront the reality that I had to face, which was that I really didn't want to be doing the job I was doing even though I did it well. In retrospect it occurred to me that it takes a lot more energy to do a job well when you really do not want to be doing it. This work is often more tiring. And maybe that extra energy would be better spent in the search for one's true vocation or calling.

In my case, I have always wanted to be a writer. And even though I have become just that and I love this work, my obsessive fears about "not being poor" have made it difficult for me to take time away from my other career, teaching and lecturing, to "just write." Susan Jeffers' book, *Feel the Fear and Do It Anyway*, has helped me to finally reach the point in my life where I can take time to "just write." Like many black women who do not come from privileged class backgrounds, who do not have family we can rely on to help if the financial going gets rough (we in fact are usually the people who are relied on), it feels very frightening to think about letting go of financial security, even for a short time, to do work one loves but may not pay the bills. In my case, even though I had worked with a self-created financial program aimed at bringing me to a point in life when I could focus solely on writing, I still found it hard to take time away. It was then that I had to tap into my deep fears of ending up poor and counter them with messages that affirm my ability to take care of myself economically irrespective of the circumstance. These fears are not irrational (though certainly mine were a bit extreme). In the last few years, I have witnessed several family members go from working as professionals to unemployment and various degrees of homelessness. Their experiences highlighted the reality that it is risky to be without secure employment and yet they also indicated that one could survive, even start all over again if need be.

My sister V. quit a job that allowed her to use excellent skills   15
because she had major conflicts with her immediate supervisor. She quit because the level of on-the-job stress had become hazardous to her mental well-being. She quit confident that she would find a job in a few months. When that did not happen, she was stunned. It had not occurred to her that she would find it practically impossible to find work in the area she most wanted to live in. Confronting racism, sexism, and a host of other unclear responses, months passed and she has not found another job. It has changed her whole life. While material survival has been difficult, she is learning more about what really matters to her in life. She is learning about "right livelihood." The grace and skill with which she has confronted her circumstance has been a wonderful example for me. With therapy, with the help of friends and loved ones, she is discovering the work she would really like to do and no longer feels the need to have a high-paying, high-status job. And she has learned more about what it means to take risks.

In *Do What You Love, the Money Will Follow*, Sinetar cautions those of us who have not been risk-takers to go slowly, to practice, to begin by taking small risks, and to plan carefully. Because I have planned carefully, I am able to finally take a year's leave from my teaching job without pay. During this time, I want to see if I enjoy working solely as a writer and if I can support myself. I want to see if (like those old-time black folks I talk about at the start of the essay) doing solely the work I feel most "called" to do will enhance my joy in living. For the past few months, I have been "just writing" and indeed, so far, I feel it is "work that makes life sweet."

The historical legacy of black women shows that we have worked hard, long, and well, yet rarely been paid what we deserve. We rarely get the recognition we deserve. However, even in the midst of domination, individual black women have found their calling, and do the work they are best suited for. Onnie Lee Logan, the Alabama midwife who tells her story in *Motherwit*, never went to high school or college, never made a lot of money in her working life, but listened to her inner voice and found her calling. Logan shares:

> I let God work the plan on my life and I am satisfied at what has happened to me in my life. The sun wasn't shinin' every time and moon wasn't either. I was in the snow and the rain at night by my lonely self. . . . There had been many dreary nights but I didn't look at em as dreary nights. I had my mind on where I was going and what I was going for.
>
> Whatever I've done, I've done as well as I could and beyond. . . . I'm satisfied at what has happened in my life. Perfectly satisfied at what my life has done for me. I was a good midwife. One of the best as they say. This book was the last thing I had planned to do until God said well done. I consider myself—in fact if I leave tomorrow—I've lived my life and I've lived it well.

The life stories of black women like Onnie Logan remind us that "right livelihood" can be found irrespective of our class position, or the level of our education.

To know the work we are "called" to do in this world, we must know ourselves. The practice of "right livelihood" invites us to become more fully aware of our reality, of the labor we do and of the way we do it. Now that I have chosen my writing more fully than at any other moment of my life, the work itself feels more joyous. I feel my whole being affirmed in the act of writing. As black women unlearn the conventional thinking about work—which views money and/or status as more important than the work we do or the way we feel about that work—we will find our way back to those moments celebrated by our ancestors, when work was a passion. We will know again that "work makes life sweet."

Endnotes

1. *Hard Times Cotton Mill Girls:* an oral history of life in southern textile mills, compiled by Victoria Byerly (b. 1949), a former mill worker.
2. *Katie Geneva Cannon:* The first black woman ordained a Presbyterian minister. She worked with Victoria Byerly, author of *Hard Times Cotton Mill Girls*.

Questions for Discussion

1. What sense of community and values made Southern black folks feel that "work makes life sweet"? Why did black women's values about the meaning of work change in the decades after the 1950s? How does hooks argue that both the older Southern traditions about the meaning of work and the philosophy of Buddhism suggest that work should be a calling rather than a vocation? (See the interview with the Dalai Lama in this chapter.)
2. Why do black women working today prefer to support themselves through work rather than being taken care of by a partner or being on welfare? How are their attitudes toward work similar to and also very different from the values of their ancestors?
3. Why have many black women been discouraged from earning, or not been allowed to earn, a B.A. degree? If they do complete a college education and achieve success, what problems do black women often bring on themselves?
4. How does hooks define and illustrate the concept of "right livelihood"? Why does she believe that it is essential for raising black women's, or any individual's, self-confidence and self-esteem? Why does hooks believe that black women today will find their way back to the values that their ancestors lived by and be able to experience work as "making life sweet"?

Ideas for Writing

1. Write an essay in which you analyze your working life to explain how hooks's concepts that "work makes life sweet" and "right livelihood" are or are not integrated into your job. Are hooks's concepts realistic in the context of your working life? If they are, what can you do to make your working

life more rewarding? Set some goals for yourself and explain to your readers how they will improve your working life.

2. Write an essay that argues against hooks's claim that it is possible to make one's "working life sweet." What is it about the conditions of modern labor that make such "sweetness" hard to attain?

The Creative Class

RICHARD FLORIDA

Richard Florida earned his B.A. from Rutgers College and his Ph.D. from Columbia University. He is the H. John Heinz III Professor of Regional Economic Development in the Heinz School of Public Policy and Management at Carnegie Mellon University and the cofounder of the school's Software Industry Center. He has been a visiting scholar at the Brookings Institution. Florida lives in Pittsburgh, Pennsylvania, and Washington, D.C. The author of many articles and books, his most widely read books include The Breakthrough Illusion: Corporate America's Failure to Move from Innovation to Mass Production *(1990) and* Industrializing Knowledge: University-Industry Links in Japan and the United States *(1999). Florida is best known for* The Rise of the Creative Class and How It's Transforming Work, Leisure, Community and Everyday Life *(2002), which provides a new perspective on the increasing value of creativity in the world's economy. The following selection from that provocative book attempts to define the nature of the new creative class in the modern company, a class that is rapidly reinventing both the products of work and the nature of work.*

———————— ✦ ————————

The rise of the Creative Economy has had a profound effect on the sorting of people into social groups or classes. Others have speculated over the years on the rise of new classes in the advanced industrial economies. During the 1960s. Peter Drucker and Fritz Machlup described the growing role and importance of the new group of workers they dubbed "knowledge workers." Writing in the 1970s, Daniel Bell pointed to a new, more meritocratic class structure of scientists, engineers, managers and administrators brought on by the shift from a manufacturing to a "postindustrial" economy. The sociologist Erik Olin Wright has written for decades about the rise of what he called a new "professional-managerial" class. Robert Reich more recently advanced the term "symbolic analysts" to describe the members of the workforce who manipulate ideas and symbols. All of these observers caught economic aspects of the emerging class structure that I describe here.

Others have examined emerging social norms and value systems. Paul Fussell presciently captured many that I now attribute to the Creative Class in his theory of the "X Class." Near the end of his 1983 book *Class*—after a witty romp through status markers that delineate, say, the upper middle class from "high proles"—Fussell noted the presence of a growing "X" group that seemed to defy existing categories:

> [Y]ou are not born an X person . . . you earn X-personhood by a strenuous effort of discovery in which curiosity and originality are indispensable. . . . The young flocking to the cities to devote themselves to "art," "writing," "creative work"—anything, virtually, that liberates them from the presence of a boss or superior—are aspirant X people. . . . If, as [C. Wright] Mills has said, the middle-class person is "always somebody's man," the X person is nobody's. . . . X people are independent-minded. . . . They adore the work they do, and they do it until they are finally carried out, "retirement" being a concept meaningful only to hired personnel or wage slaves who despise their work.

Writing in 2000, David Brooks outlined the blending of bohemian and bourgeois values in a new social grouping he dubbed the Bobos. My take on Brooks's synthesis . . . is rather different, stressing the very transcendence of these two categories in a new creative ethos.

The main point I want to make here is that the basis of the Creative Class is economic. I define it as an economic class and argue that its economic function both underpins and informs its members' social, cultural and lifestyle choices. The Creative Class consists of people who add economic value through their creativity. It thus includes a great many knowledge workers, symbolic analysts and professional and technical workers, but emphasizes their true role in the economy. My definition of class emphasizes the way people organize themselves into social groupings and common identities based principally on their economic function. Their social and cultural preferences, consumption and buying habits, and their social identities all flow from this.

I am not talking here about economic class in terms of the ownership of property, capital or the means of production. If we use class in this traditional Marxian sense, we are still talking about a basic structure of capitalists who own and control the means of production, and workers under their employ. But little analytical utility remains in these broad categories of bourgeoisie and proletarian, capitalist and worker. Most members of the Creative Class do not own and control any significant property in the physical sense. Their property—which stems from their creative capacity—is an intangible because it is literally in their heads. And it is increasingly clear from my field research and interviews that while the members of the Creative Class do not yet see themselves as a unique social grouping, they actually share many similar tastes, desires and preferences. This new class may not be as distinct in this regard as the industrial Working Class in its heyday, but it has an emerging coherence.

THE NEW CLASS STRUCTURE

5   The distinguishing characteristic of the Creative Class is that its members engage in work whose function is to "create meaningful new forms." I define the Creative Class as consisting of two components. The Super-Creative Core of this new class includes scientists and engineers, university professors, poets and novelists, artists, entertainers, actors, designers and architects, as well as the thought leadership of modern society: nonfiction writers, editors, cultural figures, think-tank researchers, analysts and other opinion-makers. Whether they are software programmers or engineers, architects or filmmakers, they fully engage in the creative process. I define the highest order of creative work as producing new forms or designs that are readily transferable and widely useful—such as designing a product that can be widely made, sold and used; coming up with a theorem or strategy that can be applied in many cases; or composing music that can be performed again and again. People at the core of the Creative Class engage in this kind of work regularly; it's what they are paid to do. Along with problem solving, their work may entail problem finding: not just building a better mousetrap, but noticing first that a better mousetrap would be a handy thing to have.

Beyond this core group, the Creative Class also includes "creative professionals" who work in a wide range of knowledge-intensive industries such as high-tech sectors, financial services, the legal and health care professions, and business management. These people engage in creative problem solving, drawing on complex bodies of knowledge to solve specific problems. Doing so typically requires a high degree of formal education and thus a high level of human capital. People who do this kind of work may sometimes come up with methods or products that turn out to be widely useful, but it's not part of the basic job description. What they *are* required to do regularly is think on their own. They apply or combine standard approaches in unique ways to fit the situation, exercise a great deal of judgment, perhaps try something radically new from time to time. Creative Class people such as physicians, lawyers and managers do this kind of work in dealing with the many varied cases they encounter. In the course of their work, they may also be involved in testing and refining new techniques, new treatment protocols, or new management methods and even develop such things themselves. As a person continues to do more of this latter work, perhaps through a career shift or promotion, that person moves up to the Super-Creative Core: producing transferable, widely usable new forms is now their primary function.

Much the same is true of the growing number of technicians and others who apply complex bodies of knowledge to working with physical materials. And they are sufficiently engaged in creative problem solving that I have included a large subset of them in the Creative Class. In an insightful 1996 study, Stephen Barley of Stanford University emphasized the growing importance and influence of this group of workers. In fields such as medicine and scientific research, technicians are taking on increased responsibility to interpret their work and make decisions, blurring the old distinction between white-collar work (done by decisionmakers) and blue-collar work (done by those who follow orders). Barley notes that in medicine, for instance, "emergency medical technicians take action on the basis of diagnoses made at the site," while sonographers and radiology technicians draw on "knowledge of biological systems, pharmacology, and disease processes to render diagnostically useful information"—all of which encroaches on turf once reserved for the M.D.

Barley also found that in some areas of biomedical work, like the breeding of monoclonal antibodies, labs have had increasing difficulty duplicating each other's work: They might use the same formulas and well-documented procedures but not get the same results. The reason is that although the lead scientists at the labs might be working from the same theories, the lab technicians are called upon to make myriad interpretations and on-the-spot decisions. And while different technicians might all do these things according to accepted standards, they do them differently. Each is drawing on an arcane knowledge base and exercising his or her own judgment, by individual thought processes so complex and elusive that they could not easily be documented or communicated. Though counterproductive in this case, this individuality happens to be one of the hallmarks of creative work. Lest you think this sort of thing happens only in the rarefied world of the biomedical laboratory, Barley notes a similar phenomenon among technicians who repair and maintain copying machines. They acquire their own arcane bodies of knowledge and develop their own unique ways of doing the job.

As the creative content of other lines of work increases—as the relevant body of knowledge becomes more complex, and people are more valued for their ingenuity in applying it—some now in the Working Class or Service Class may move into the Creative Class and even the Super-Creative Core. Alongside the growth in essentially creative occupations, then, we are also seeing growth in creative content across other occupations. A prime example is the secretary in today's pared-down offices. In many cases this person not only takes on a host of tasks once performed by a large secretarial staff, but becomes a true office manager—channeling flows of information, devising and setting up new systems, often making key decisions on the fly. This person contributes more than "intelligence" or computer skills. She or he adds creative value. Everywhere we look, creativity is increasingly valued. Firms and organizations value it for the results that it can produce and individuals value it as a route to self-expression and job satisfaction. Bottom line: As creativity becomes more valued, the Creative Class grows.

10   Not all workers are on track to join, however. For instance in many lower-end service jobs we find the trend running the opposite way; the jobs continue to be "de-skilled" or "de-creatified." For a counter worker at a fast-food chain, literally every word and move is dictated by a corporate template: "Welcome to Food Fix, sir, may I take your order? Would you like nachos with that?" This job has been thoroughly taylorized—the worker is given far less latitude for exercising creativity than the waitress at the old, independent neighborhood diner enjoyed. Worse yet, there are many people who do not have jobs, and who are being left behind because they do not have the background and training to be part of this new system.

Growing alongside the Creative Class is another social grouping I call the Service Class—which contains low-end, typically low-wage and low-autonomy occupations in the so-called "service sector" of the economy: food-service workers, janitors and groundskeepers, personal care attendants, secretaries and clerical workers, and security guards and other service occupations.

In U.S. Bureau of Labor Statistics projections from the late 1990s and 2000, the fastest-growing job categories included "janitors and cleaners" and "waiters and waitresses" alongside "computer support specialists" and "systems analysts." The growth of this Service Class is in large measure a response to the demands of the Creative Economy. Members of the Creative Class, because they are well compensated and work long and unpredictable hours, require a growing pool of low-end service workers to take care of them and do their chores. This class has thus been created out of economic necessity because of the way the Creative Economy operates. Some people are temporary members of the Service Class, have high upward mobility and will soon move into the Creative Class—college students working nights or summers as food clerks or office cleaners, and highly educated recent immigrants driving cabs in New York City or Washington, D.C. A few, entrepreneurial ones may be successful enough to open their own restaurants, lawn and garden services and the like. But many others have no way out and are stuck for life in menial jobs as food-service help, janitors, nursing home orderlies, security guards and delivery drivers. At its minimum-wage worst, life in the Service Class is a grueling struggle for existence amid the wealth of others. By going "undercover" as a service worker, Barbara Ehrenreich provided a moving chronicle of what life is like for people in these roles in her book *Nickel and Dimed*.

A study of the Austin, Texas, economy sheds light on the growing gaps between the Creative and Service Classes. Austin is a leading center of the Creative Economy and consistently ranks among the top regions on my indicators. A study by Robert Cushing and Musseref Yetim of the University of Texas compared Austin, which in 1999 had a whopping 38 percent of its private-sector workforce in high-tech industries, to other regions in the state. Between 1990 and 1999, average private-sector wages in Austin grew by 65 percent, far and away the most in the state. During that same time, the gap between wages earned by the top fifth and the bottom fifth of the people in Austin grew by 70 percent—also far and away the most in the state. Remove the high-tech sector from the equation and both effects go away. There is a perfectly logical reason for the gap: High-tech specialists were in short supply so their wages were bid up. And in fairness, it should be noted that Austin's bottom fifth of wage earners weren't left out entirely. Their income did go up from 1990 to 1999, and more than for their counterparts in other Texas regions. Apparently Austin had a growing need for their services, too. But these trends do more than illustrate a widening income gap. They point to a real divide in terms of what people do with their lives—with the economic positions and lifestyle choices of some people driving and perpetuating the types of choices available to others. . . .

CREATIVE CLASS VALUES

The rise of the Creative Class is reflected in powerful and significant shifts in values, norms and attitudes. Although these changes are still in process and certainly not fully played out, a number of key trends have been discerned by researchers who study values, and I have seen them displayed in my field research across the United States. Not all of these attitudes break with the past: Some represent a melding of traditional values and newer ones. They are also values that have long been associated with more highly educated and creative people. On the basis of my own interviews and focus groups, along with a close reading of statistical surveys conducted by others, I cluster these values along three basic lines.

Individuality

The members of the Creative Class exhibit a strong preference for individuality and self-statement. They do not want to conform to organizational or institutional directives and resist traditional group-oriented norms. This has always been the case among creative people from "quirky" artists to "eccentric" scientists. But it has now become far more pervasive. In this sense, the increasing nonconformity to organizational norms may represent a new mainstream value. Members of the Creative Class endeavor to create individualistic identities that reflect their creativity. This can entail a mixing of multiple creative identities.

Meritocracy

15   Merit is very strongly valued by the Creative Class, a quality shared with Whyte's class of organization men. The Creative Class favors hard work, challenge and stimulation. Its members have a propensity for goal-setting and achievement. They want to get ahead because they are good at what they do.

Creative Class people no longer define themselves mainly by the amount of money they make or their position in a financially delineated status order. While money may be looked upon as a marker of achievement, it is not the whole story. In interviews and focus groups, I consistently come across people valiantly trying to defy an economic class into which they were born. This is particularly true of the young descendants of the truly wealthy—the capitalist class—who frequently describe themselves as just "ordinary" creative people working on music, film or intellectual endeavors of one sort or another. Having absorbed the Creative Class value of merit, they no longer find true status in their wealth and thus try to downplay it.

There are many reasons for the emphasis on merit. Creative Class people are ambitious and want to move up based on their abilities and effort. Creative people have always been motivated by the respect of their peers. The companies that employ them are often under tremendous competitive pressure and thus cannot afford much dead wood on staff: Everyone has to contribute. The pressure is more intense than ever to hire the best people regardless of race, creed, sexual preference or other factors.

But meritocracy also has its dark side. Qualities that confer merit, such as technical knowledge and mental discipline, are socially acquired and cultivated. Yet those who have these qualities may easily start thinking they were born with them, or acquired them all on their own, or that others just "don't have it." By papering over the causes of cultural and educational advantage, meritocracy may subtly perpetuate the very prejudices it claims to renounce. On the bright side, of course, meritocracy ties into a host of values and beliefs we'd all agree are positive—from faith that virtue will be rewarded, to valuing self-determination and mistrusting rigid caste systems. Researchers have found such values to be on the rise, not only among the Creative Class in the United States, but throughout our society and other societies.

Diversity and Openness

Diversity has become a politically charged buzzword. To some it is an ideal and rallying cry, to other a Trojan-horse concept that has brought us affirmative action and other liberal abominations. The Creative Class people I study use the word a lot, but not to press any political hot buttons. Diversity is simply something they value in all its manifestations. This is spoken of so often, and so matter-of-factly, that I take it to be a fundamental marker of Creative Class values. As my focus groups and interview reveal, members of this class strongly favor organizations and environments in which they feel that anyone can fit in and can get ahead.

20   Diversity of peoples is favored first of all out of self-interest. Diversity can be a signal of meritocratic norms at work. Talented people defy classification based on race, ethnicity, gender, sexual preference or appearance. One indicator of this preference for diversity is reflected in the fact that Creative Class people tell me that at job interviews they like to ask if the company offers same-sex partner benefits, even when they are not themselves gay. What they're seeking is an environment open to differences. Many highly creative people, regardless of ethnic background or sexual orientation, grew up feeling like outsiders, different is some way from most of their schoolmates. They may have odd personal habits or extreme styles of dress. Also, Creative Class people are mobile and tend to move around to different parts of the country; they may not be "natives" of the place they live even if they are American-born. When they are sizing up a new company and community, acceptance of diversity and of gays in particular is a sign that reads "nonstandard people welcome here." It also registers itself in changed behaviors and organizational policies. For example, in some Creative Class centers like Silicon Valley and Austin, the traditional office Christmas party is giving way to more secular, inclusive celebrations. The big event at many firms is now the Halloween party: Just about anyone can relate to a holiday that involves dressing up in costume.

While the Creative Class favors openness and diversity, to some degree it is a diversity of elites, limited to highly educated, creative people. Even though the rise of the Creative Class has opened up new avenues of advancement for women and members of ethnic minorities, its existence has certainly failed to put an end to long-standing divisions of race and gender. Within high-tech industries in particular these divisions still seem to hold. The world of high-tech creativity doesn't include many African-Americans. Several of my interviews noted that a typical high-tech company "looks like the United Nations minus the black faces." This is unfortunate but not surprising. For several reasons, U.S. blacks are underrepresented in many professions, and this may be compounded today by the so-called digital divide—black families in the United States tend to be poorer than average, and thus their children are less likely to have access to computers. My own research shows a negative statistical correlation between concentrations of high-tech firms in a region and non-whites as a percentage of the population, which is particularly disturbing in light of my other findings on the positive relationship between high-tech and other kinds of diversity—from foreign-born people to gays.

There are intriguing challenges to this kind of diversity that the members of the Creative Class are drawn to. Speaking of a small software company that had the usual assortment of Indian, Chinese, Arabic and other employees, an Indian technology professional said: "That's not diversity! They're all software engineers." Yet despite the holes in the picture, distinctive value changes are indeed afoot, as other researchers have clearly found.

THE POST-SCARCITY EFFECT

Ronald Inglehart, a political science professor at the University of Michigan, has documented the powerful shift in values and attitudes across the world in more than two decades of careful research. In three periods over the past twenty years, researchers participating in Inglehart's World Values Survey administered detailed questionnaires to random samples of adults in countries around the world. By 1995–1998, the last survey period, the number of nations studied had grown to sixty-five, including about 75 percent of the world's population. Along with specific issues like divorce, abortion and suicide, the survey delved into matters such as deference to authority versus deciding for oneself, openness versus insularity (can strangers be trusted?), and what, ultimately, is important in life. Inglehart and his colleagues have sifted the resulting data to look for internal correlations (which kind of values tend to go together) and for correlations with economic and social factors such as a nation's level of economic development, from of government and religious heritage. The researchers compared nations to one another, mapping out various similarities and differences—and they also looked for change over time.

Among other things, Inglehart found a worldwide shift from economic growth issues to lifestyle values, which he sometime refers to as shift from "survival" to "self-expression" values. Moreover where lifestyle issues are rising or dominant, as in the United States and most European societies, people tend to be relatively tolerant of other groups and in favor of gender equality. This is very much in line with Creative Class values. In everything from sexual norms and gender roles to environmental values, Inglehart finds a continued movement away from traditional norms to more progressive ones. Furthermore, as economies grow, living standards improve and people grow less attached to large institutions, they become more open and tolerant in their views on personal relationships. Inglehart believes this new value system reflects a "shift in what people want out of life, transforming basic norms governing politics, work, religion, family and sexual behavior."

25   In their 2000 book *The Cultural Creatives*, sociologist Paul H. Ray and psychologist Ruth Anderson report similar conclusions. They estimate that some 50 million Americans fall into the category of cultural creatives, having neither "traditional' nor conventionally "modern" values. These people tend to be socially active on issues that concern them pro-environment and in favor or gender equality. Many are spiritually oriented, though rejecting mainstream religious beliefs. Members of this group are more likely than others to be interested in personal development and relationships, have eclectic tastes, enjoy "foreign and exotic" experiences, and identify themselves as being "not financially materialistic." In short, these cultural creatives have values that Inglehart refers to as "postmaterialist."

This shift in values and attitudes, Inglehart argues, is driven by changes in our material conditions. In agricultural societies and even for much of the industrial age, people basically lived under conditions of scarcity. We had to work simply to survive. The rise of an affluent or "post-scarcity" economy means that we no longer have to devote all our energies just to staying alive, but have the wealth, time and ability to enjoy other aspects of life. This in turn affords us choices we did not have before. "Precisely because they attained high levels of economic security," writes Inglehart, "the Western societies that were the first to industrialize have gradually come to emphasize post-materialist values, giving higher priority to the quality of life than to economic growth. In this respect, the rise of post-materialist values reverses the rise of the Protestant ethic." The overriding trend appears to be

> an intergenerational shift from emphasis on economic and physical security toward increasing emphasis on self-expression, subjective well-being, and quality of life. . . . This cultural shift is found throughout advanced industrial societies; it seems to emerge among birth cohorts that have grown up under conditions in which survival is taken for granted.

The Nobel Prize-winning economist Robert Fogel concurs: "Today, people are increasingly concerned with what life is all about. That was not true for the ordinary individual in 1885 when nearly the whole day was devoted to earning the food, clothing, and shelter needed to sustain life." Even though many conservative commentators bemoan these shifts as hedonistic, narcissistic and damaging to society, the Creative Class is anything but radical or nonconformist. On the one hand, its members have taken what looked to be alternative values and made them mainstream. On the other, many of these values—such as the commitment to meritocracy and to hard work—are quite traditional and system-reinforcing. In my interviews, members of the Creative Class resist characterization as alternative or bohemian. These labels suggest being outside or even against the prevailing culture, and they insist they are part of the culture, working and living inside it. In this regard, the Creative Class has made certain symbols of nonconformity acceptable—even conformist. It is in this sense that they represent not an alternative group but a new and increasingly norm-setting mainstream of society.

Perhaps we are indeed witnessing the rise of what Mokyr calls *homo creativus*. We live differently and pursue new lifestyles because we see ourselves as a new kind of person. We are more tolerant and more liberal both because our material conditions allow it and because the new Creative Age tells us to be so. A new social class, in short, has risen to a position of dominance in the last two decades, and this shift has fundamentally transformed our economy and society—and continues to do so. The rest of this book will look at how these changes in our economy and society, in the class structure and in our values and identity are playing themselves out in the way we work and live in this new age.

Questions for Discussion

1. According to Florida, what is the "Creative Class" and what is its "basis"?
2. What are the "two components" of the Creative Class? What types of professions are included in each group? What do these two groups have most in common?
3. Why is creativity becoming more important to employers? How has and how will this demand affect the future of the Creative Class?
4. What are the main values of people in the Creative Class? How has our "post-scarcity" society contributed to the shaping of these values?

Ideas for Writing

1. Based on this reading's perspective as well as other sociological or economic perspectives, write an essay about the rise of the Creative Class and its future. In your essay consider the following issues: What types of people and which professions make up this class? What are its values? Why is this class growing so rapidly, and how big do you think it will become? Do you know

any people who belong to the Creative Class? Is this a type of work that you would like to pursue?

2. Write an essay arguing for or against the values of the Creative Class. Consider how the group can have a beneficial or detrimental affect on society. How has "post-scarcity" helped create these values? How will "post-scarcity" affect the workplace?

Second-Grade Teacher
KATY BRACKEN

This reading is included in Gig: Americans Talk about Their Jobs at the Turn of the Millennium *(2000), edited by Marisa Bowe, John Bowe, and Sabin Streeter. The original articles in this collection of over 120 first-person narratives on work were conceived as a tribute to the essays found in Studs Terkel's classic book,* Working *(1972), which was also a compilation of varied workers' oral histories. The following article, "Second-Grade Teacher," tells us the story of Katy Bracken and how she became an educator. The account is given in Bracken's own words, and her language is informal and conversational. Her narrative provides us with a useful and engaging glimpse into the inside world of elementary school teaching and the rewarding nature of this type of work.*

⬥

I was one of those people who was pretty much totally unable to decide what they wanted to do with themselves, When I graduated from college, I moved to Chicago. Why? I was dancing a lot and I just wanted to be in a city. Any city, it didn't matter. I didn't have any kind of long-term plan or anything. Then I started waitressing. [Laughs] That sobered me up a bit. I was too tired to think, much less dance. So I was like, "Okay, I'm going to get a normal job where I'm not running around all night, so I can do the dancing thing." And right away, I saw this teaching position advertised, an assistant for second grade. I lived right near the school, and it was in this old building and I thought that was cool, so I interviewed, and they hired me. And that's how I got into teaching [laughs]—randomly.

But I was so thrilled by it. I mean, there were problems—that first school was kind of weird. It was sort of going bankrupt and it had some very bizarre children—tough kids—a boy who'd been adopted that year, when he was nine, who had something seriously wrong and really didn't talk. Another boy who was always grabbing and fighting with other kids. It wasn't the best situation. But I just loved the teaching thing—with even the worst kids there was something interesting and kind of lovely. I was really into it in a way that I just hadn't been into anything before. So I started looking for another school and I found this place where I've been the last seven years. I had a friend who used to teach here and she got me an interview and I walked in and it was like I couldn't believe I'd been at the other place that was so dilapidated. This school has so much energy, so many happy kids. I just knew I had to work here. And, fortunately, I got along very well with the woman who interviewed me.

I started in the library, because that was the only position open, but I made sure that during every free moment, I went into classrooms and helped out with the kids—reading books with them and stuff. And after two months, a woman that I had been helping a lot was, like, "I want her to be my assistant." So I went into her classroom as an assistant teacher and I guess I did very well at that because, at the end of the year, I was offered a head teacher job for the next fall.

And suddenly, things got very weird because I wanted to do the job—it was totally my ambition by that point—but I was terrified. Absolutely terrified. Because I knew what a big deal it was.

Being a head teacher is incredibly challenging. It's all up to 5 you. There's twenty kids and you don't have any breaks during the day. You eat lunch with the kids, you're with them constantly, and you're responsible for everything. There are times, even as an assistant, where I'd be like, "I don't know how I'm going to make it." Like I want to go the bathroom just to get a minute's peace. The level of exhaustion is that high. There's also times when your responsibility is just overwhelming, like being responsible for their safety. Like three weeks ago I couldn't find a kid in the park. And I just—my whole life was flashing—this kid's been kidnapped and—life is now over. [Laughs] I mean, she was just away collecting sticks. But there are these moments of intense stress.

So I was just scared shitless to become a head teacher. And all that summer before I had to actually start doing it, I took classes at a teacher's education program to kind of prepare me. It was a very hands-on program, but still, I was totally nervous. I was inheriting my classroom from this woman who'd taught here for twenty-five years. She hadn't cleaned her room out, so the weeks before school began, I would go in each day and try to whittle down her stuff to what I wanted for my teaching. I was wading through like twenty-year-old mimeographs and just losing it because I couldn't make any decisions. I had, like, tremendous insomnia. I was crying a lot. I would ask the most ridiculous questions to every other teacher I could get my hands on: "Do you put the lined paper above the white paper? The white paper near the construction paper? What kind of sign should I have on the door?"

It was ridiculous. I was deluded. I mean, these things are important, but at the same time, once you get them down, it's like who cares? [Laughs] But there's a lot of obsessiveness in that first year being a head teacher. And, you know, just generally, I think I've always been a kind of anxious person—like I said, a little afraid of deciding what I want to do. My dad is a very successful pediatrician and he's great, very supportive and all that but, well, I've always felt one of the biggest crises of my life was deciding that I didn't want to do exactly what he does—even if that meant I didn't know what I wanted to do. I mean, I'll never forget the college thing of my dad— he thought I could do anything—and so I would go home on vacations from college and get infused by his confidence in me being able to be a doctor or whatever. I would be, like, "Right. I'm going to do the pre-med thing!" But then, back among my friends, I would be like, "I have no desire to do that. I want to dance or act or write poetry, or whatever," you know? It just took a while to just get past him—and realize that I was doing it fine the way I was going along.

Anyway, a lot of this kind of thing came to a head that summer before I became a head teacher. [Laughs] I was a wreck. But then, somehow, I finally set up my classroom and then my first year came. [Laughs] And I got a new bunch of problems.

This is a private school. And it's kind of known for artsiness, for letting the kids excel in the things that they're naturally good at. Our director doesn't like to hire people with education degrees—she wants people who are going to teach what they are passionate about. But what happened to me my first year is I was having these conflicting ideas because I'd gone to this summer teacher's ed program that was kind of philosophically entrenched. It was like you teach kids first what's around them and then what's far away. They actually had a code phrase for this that they said all the time: "Here now, far tomorrow." It meant that you first teach the here and now and then you teach the faraway. So you don't teach Native Americans first, you teach Lake Michigan. Because that's what's right here.

10 So I got very excited about teaching the kids about Lake Michigan. I did this unit on it and we went there a couple of times

and it was okay, but it seemed to go on too long. The kids weren't that excited about it. And our director wasn't into it at all because she hates that "here now" philosophy. She feels like it deprives kids of their imagination, because the here and now is so concrete. So then my second semester that first year I hadn't planned to do this, but I decided to do India. Which was instantly a huge success. Like it was so full of color and sexiness for the kids. I'd get these dance videos from the library that were amazing and I brought in all this Indian music and stuff and it just went great. It was basically my salvation. I've taught India every year since then. [Laughs] It's gotten to the point where parents often think I'm Indian, because of my [laughs] skin color and I'm so into it. And I'm not Indian at all, but so what?

The Indian gods are really exciting. I love them. I always start with Ganesh because he's a fat elephant who loves eating sweets and stuff. Very kid-friendly. And then the other Indian gods and goddesses, they're very nongendered—everyone wears makeup and there's these awesome warrior goddess women. There's just a lot of imaginative things to tap into with them. And there's also yoga— that's another way I get them into it. I do a lot of yoga, and all the stories and all the gods are related to physical poses in yoga. So that's instantly something to get the kids moving, you know, doing the Shiva's bow, which gets them involved.

It's been great. Over the years, I've just become more and more at ease. I mean, each summer I go through this anxiety about starting again. And I feel like, oh, my God, the kid's are going to hate it, or I'm going to get tired of teaching the same thing. But it always works out. It's always so enjoyable.

I've had some years that were less good then others. Three years ago, the character of that class was much more athletic, and the boys were—you know, it was the furor of the Bulls. The Chicago Bulls. [Laughs] So the boys were kind of macho and I could tell they weren't all that into this Indian stuff. But still, they had so much energy and they got into some of the dance and music. And I got through that year fine. I'm pretty confident that, now, given the time, I can make almost anything okay—at least in my classroom.

I really get along with kids this age. And I feel like this is a little bit weird, but I love their love. I don't know if I want to have kids or not, I can't picture it for many, many years. [Laughs] Because I don't really know how I'd do it—how I'd manage it. But I love the brand of love that comes from this age of kid. And I sometimes think that I'm being duped, because I experience such mutual adoration—me toward them and them toward me—and then I get into, like, the adult world where people don't do it anymore. Like they just—life is not about loving. Like in that direct way. Like there's no spontaneous hugging [laughs] which happens with these second-graders.

15   Sometimes I get done with a day and go home and I just miss that affection, that closeness. Like in a certain way, I just feel very blessed to have these kids, you know, in my life. They teach me, you know, they make me less nervous or something.

I think my ability to be affectionate has been very deeply influenced by this job, by being able to experience affection that's not sexual during the day. I have a lot of nonsexual affection with my friends now. Which is so healthy. I guess, basically, I just feel more comfortable with the world since I started teaching—and that comfort comes from, you know, hanging around with kids. It's had such an affect on me. I'm just, you know, comfortable. I feel like I'm in a good place, Like I like my job a lot. It's tiring and blah, blah, blah, but I don't have any long-term plans except this.

And it's funny, because last summer, I didn't plan to do it, but there's this two-week intensive dance class here with this semi-famous guy—and at the last minute, I decided to take it. And I was shot back in my head to those times before I started teaching when I was dancing all the time and I was all conflicted about what I wanted to do with my life. It was the scariest thing because at first I felt this euphoria. I felt like so powerful and so, like, I don't know—I just felt like I didn't need anybody. Like I wanted to get back into dance again. But then, somewhere in the middle of the two weeks, I just got totally sickened by it and scared by the selfishness of it. And I realized that I've been, like, redeemed by teaching. Like teaching was right for me. I'm a person that should be a teacher.

Questions for Discussion

1. Why was Katy Bracken excited by her first experience as a teacher? What was it about the job that made her so happy? What problems did she encounter in her work? What made her continue on as a teacher despite these challenges?
2. Bracken was initially anxious when she became a head teacher. What did she do to overcome her fears? Have you ever had to face this type of anxiety in relation to work? How did you succeed?
3. What are some of the specific duties that Bracken needs to perform as a second-grade teacher? What skills does an elementary school teacher need to have? Why is teaching challenging? What are some of its rewards?

4. Why does Bracken say that she was "redeemed by teaching?" What do you think she means by this statement? What does she love the most about being a second-grade teacher and what has she learned from being a teacher?

Ideas for Writing

1. Write an essay on your own sense of indecision and confusion about choosing a job and how you overcame it. Bracken begins her essay by saying that she was "one of those people who was pretty much totally unable to decide what they wanted to do with themselves." Does her initial indecision make her success seem more significant? Have you ever felt like Bracken? How did you eventually make a decision? Why do you think it is so difficult for many people in our culture to make work-related choices?
2. Interview a K-12 teacher and do some research on the profession. Write an essay about the positive and negative aspects of being an educator. What type of person is more likely to enjoy teaching and to continue to improve as a teacher while working in this profession? Ask one of your teachers about the pros and cons of his or her job. Do you think that teaching is a profession that you would be interested in? Include direct quotes from your interview to support your conclusions.

Extending the Theme

1. The authors in this chapter suggest a number of reasons for valuing work. Write an essay that integrates the ideas of those writers with whom you agree or strongly disagree as you shape your own theory about the value of work.
2. Referring to as many of the selections in this chapter as are relevant, write your own extended definition of the meaning of work. Be sure to also refer to your own experiences and observations, as well as doing more research on the meaning or definitions of work in America today.
3. Considering the ideas brought up in this chapter's selections, write an essay that presents your interpretation of how the value and meaning of work have already changed and will continue to be transformed by our changing social values and culture.
4. From reading the selections, how do you think an individual can make his or her outlook and approach to work more positive and rewarding? Analyze your own work experiences, and your ideas, and feelings about working, and try to come up with a way to make your own attitude toward your working life more positive, productive, and fulfilling.

CHAPTER 2

Work and Family Life

The decade of the 1960s marked a turning point in American family. The gender-specific family roles of the 1950s, when men went to work and mothers stayed home to raise their children and maintain their homes, were coming to an end. Feminists challenged mothers to think about their identities outside of their mothering, their relationships with their husbands, their children, to the public world of work and politics. Many women who had children returned to work but did not give up their responsibilities to their children. In this same decade, divorces became easier to obtain, and the sexual revolution changed the way women thought about and acted on their sexual feelings. At the same time, more and more immigrant families came to the United States with different values about the meaning of family life, and gays as well began to engage in long-term relationships and to demand the right to raise children. After more than forty years of social unrest and political change, the American family in the new millennium is dramatically different from the American family of the 1950s.

This chapter focuses on how work and family life reveal the new values and challenges as well as how many of the traditional assumptions about work and family life have endured. Today's generation of parents has many questions to consider and dilemmas to face as they balance their working lives in the workplace and their working lives caring for their children. If one parent works, then the other will have to teach their children how to adjust to life at school and to discriminate within our consumer culture and media, and he or she will have to do all the work required to make sure that their children remain healthy, continue to learn, and develop a sense of security and happiness. If both parents work, their lives may be more hectic, but the parent who does not stay at home will not experience the stigma of not working, will not have to feel dependent on a partner for money, will not have to deal with the day-to-day issues involved in raising children. Many upper- and middle-class families have to decide if both parents should work or if one parent should stay home to care for the children—and then which parent will it be?

Our first reading, "She Works, He Doesn't," by journalists Peg Tyre and Daniel McGinn, explores the different scenarios that mothers and fathers grapple with as they decide who is going to work. We learn about the frustrations and joys of middle-class and working-class stay-at-home dads as well as the expectations of the mother who works full-time to support her family. This article suggests that children are happy with either mom or dad at home, and that those children who do not have two careerists as parents get more love and attention. Thinking about the case histories featured in this article, we can see that family life is happier if both parents have flexible jobs. However, the many corporations and workplaces not willing to accommodate the needs of parents with children at home remain obstacles to a balanced work and family solution.

In our next selection by Ginia Bellafante, "Two Fathers, with One Happy to Stay at Home," we learn how career-track parents may decide to live on one salary—the salary of the parent who makes the most money, while the other stays home—regardless of gender. Although this essay is about two gay career fathers, the issues related to the status of the parent who works and the parent who does not are the same as in heterosexual career families.

Our next selection, "Doctor's Daughter" by Julia McMurray, is written by a woman whose parents were both doctors but her mother had to give up her career to take care of the family. A physician herself, McMurry rethinks her mother's decisions to stay at home while she struggles to balance work and family life. Her reminiscences about her life as a daughter bring depth to her understanding of being a working mother as she realizes that there are no simple solutions for families with two working parents.

The problems that single mothers face are even more serious. In "Children Left Behind," journalist Stephanie Mencimer focuses on the extreme instability of working-class single-parent families. Her disturbing facts and narratives demonstrate that single mothers need more help with child care. Mencimer argues for national support of quality child care for all classes of children. Her argument points out that we all live with the negative consequences of what happens when children do not have appropriate supervision.

Although there are an increasing number of single-parent families in our country, immigrant extended families have helped us develop a new perspective on American work. Despite the closeness of such families, until recently immigrant families encouraged children to move on to mainstream careers after putting them through school with funds raised from family-owned businesses. Recently, however, the immigrant family has become more of a communal enterprise, as children are returning to family businesses after college to modernize the workplace and to make the companies more productive and more lucrative. In the essay "Legacy of Dreams" by *Time* magazine reporter Lisa Takeuchi Cullen, we learn how the children of immigrants are bringing American cultural ideas to their businesses and helping them to succeed.

The selections we have included in this chapter demonstrate the need for social change in the workplace to accommodate the real needs of parents and their children. We believe that these readings will also convince you that both national and state governments must provide more support for families who work and pay taxes.

She Works, He Doesn't
PEG TYRE AND DANIEL McGINN

Peg Tyre graduated from Brown University with a degree in English literature. She is a reporter who has written for CNN, New York Newsday, Columbia Journalism Review, New York Magazine, *and* Ladies' Home Journal. *Since 2001 she has written for and worked as a general editor at* Newsweek, *where she has covered stories on criminal justice, media, and social trends. Tyre also coauthored* Two Seconds Under the World, *a non-fiction account of the 1993 World Trade Center Bombing. Daniel McGinn is a* Newsweek *national correspondent who has worked for the magazine since 1992. He has written for* The New York Times, The Boston Globe Sunday Magazine, Bloomberg Personal Finance, *and other magazines, focusing primarily on issues related to business and economics. McGinn has appeared as a guest on NBC's* Today Show, *NPR, CNBC, and MSNBC. The following* Newsweek *story by Tyre and McGinn, "She Works, He Doesn't" (2003), examines the flexible child-care patterns of middle-class couples who are adjusting to situations in*

*which the wife is the primary breadwinner and the husband finds
fulfillment in staying at home with the children.*

———————————— ✦ ————————————

Since the beginning of time, anthropologists believe, women
have been programmed to seek a mate who can provide for a
family—whether that means dragging the mastodon back to the
cave or making the payments on the Volvo. So when Laurie Earp
walked down the aisle, she joined hands with a man most brides
would consider a good catch: a lawyer. "By marrying a lawyer,"
she says, "I thought he'd be able to bring in money." Freed from
the need to earn a big paycheck, Laurie imagined herself in a
part-time job, one that allowed her to spend long afternoons with
their children.

For a time the Earps realized that vision. Jonathan earned a six-
figure salary as a lawyer at Napster, while Laurie worked leisurely
hours as a fund-raising consultant. But last May Jonathan was laid
off; he still can't find work. So, reluctantly, Laurie has become the
breadwinner. On a recent evening their son, Dylan, 5, skipped
through their home in Oakland, Calif., praising how well his stay-
at-home dad cares for him. But Dylan is the only one pleased with
the turnabout. "This is not the life I wanted," says Laurie, who's
heading off to an after-dinner meeting with clients. Meanwhile,
Jonathan spends his days doing housework and preparing badly
cooked dinners. "I hate it all," he says.

Like several million American families, the Earps are experiencing the quiet, often painful transformation that takes place
when Dad comes home with a severance package. The unemployment rate hit 6 percent last month, and while that's low by historical standards, some economists say it underestimates the difficulties facing laid-off workers—especially white-collar men who've
been victimized by corporate downsizings. Despite Alan Green-
span's predictions of rosier times on the horizon, some experts talk
of a growing problem of "underemployment" that goes beyond the
nation's 8.8 million jobless. Their numbers include people forced to
accept part-time work, all those newfound "consultants" who are
playing computer solitaire but producing little income, and "discouraged workers" who've given up job hunting altogether.

The good news, at least for the 1.7 million unemployed men
who are married, is that their wives are better equipped than any
generation in history to pick up the financial slack. Women are
currently earning more college degrees and M.B.A.s than men.
In 1983, women made up 34 percent of high-paying "executive,

administrative and managerial" occupations; in 2001 they were nearly half of that category. They've also weathered the recession better than men, because traditionally female industries like health care and education have suffered less than male-dominated businesses like manufacturing. Although the average woman's wage still trails a man's (78 cents to the dollar), enough women are breaking into better-paying professions that in 30.7 percent of married households with a working wife, the wife's earnings exceeded the husband's in 2001. Many of these women were born and bred for the office; they wouldn't want it any other way.

5   Within these homes, some of the husbands have voluntarily dialed back their careers (or quit work entirely) to care for kids and live off their wives' income. Some experts use a new phrase to describe high-income female providers: Alpha Earners. For some families, this shift works wonderfully; for others (especially those forced into it by layoffs), it creates tensions. Regardless, it's a trend we'd better get used to. Like runners passing the baton in a track event, many 21st-century couples will take turns being the primary breadwinner and the domestic god or goddess as their careers ebb and flow. Says marriage historian Stephanie Coontz: "These couples are doing, in a more extreme form, what most couples will have to do in the course of their working lives."

Most experts believe the number of families converting to the "Mr. Mom" lifestyle remains quite small. According to the Bureau of Labor Statistics, just 5.6 percent of married couples feature a wife who works and a husband who doesn't. But that information is misleading: most of those nonworking husbands are retired, disabled or full-time students, not househusbands who care for the kids. On the other hand, many of the men who have put their careers on the back burner to watch the kids still have part-time or entrepreneurial gigs of some sort, so they don't show up in that number. So to better understand the Alpha Earner phenomenon, some researchers focus instead on those households where the wife outearns the husband. They're crunching the data to eliminate men who are retirees or students, and to seek families where the wife's career appears dominant (by finding, say, households where the wife earns 60 percent or more of the family income). Until the 1990s these numbers were tiny. But University of Maryland demographer Suzanne Bianchi recently began analyzing new 2001 data. Her initial results suggest that 11 percent of marriages feature an Alpha Earner wife. There's probably one in your neighborhood: in a *Newsweek* poll, 54 percent of Americans said they "personally know a couple where the woman is clearly the major wage earner and the man's career is secondary."

The shift is showing up more frequently in pop culture, too. "Friends" fans spent much of this season watching Monica support her unemployed husband, Chandler. (To recycle an old Thursday-night catchphrase: "Not that there's anything wrong with that.") Eddie Murphy hits theaters this week in "Daddy Day Care," in which he plays a laid-off dad whose wife becomes the primary breadwinner. In bookstores, Alpha Earners are at the heart of Allison Pearson's novel "I Don't Know How She Does It" and "The Bitch in the House," a collection of feminist essays. "There are few things that make a man less attractive to women than financial instability," writes one contributor. "We can deal with men in therapy, we can deal with men crying, but I don't think gender equality will ever reach the point where we can deal with men broke."

Fathers who voluntarily choose the househusband role are challenging that sensibility. Last month three Chicago men gathered for breakfast at a suburban strip mall. Each has a wife with a lucrative job—two in finance, one in market research—and each man had achieved enough workplace success that he felt able to ease off the throttle. Ron Susser, 43, was chief financial officer for a consulting firm; today he practices the 4 O'Clock Shuffle, his name for his frantic afternoon cleaning binge. "When my wife comes home, she expects the pantry to be stocked, the house to be in order and dinner cooked—I consider that my job," Susser says. David Burns, 49, was a computer consultant; today he's a Brownie leader. Scott Keeve, 52, oversaw 150 employees for a food distributor. When the nanny told his two kids she'd quit if they didn't behave, Keeve took the job himself. Like so many women before them, these guys are learning to adapt to a job without paychecks, business lunches or "attaboys." You get the sense that if the Lifetime cable channel installed cameras in their homes, there's a ready-made reality show to be found in their bouts of ambivalence.

For Bill Laut, a former real-estate appraiser, those moments come frequently. While his wife, Sheila, racks up frequent-flier miles as a business-development executive, Bill hauls their 6-year-old triplets to the grocery store, where strangers gawk. "Your poor wife," they say, to which Laut has a standard reply: "I look around very dramatically and then ask them, 'Do you see her here?'" When his kids were younger, he'd be watching football with friends, and talk would inevitably turn to work. "I changed 27 diapers today," Bill would interject, only to be heckled: "Get a job!" "At parties I feel like an outcast," Bill says. "I tell people what I do and some of them are thinking, 'What a freeloader.' Everyone pats you on the back, but I wonder, are they patronizing me or being sincere?"

10   But on good days, many househusband-by-choice families are so jubilant about their lifestyle they sound like the "after" example in an ad for antidepressants. Dan and Lynn Murray were both Chicago lawyers when Lynn became pregnant with their triplets. Assessing their lives, they decided Lynn was happier in the office. "I'm sort of a type-A personality who likes to control my environment, and there's more of that at work than at home," she says. Today Dan cares for their five children; Lynn hopes he never returns to work. Brian and Maria Sullivan of Highland Park, Ill., saw their income drop 40 percent when Brian quit his sales job to care for their two kids, now 5 and 3 (Maria's a VP with a big computer company). Brian had resisted quitting, but now he sees the upside. "How many dads get to potty-train their kids?" he says. When they're teenagers, Brian would like to spend some afternoons on the golf course. "That's fine as long as he's chaperoning every field trip and is there at every sports practice," Maria says.

Many such couples have simply decided that no matter how much lip service companies pay to "family friendly" policies, it's simply not possible to integrate two fast-track careers and kids without huge sacrifices. So they do a cold-eyed calculation, measuring the size and upside potential of each parent's paycheck, and opting to keep whoever's is larger. For the highest-achieving women, the trend is striking. Last fall *Fortune* reported that more than one third of its "50 Most Powerful Women in Business" have a stay-at-home man (it dubbed them "trophy husbands"). But this trend reaches women far below the executive-vice-president rank. Patty Lewis, 42, is a video producer and meeting planner in east Dallas; her husband, Spencer Prokop, 45, is an actor. When son Chase arrived, her income was steadier, so Prokop stayed home. Dad feels isolated, and he's given up on lugging Chase along to occasional auditions. "This notion that I would have time to work on myself—well, that goes right out the window," says Prokop, who misses the luxury of uninterrupted bathroom time. After Lewis's 12-hour workdays, she's often too beat for spousal conversation. Sometimes Prokop thinks he's nagging his wife the same way his stay-at-home mom nagged his father. While they've no regrets that Chase enjoyed a full-time dad for 3½ years, Prokop is ready for a change. Their son started day care two weeks ago.

The wives of these househusbands have one universal regret: they spend too little time with their children. Of course, two-career couples with kids in day care express similar sentiments. Still, becoming the family's only revenue stream can add a dose of anxiety, even to a job you love. "I feel an intense pressure being the sole wage earner," says Sally Williams, 28, a Philadelphia lawyer with a 4-year-old daughter and a stay-at-home husband. "The house, the car—everything is riding on my shoulders." Some Alpha Earners say colleagues assume that their husbands are deadbeats who can't hold jobs. They also complain about the other extreme: how the novelty of Dad's dialing back can lead people to lavish him with too much praise. Says Beth Burkstrand-Reid, a lawyer in Washington, D.C.: "I'm doing a good job of supporting the family, [but] no one is giving me a pat on the back."

Feminists see the emerging era—when it's no longer the default choice that the kids will be watched by Mom, the nanny or a day-care center—as a necessary evolution. "The first half [of the feminist vision] was to liberate women from domestic servitude," says Suzanne Levine, a founding editor of *Ms. Magazine* and author of "Father Courage: What Happens When Men Put Family First." "The second half was to integrate the men back into the family." But while many dads now help with 3 a.m. feedings, it hasn't led to wholesale acceptance of wives as breadwinners. In the *Newsweek* poll, 41 percent of Americans agreed that "it is much better for everyone involved if the man is the achiever outside the home and the woman takes care of the home and family." One in four said it was "generally not acceptable" for a woman to be the major wage earner in a marriage.

While those attitudes may fester, the data suggest women's economic power will only grow. And as you plot out those trend lines a few decades, it's easy to imagine more-dramatic implications. For example, conventional wisdom is that once a man earns a certain income, whether his wife works becomes optional. Does that mean work will become equally optional for men whose wives bring home big paychecks? For many families, it appears so: in the *Newsweek* poll, 34 percent of men said that in their relationship, if the wife landed a big pay raise, the husband would consider not working or reducing his hours.

Here's a related twist: we know many women consider a man's   15
earning potential when choosing spouses. (Why do you think they're hiding the bachelors' occupations on "Mr. Personality"?) But as women's earnings rise, are more men paying attention to women's earning potential when they choose a mate? Yes, says University of Wisconsin economist Maria Cancian, who believes high-earning women are starting to be seen by men as a "good catch." As for high-powered women, Cancian wonders if their view may be changing,

too. "Are we now in a situation where very career-oriented women might look for husbands that are less career-oriented" and better equipped to nurture the kids full time?

Those questions will take years to answer. In the short term, there are aspects of this role reversal that are less cheery. By all accounts, the shift to wife as breadwinner is far more difficult when it's forced on couples because of Hubby's layoff. Predicting which families will suffer most is largely intuitive. Men who identify closely with their jobs or believe in traditional gender roles are hit hardest. Younger couples—the ones who grew up listening to "Free to Be . . . You and Me" while their moms were at work tend to take the turnabout more in stride . . .

But there are also wrinkles that aren't obvious. Working-class families may suffer less psychic whiplash because lesser-skilled workers have always been more susceptible to layoffs. As layoffs have crept up into white-collar ranks, they've taken more families by surprise. "When transitions are unexpected, then people are more likely to think it's somehow your fault, and that compounds the problems," says University of California, Berkeley, marriage researcher Philip Cowan.

Sherie Zebroswki was so unprepared for her husband Sean's layoff that she thought he was kidding when he came home with the news. The $80,000-plus-commissions he'd earned as an Austin, Texas, software salesman had allowed Sherie to care for their two children, train for triathlons and teach Sunday school. After his layoff two years ago, Sean spent months unsuccessfully looking for a similar job. For a while, the couple just hung on. "I tried not to fault him—he was good at what he did," Sherie says. "But after a while, you can't help but question: Is he looking in the right places? Could he be doing more?" To pay the bills, Sherie began turning her hobby—decorative painting—into a business. Soon she was working 10-hour days—and doing most of the housework while Sean surfed the Web. When their parish priest asked how they were doing, Sherie burst into tears. She told the priest: "I understand how the stress of being unemployed can break up a marriage."

So the Zebrowskis sat down for what they recall as The Talk. "I said, 'Either get a job at a checkout counter or you have to help me,' " Sherie says. So Sean created a marketing plan for her painting business. He began estimating jobs and boosting prices. They began hiring subcontractors. They're surviving, but it's far from ideal. "I'm still looking for a job," Sean says. "When I get it, Sherie can go back to sleeping in. This is not what I want to do, but I like to eat. I will get back to selling software. It's just a matter of when."

One element of the Zebrowskis' experience is near universal: 20 among these couples, who does the housework becomes a battle-field. Some men claim wives develop bionic eyesight once the husband is home all day. "I don't tend to see dirt, but she can spot a single molecule," says Brian Reid, a former reporter who now cares for daughter Clio while his wife practices law. Sociologists speculate that some men actually do less housework when they stop working. Why? Being out of work already threatens their manhood, and taking on "feminine" tasks like cleaning the toilet might only make them feel worse.

For families of laid-off househusbands, there's a more obvi-ous source of marital tension: money. During the Internet boom, Gregg Wetterman prospered by organizing networking parties for Dallas techies. His wife, Jennie, remembers those days fondly. "The summer of 2001, I was at the pool every day," Jennie says. "I went scuba diving, sky diving—I must have read 30 books that summer." But when the tech bubble burst, Gregg bounced through a series of unstable jobs. As his career outlook became bleaker, an old boss of Jennie's called and asked if she wanted a management job at Old Navy. Says Gregg: "When she got the op-portunity, I said, 'You don't have to,' but inside I was saying, 'Please, please, please. . . .' "

While Jennie works 50 hours a week, Gregg carts their kids to school and works on documentary films (he hasn't sold anything yet). Their two cars have a combined 286,000 miles; they've ditched their cell phones to cut expenses. At the kitchen table, the tension is palpable. Gregg argues it's smarter for him to keep pursuing nonpaying opportunities related to his aspirations—filmmaking and technology marketing—than to take an unpleasant job just to pay the bills. When the economy picks up, he figures he'll find something that pays well in his field. But he realizes the family can't wait forever. "I'm not pulling my weight financially," he says. Jennie is sometimes resentful. "I would just like for every-body to do their part," she says. "I don't want to be in this situa-tion two years down the road. I'll have to put my foot down." Gregg says it may not come to that. "There's no telling," he says. "Jennie could get a better job."

For many couples, switching in and out of roles may become a routine part of life. Counselors say that 21st-century careers will involve more jumps between industries and more time out of work for retraining or as a result of downsizing. Ted and Jenny Cater, 40 and 43, already have that routine down pat. In 1999 Ted, a salesman, relocated to San Francisco with his company. When his employer went bankrupt, Jenny, who works in marketing, immediately received a call about a $100,000-a-year job in Atlanta. So they moved her career to the front burner; Ted stayed at home with daughter Megan. Then two months ago Jenny was laid off. They're expecting a baby next month, but by July they'll both be job hunting. "Whoever wins the best position wins a ticket back to coffee breaks and time to check e-mail," Jenny says. "Not that we don't want to stay at home with the kids, but we are both geared for working."

Some younger couples are talking about these issues long before kids or joblessness enters their lives. Jennifer McCaskill is a 33-year-old Washington, D.C., lawyer; Ryan Schock, 28, is an accountant. As they look ahead to their September wedding, they're already talking about who might care for their future children. "Quite honestly, I don't want to stay at home," McCaskill says. "I won't make partner if I'm not working full time—and my earnings potential is higher." Schock's response: he'd love to be a full-time father. "He has a lot more patience than I do," McCaskill says. "I think he would be a better parent for our kids." With his master's degree and experience, Schock doesn't think a few years off would kill his career. "She would lose more than I would," Schock says. As more Alpha Earners roam the earth, that kind of outlook may be worth a premium. Forget doctors or lawyers. For a certain kind of woman, a laid-back guy like Ryan Schock may become the ultimate good catch.

Questions for Discussion

1. In the context of the author's opening examples, what is ironic about Laurie Earp's decision to go back to work after her child is born? Discuss the implications of this irony for an entire generation of parents who thought that the man would be the family's primary breadwinner.
2. What is an Alpha Earner? Why are there more Alpha Earners than ever before? Why is this both a positive and negative turn of events?
3. How do very successful men adjust to the role of Mr. Mom in contrast to less ambitious men who accept the role of primary nurturer and housekeeper? How are children affected having Mr. Mom fathers?
4. What range of reactions do breadwinner mothers experience about their husbands who have become Mr. Mom? Do you think that this trend in reversed family roles will continue to grow? Explain.

Ideas for Writing

1. Do some additional research to find out more about the increasing number of men who assume the role of Mr. Mom and the increasing number of women who are becoming the family's primary breadwinner. Do sociologists' studies suggest that this will improve the quality of family life and make men and women more equal partners in raising their children? Write an essay about what you have learned from researching this topic.
2. If you are a male, imagine that you have become a Mr. Mom. How would you adjust to your new role? What would be the biggest challenges? What would you like most? If you are a female, imagine that you have become the family's primary breadwinner. How would you adjust to your new role? What would be the biggest challenges? What would you like most? Write an essay or short story about one of these scenarios.

Two Fathers, with One Happy to Stay at Home
GINIA BELLAFANTE

Ginia Bellafante is a reporter for Time *magazine and* The New York Times; *she has written over 300 articles for the* Times *on cultural style, film, and fashion. For* Time *she has written controversial articles on feminism and current media role models for women. The following article, which presents facts and case histories related to gay fathers who stay home with their children, appeared in* The New York Times *in 2003.*

———————— ✦ ————————

Right before Christmas, Jamie McConnell arrived at the Lake Country School here, as he does most days of the week, to pick up his son, Ben, 3. Hardly short on spunk, Ben made his way out to the snowy playground, and Mr. McConnell, as parents have done since the dawn of swings and monkey bars, trailed behind.

Mr. McConnell had plenty of time to watch Ben romp and to invite one of his classmates and his mother home for peanut butter and jelly sandwiches.

For years, Mr. McConnell ate very different lunches. He was a corporate litigator at Dorsey & Whitney, among the country's most prestigious law firms. But since he and Dr. Bill Atmore, an anesthesiologist, adopted Ben as an infant, taking care of the child has been his full-time job. Dr. Atmore, his partner of eight years, works full time.

In assuming those roles, demographers say, the two are part of an emerging population of gay men who are not only raising children but are also committed to the idea that one parent should leave the workplace to do it. Of 9,328 same-sex couples with children whose census returns were randomly selected for analysis by the Census Bureau, 26 percent of the male couples included a stay-at-home parent, said Gary Gates, a demographer with the Urban Institute, a nonpartisan research organization in Washington. That figure is one percentage point more than for married couples with children and four percentage points higher than for female couples, said Mr. Gates, who performed the analysis for this article.

5   The percentage of men who stay at home is significantly smaller among married heterosexual couples, Mr. Gates said.

The obstacles of finding surrogate mothers and of discriminatory adoption laws that favor heterosexual couples have led some gay men to pursue parenthood with fervor.

"Being a planned gay father is such a project in itself," said Judith Stacey, a professor of sociology at New York University and a senior scholar at the Council on Contemporary Families, a research organization. Often, Professor Stacey said, gay fathers or those aspiring to be "remain very judgmental of parents who don't stay home."

To some gay men, the idea of entrusting the care of a hard-won child to someone else seems to defeat the purpose of parenthood.

Ray Friedmann, of Portland, Ore., gave up an accounting job at a credit union after he and his partner adopted their daughter, Ceriwen, now six months old. Unable to join his partner's medical plan because it does not provide for domestic partners, Mr. Friedmann, like many other gay fathers, pays for his own health insurance.

10   "We never thought we'd even be able to have this child," Mr. Friedmann said. "When we had the opportunity to do it, we wanted to give her the best attention and love."

Four years ago, after Bernie Cummings and his partner, Ernie Johnston, a marketing executive at Warner Brothers, had a baby girl, Caelan, through a surrogate mother, Mr. Cummings left his job as a managing director at Ogilvy Public Relations. Since then, they have added twins to their family, also through surrogacy.

"I've taken myself out of an industry that moves pretty quickly," said Mr. Cummings, who lives in Los Angeles. "But if I were working, I'd miss that moment when Caelan was just getting up from her nap, grabbing and holding on to me."

Same-sex couples with a stay-at-home parent are doing this even though census figures show that their median household income, $35,000, is lower than the $45,000 for a heterosexual married couple with a stay-at-home parent, Mr. Gates of the Urban Institute said.

The 2000 census found that there were some 60,000 male couple households with children in America, and close to 96,000 female couple households. Those figures are about 20 percent of all male couples and a third of all female couples.

Rob Calhoun and his partner refinanced their home in subur-   15
ban Atlanta when Mr. Calhoun quit his job as a social worker to stay home with their baby daughter. "We really couldn't afford it," Mr. Calhoun said.

Sociologists, gender researchers and gay parents themselves say that because gay men are liberated from the cultural expectations and pressures that women face to balance work and family life, they may approach raising children with a greater sense of freedom and choice.

They may also not fear stigmatization in these new roles, said Ellen Lewin, chairwoman of the women's studies department at the University of Iowa. Professor Lewin is the author of "Lesbian Mothers" (Cornell University Press, 1993) and is working on a study of gay fathers.

Conversely, feminism's legacy may leave lesbians more ideologically committed to equality in their relationships, said Christopher Carrington, a professor of sociology at San Francisco State University and the author of "No Place Like Home" (University of Chicago Press, 2002), which examines how gay and lesbian couples divide household labor.

That staying at home constitutes the just and noble course of parenthood was a sentiment echoed again and again in more than a dozen interviews with gay fathers.

Mike Farina, 40, left his job as an engineer in Anaheim, Calif.,   20
after adopting twins with his partner in 1998.

"In the beginning, I was even pig-headed about it," said Mr. Farina, who now has four children with his partner. "I wanted the kids to bond with us. I didn't want any help. In those first few years, I didn't even get baby sitters. I thought, 'That's my job.'"

Though many gay fathers may enter into domesticity with few conflicts or reservations, the pressures of starting a new life stripped of professional status can mirror those faced by nonworking mothers. The transition may be even rockier, given that male identity is largely defined by achievements outside the confines of nurseries, mud rooms and kitchens.

Professor Carrington said some of the domestically oriented men he observed struggled with self-esteem. "Men who make these choices really grapple with how to portray their lives to their friends, families, to service people and repairmen," he said.

For Tom Howard, a stay-at-home father of three adopted children, all younger than 4, the consequence of his decision struck two years ago, just before April 15. "I was filling out our tax returns for the first entire calendar year I was not working, and my occupation went from 'professor' to 'homemaker.' I felt like someone had put a knife in my stomach and twisted it."

25   For the preceding 10 years, Mr. Howard, who has a doctorate in microbiology, had worked at the University of Southern California, first as a researcher at its virology laboratory and then also as a professor at its medical school. "I can truly empathize with the women's movement now," Mr. Howard said. "I know that I've committed career suicide."

After the birth of his first child, Emma, Mr. Howard, now 47, took a three-month paid paternity leave from the university, returning to work in February 2000. At the same time, his partner of 17 years, Ken Yood, 40, was working his way to a partnership at a Los Angeles law firm. "We realized pretty quickly that Ken's pay scale was going to support the family," he said.

No matter how fair-minded the intentions of partners may be, the myriad obligations of home stewardship invariably fall to the partner who remains at home.

After Tom Seid, 47, and his partner, Howard Ronder, the creative director of Gaiam, a lifestyle company in Boulder, Colo., adopted their son, Matthew, four years ago, Mr. Seid left his career as a feature-film editor. Their shift to a single income meant that they could no longer afford a housekeeper. Now, Mr. Seid's day consists of shopping, cleaning and dropping off and picking up his son from school.

The choice leaves many facing a loss of financial independence that may result in a suddenly dismal credit rating or strong feelings of guilt about buying a CD or sweater.

30   "I have a problem asking for money, and I have to ask for money every time we're paying the bills," said Bill Koch, who stays at home with his 4-year-old son, Frankie, while his partner of eight years, Paul Lennander, works as an investigator at a children's social service agency here.

Mr. Koch, who previously worked in internal technology at General Mills, said that a lack of income had left him feeling invisible.

"After I'd been home a few months, we went to lease a car," Mr. Koch recalled. "We'd sold my car to come up with the money, and the whole time the salesman is only talking to Paul. The guy just looked right through me. Only Paul's name could appear on the lease, and I was just sitting there the whole time twirling my pearls, so to speak."

Still, Mr. Koch, like many of the other gay fathers interviewed, did not betray any eagerness to return to the work world soon.

As Peter Vitale, a gay stay-at-home father in the Twin Cities, put it, "If I were honest, I'd say that I want to do an excellent job at this because I know the world has me under a microscope."

Questions for Discussion

1. Based on statistics of families of male couples with a child, 26 percent have one parent who stays home full-time. In the families of male/female couples, 25 percent have one parent who stays home full-time, whereas in families of female couples, 22 percent have one parent who stays home full-time. In the families of male/female couples, the male is much less likely to stay home. How does Judith Stacey, Professor of Sociology, interpret these statistics and how do you interpret them?

2. Why does one member of a gay couple with a child or children often have to pay for his or her own medical insurance if he or she is not working? Why does that person stay at home? Do you think the law governing insurance for gay partners should be made by the national government or by state governments? Explain your point of view.

3. Many stay-at-home gay fathers believe that remaining with their children is "the just and normal course of parenthood." In spite of their convictions, what conflicts do some gay fathers experience about staying home?

4. Gay fathers who stay at home suffer a similar loss of self-esteem as do stay-at-home mothers: Besides other issues, they often feel "invisible." What conclusions do you draw from this information? What social changes could be implemented to make stay-at-home parents feel better about their work?

Ideas for Writing

1. Write an essay in support of gay marriage or in opposition to it. First do a significant amount of research on the topic, which will help you to clarify your thinking. Be sure to acknowledge your opponent's point of view.

2. Interview a gay couple who have a child or children. Try to learn as much as you can about the struggles and joys that they face as parents. Then write an essay that explains what you learned from your interview. Consider the following issues: What are the most difficult issues facing gay parents? How do you feel about the problems that stay-at-home parents face? How has your opinion on gay marriage changed as a result of doing the interview? What social changes might make the lives of stay-at-home parents more rewarding?

Doctor's Daughter
JULIA McMURRAY

Julia McMurray attended medical school at the University of North Carolina, completed her internship and residency at the Medical Center in the Bronx, and earned a fellowship to practice at Mount Sinai Medical Center in New York City. She then moved back to Wisconsin where she practices medicine at the University Station Clinic in the Internal Medicine Department at the University of Wisconsin. McMurray, an associate professor, is well known for her interest in women's health issues. She has published numerous articles in different medical journals, most notably in the Journal of American Medical Women's Association *(JAMWA) and* Women's Health. *Her decision to become a doctor while raising a family has its roots in her childhood experiences growing up in a family where her father was a physician and her mother dropped out of medical school.*

✦

As a small child, I often stood on the stairway in my home, looking up at the pictures of my mother. O.U. School of Medicine, class of 1945. I counted the 69 sepia-toned faces many times, always coming back to my mother's in the oval composite photograph. My mother is one of only three women, and her countenance is serious and composed; the hair in a long, wavy cut typical of the period. In an old picture from the local newspaper, written the year before my birth, my mother is sitting at a desk, wearing a white lab coat, staring out at the camera from her desk at the sexually transmitted diseases clinic where she worked. "Young Doctor Works in Town," reads the headline.

"How come you never worked as a doctor, Mama?" I asked frequently. I often went on rounds with my physician-father in

the early morning at the community hospital in the small southern town where we lived. In one minute flat, he could tap a chest,
letting the straw-colored liquid rush through the brown rubber
tubing to puddle in the glass vacuum bottle on the bed. The
nurses stood by at attention, in their starched white dresses and
peaked caps. In the small emergency area, my father would casually flip his tie over his shoulder and insert the needle for the lumbar puncture that would diagnose the subarachnoid bleeding in
his patient. Afterward, we would drive home to the house, where
my mother would be standing in front of the stove, scrambling
eggs for my three brothers, who sat watching Saturday morning
cartoons. My mother was always home.

"Well, I loved you children and felt you needed me at home.
You would start sucking your thumbs or the babysitter would
quit." On the day I was born in an army barracks hospital, a psy-
chotic WAC ran amok in the maternity area brandishing a
butcher knife. My mother hid me behind her body next to the wall
and called my father to come take us home. Later on, a German
war bride would sometimes baby-sit for my brother and me in a
pinch so my mother could work. After the war, while my father
was in fellowship training, there was a job for her at the public
health department. The syphilis patients would sit on a long row
of stools with their hospital gowns open in the back while she
went from one to the other, performing the lumbar punctures for
diagnosis or test of cure. It was the last clinical job she ever had.

Such were the stories of my childhood. In the small town
near the mountains, my father worked first in solo practice, then
with a gradually increasing number of partners. He was on call
every second or third night for most of my childhood and was
rarely home. The special office phone at home, one that we were
never to answer, rang off the hook each call night. Ventricular
tachycardia, acute myocardial infarctions, diabetic ketoacidosis,
and acute leukemia were never discussed at the dinner table but
were nonetheless an integral part of the household. His cotton
shirts were ironed every afternoon, and a sandwich was always
waiting on the table for the 20-minute lunch break he took every
day as he read his mail. On Sunday afternoons, I would go into
the office with him while he saw patients. Using his secret name
for me, I would pick up the phone and say gleefully, "Doctor
McMurray's office, Miss Bird speaking," to neighbors and patients
who knew me only as a quiet, well-behaved child.

My mother, on the other hand, was at home for us every day   5
after school, cooking dinner in the evenings when my father

walked in after rounds. She kept the family in clothes, helped with homework, played music to dance to on rainy afternoons, ferried us all to swimming and music lessons, met with the teacher when my brothers got into trouble at school, and always made it to recitals. She was president of the local mental health society, gave the embarrassing sex talks in schools, and thrilled us all once with a hole-in-one on the golf course. A gifted amateur naturalist, she admonished me not to be squeamish while helping me dissect fish eyes at the lake in the summers. Almost none of the other women in her circle of friends worked; most had never been to college. In the evenings she read all the "Great Books," and she loved nonfiction on almost any subject. I would crawl around her under the covers as she lay reading in bed, feeling the safety and security of her body.

The first crack in her armor of stoicism came when Betty Friedan's *The Feminine Mystique* was published. After reading the book, she refused to cook dinner for 3 days. She looked at me that afternoon and said, "I was smart; I could have done some things." I urged her to work out a way to drive the 3 hours to the nearest medical school in the state in order to get back into practice. But there were four children at home and one demanding, full-time private practice to support. Secretly, I chided my father for what I took to be his inflexibility in this regard; my mother simply said it couldn't be done.

I grew up, did well in school, and was a pre-medicine major in college. My father was emphatic in his support and unambivalent in his enthusiasm for medicine. "It's a great job. Easy, really. You just hang up your shingle and do things any way you like. People will come to see a woman physician. I wish your mother could have done it."

My mother was more cautious. "Whatever you want to do is fine; don't do it for me."

"How did you decide to become a doctor?" I once asked.

10 She responded in her typical low-key way, "I grew up in dust-bowl Oklahoma in the middle of the Depression. We had no money whatsoever. My father ran a garage, but I went to the state university. I was a chemistry major planning on going to pharmacy school, when a local couple urged me to go on to medical school. It was pretty simple, really. I just did it."

When my letter of acceptance came from medical school, she sent me a medical dictionary inscribed, "From one to another." Once in my clinical years, I began using her battered brown medical bag. Medical school was overwhelming, but memories of time spent with my father on house calls and in his office sustained me. I fell in and out of love a half dozen times, married during my residency, and ultimately started a family. My first job was exciting and utterly absorbing. Before the baby came, I was in every morning at 7:00 a.m., staying until late at night. No part-time work for me! Child care would be easy in the city where I lived, and my physician-husband was deeply committed to being involved as a father. It would all work out so easily. Why couldn't my mother have done this? I emulated my father at this point. My profession came first.

When my 4-month-old began reaching for his child care person instead of me and started sucking his thumb, I felt he needed me, as we had needed my mother. I cut back to part-time. Sitting with my child on my lap, I asked my mother, "Couldn't you have worked part-time?" This time, the stories were about the refusal of all the practices in town to hire anyone less than full-time. In fact, the only acceptable full-time jobs for women in her social strata were those of teacher or nurse. It wasn't considered acceptable otherwise.

My second child was born, and life got more complex. I would feel crazed with worry and guilt when a waiting room full of patients were waiting for me at the hospital while I sat helplessly in the pediatrician's office with a sick child. The nannies didn't want to work more than 8 to 10 hours a day, and the consultants always seemed to page me in the late afternoon while I was swinging the children out in the back yard. It was difficult to discuss the cardiac ejection fractions of patients receiving chemotherapy with the children squabbling in the background.

As I contemplated my own difficulties, I seemed to be headed down the same road as my mother and began to think more and more about the mystery of her lost medicine. I couldn't believe things had been so cut and dried, so matter of fact. How could she have avoided the gut-wrenching feelings of guilt, love, and inadequacy that I myself so often felt? And so I became instantly alert one hot summer day, as I sat by a pool with my mother and watched my two small children swim.

The question was innocent enough. "So, Mom, just how far 15 did you get in residency exactly? What kind of doctor were you planning to be?"

At her answer I felt a sudden stillness, the sounds of the summer cicadas buzzing loudly in my ears. "I wanted to be a pediatrician, but I got sick."

Sick? My mother was robustly healthy and had not been sick a day in her life. "What do you mean sick, Mother? What kind of sick?"

She answered, "It was stress, I guess." And for the first time she told me the story of how she started in a pediatric residency during the war. Four men, one woman. All the men were married and lived with their families. My mother was given a small room for living quarters on the tuberculosis ward. Being skin-test negative, she was terrified of contracting tuberculosis and asked to be moved. She was then put in a room at the end of the hall in the nurses' quarters. "It was just too much," my mother said in a voice devoid of emotion. She moved to the town where her sister lived, met my father, and married. There it was. A shaky start in the profession: scared, unsupported, possibly unwanted in medicine. The other answer had been in front of me all my life: the demands of mothering, needs of a busy physician-husband, a reluctant profession, and small-town social mores that made employment difficult for a woman physician who wanted a home in addition to a career.

My father retired at the age of 62. After 40 years of working, he told me that he hadn't had a summer off since the third grade. A poem came from him once that said, "I wish I had picked more daisies." Although he would say that he had been more successful than he had ever dreamed, in other moments he would speak of "being sucked dry" by patients or mention fears and anxieties that kept him awake at night, shared with no one. My mother would bask in the glories of her grandchildren and never once mention her lost medicine.

20   As for me, I have come through. I am fortunate to have been able to work part-time and to have a physician-husband willing and able to be fully engaged as a partner in our enterprise of work and home. But the challenges have been formidable and not simply a matter of more child care, more housecleaning help, or take-out food. Children's needs are not always so easily postponed until after hours, and relationships need constant tending. More equal measures of love and work sustain me, options that were not available to my mother.

Indeed, my mother "could have done some things." She earned her career, working hard in difficult times. Because she was one of only three women in a medical school class, there is a temptation to say she was obligated to continue, no matter what. But as this doctor's daughter, I benefited from her choices and her sacrifices. "From one to another," she passed on to me a legacy of competence and a courage tempered with love, a battered brown medical bag and a dictionary. I understand what I did not see before.

Questions for Discussion

1. What values guided Julia's parents as they raised her? Why was the publication of Betty Friedan's *The Feminine Mystique* especially influential in Julia's mother's decisions to change the way she raised Julia? Who is the happier parent: Julia's mother or her father? Why?
2. Why does McMurray decide to attend medical school? In what ways is her decision related to her mother's decision to drop out of medical school?
3. Why does Julia understand her mother's decision not to practice medicine when she becomes a mother herself?
4. How was working and raising a family different for Julia and for her mother?

Ideas for Writing

1. Develop a set of questions that target the challenges women doctors who have families face today. Discuss your questions with your instructor, before interviewing a woman doctor in your community. Alternatively, you can interview several women doctors. Write up the information you have learned in the form of an essay that includes quotes from the woman or women doctors with whom you have spoken.
2. Do some research into the challenges that women doctors who are also raising a family face. Write a paper that presents these challenges and ways that the medical profession is changing to accommodate the realities of women doctors with families.

Children Left Behind

STEPHANIE MENCIMER

Currently a contributing editor at the Washington Monthly, *Stephanie Mencimer has worked as an investigative reporter for* The Washington Post *and contributes articles on a regular basis to such liberal magazines as* The American Prospect *and* Mother Jones. *She also publishes fiction on political and social subjects. In 2000 Mencimer was given the Harry Chapin Media Award for her reporting on hunger and poverty. In the article that follows, originally published in* The American Prospect *(2002), Mencimer*

*reveals the current quality of child care that is available for work-
ing-class women and/or families and makes a cogent argument for
the urgent need to make child-care reform a part of the national political debate.*

———————————— ✦ ————————————

In early October, Nakia Burgess had just gotten a job as a tran-
scriber in Atlanta. She had already lost two other jobs because
of her inability to secure reliable and affordable child care for her
3-year-old daughter, Asan'te, who had Down syndrome. So when
the temp agency she had signed up with sent her out for a new assignment, Burgess was desperate to hang on to the position. But
on her second day, her child-care arrangement fell through. She
took Asan'te to work with her and left the girl in the car on the
company's parking deck. Burgess came out periodically to check
on the child, but after only 90 minutes, Asan'te was unconscious.
The temperature that day had risen to 85 degrees, and it was even
higher inside the car. When Asan'te reached the hospital, her
temperature registered 108 and she was pronounced dead from
hyperthermia.

The story provoked gasps of horror in the Atlanta area, where
Burgess was charged with murder even as she drew sympathy
from thousands of working parents who understood her difficulties
in finding child care. (The charges against Burgess have been
changed from felony murder and cruelty to children to involuntary
manslaughter and reckless conduct.) The media treated the story
as if it were a freak accident, but the incident was far from unusual.
A car is increasingly becoming a child-care arrangement of last re-
sort. In 1998, for instance, a 23-year-old mother in Wisconsin was
sentenced to six months in prison after leaving her 2-year-old son in
the trunk while she worked because she couldn't afford child care.

In November 2000, Rosmarie Radovan was arrested for locking her 5- and 7-year-old sons in the trunk of her car while she
worked. A single parent who was owed at least $41,000 in back
child-support payments and who was working two jobs to care for
her boys, Radovan argued in court that she could not find affordable child care for the children on the nights and weekends when
she worked. California's Santa Clara County, where she lived, had
at least 8,000 families on the waiting list for child-care openings
at the time, according to news reports. Nonetheless, Radovan was
sentenced to three months in jail for child endangerment.

The demand for quality, affordable child care has grown acute.
In Georgia, where Burgess lived, more than 16,000 people are on

the waiting list for a subsidy that would offset the cost of child care, which can run between $5,000 and $10,000 a year. A similar situation exists throughout much of America. Nineteen states currently have long waiting lists for child-care subsidies. (At the end of 2001, California had 200,000 families waiting, Florida had more than 46,000 and Texas had more than 36,000.) What's more, those families generally spend 50 percent of their incomes on child care.

As Burgess and others have demonstrated, desperate people   5
will do desperate things when they must work but can't find care for their children. With all the talk in this country about caring for children—right down to the fetus—you'd think Nakia Burgess' story would have sparked cries to address the nation's child-care crisis. But you'd be wrong. Instead, the Bush administration, which promises to "leave no child behind," has proposed forcing more women on welfare into the workforce while failing to provide even a cost-of-living increase in the federal child-care budget. Meanwhile, the economic downturn and state budget crises are forcing states to slash spending on all child-care services. Without additional funds, nearly half the states will need to scale back federally funded child-care programs by fiscal 2003, according to the Children's Defense Fund—all indications that stories such as Burgess' are likely to become depressingly more common.

The recent shortage of affordable child care is nothing new. When Marian Wright Edelman of the Children's Defense Fund testified before Congress in 1988 in support of the Act for Better Child Care Services, she told the story of Sandra James, a part-time housekeeper who lived in a community that had 5,000 young children competing for 453 day-care slots. James and her husband both worked and were unable to find care for their two children. One day, James left her 6-year-old son and his friend in the care of her 8-year-old daughter. A fire broke out in their apartment, and James' daughter ran for help, inadvertently locking the two younger children in the apartment. Both died in the fire.

Edelman laid out a host of similar horror stories, including those of substandard day-care centers, and implored Congress to take action to correct the problem. The situation is slightly better today—states are spending a record amount of money trying to improve child care—but progress has been slowed by the increased demand due to the welfare-reform legislation passed in 1996. Since then, employment among low-income single mothers with young children grew from 44 percent to 59 percent in 2000, according to the U.S. Department of Health and Human Services, creating a dire need for affordable child care.

. . .

Despite more than a decade's worth of tragedies, though, child care rarely prompts a sense of urgency among elected officials. Certainly it's been a divisive issue in this country because of the "culture wars," as conservatives have objected to women (at least white, middle-class women) moving into the workforce and have fought liberals over expanding child-care availability on the grounds that it only encourages more women to abandon their traditional gender roles in the home. But economics have largely silenced the last two decades' debates over mothers in the workforce. Most reasonable people now agree that work is a necessity for most parents.

The biggest political obstacle to addressing the child-care crisis, according to many on Capitol Hill, is simply the cost. In her recent book, *America's Childcare Problem: A Way Out*, economist Barbara Bergmann estimates that creating a national child-care program that would offer both quality and affordable care would cost about $50 billion annually—$30 billion more than the country spends now through Head Start, Title XX, the federal child-care block grant and state child-care subsidies combined. "It is daunting when you think of the size of the problem," says the Urban Institute's Gina Adams.

10   Rather than attempt a comprehensive approach that would invariably be tagged as expanding "big government," elected officials have preferred to let parents pick up the hefty tab for what most other industrialized countries consider a public obligation. While child care for young children routinely costs parents or guardians more than public university tuition, the government pays for 77 percent of the cost of higher education, according to the Children's Defense Fund, whereas parents assume 60 percent of child-care costs.

Middle-class parents have rarely squawked about this burden, reflecting a national ambivalence about the government's role in caring for children. "This is a country very focused on parental responsibility," says Adams. While seniors may feel entitled to prescription-drug benefits, parents of young children are reluctant to ask for government support, although most would welcome it. And because children (and their harried parents, often) don't vote, they're a demographic that politicians can ignore without risk.

A "POVERTY PROGRAM"

The silence of middle-class parents combined with the conservative political climate has left the issue of child care to anti-poverty groups, who rightly see it as inextricable from welfare reform. In fact, the relationship between welfare and child care is not a new one. During World War II, the government set up a network of child-care centers to allow women to contribute to the war effort while men served in the military. When the war ended, much of the industrialized world built on similar child-care infrastructures, developing nonparental centers and preschools that extended public schooling down to 3- and 4-year-olds. The United States, however, disbanded the centers and sent working mothers home. Rather than use child care to address the problem of mothers without husbands, the government created subsidies so that women could stay home and raise children. Those subsidies later became known as "welfare."

In the 1970s, as the conservative argument that welfare laws fueled increases in unwed motherhood gained political traction, Congress and various administrations attempted to "reform" welfare and force mothers into the workforce. But nearly every one of those early reform efforts failed, primarily because they neglected to factor in the need for child care. Congress seemed to have learned that lesson when it passed the 1996 welfare-reform effort and encouraged states to use surplus welfare funds to address the child-care problem. Child-care subsidies have increased since then, from about $4 billion in 1997 to about $8 billion last year, according to the Center for Law and Social Policy. Progressive states, which must match the federal grant, have also used some of their surplus welfare funds to expand the subsidies to cover some working families at risk of going on welfare.

The subsidies, though, are vastly inadequate for the need, and also immensely complicated to procure, as Nakia Burgess discovered when she inquired about them in Georgia. (She was told that the money had run out—and it had—so she never bothered to even apply.) In many states, the subsidies don't actually cover the full cost of providing day care, so many providers won't take kids who use them, as doing so would mean that the providers lose money. "The people who get them are the ones who can navigate the byzantine system to get it," says Ruby Takanishi, president of the Foundation for Child Development. "It's often so bad that people say, 'Forget it, I'm going to leave my kids in the car.'"

Today, only one out of seven eligible children actually gets   15
the subsidies, and the Congressional Budget Office estimates that the program will need an additional $5 billion or so over the next five years just to maintain the current slots. In the recent debate over reauthorizing the welfare-reform law, Senate Democrats lobbied to increase child-care funding by $11 billion

over the next half-decade—but ended up with a bill that would increase it by $5.5 billion. House Republicans passed their own version, which would only increase the funding by $1 billion. The whole reauthorization package stalled, and Congress will have to revisit the issue again next year.

The focus on subsidies as a substitute for a larger national debate on the crisis limits child care's prominence as a political issue. "Because subsidies are so narrowly focused, there is no organized constituency except for those particular advocacy groups [for the poor]," says Takanishi. Mustering political support for increased subsidies for welfare recipients is difficult when those being asked to support—and pay for—them are also struggling with their own child-care burdens. "Most people view child care as a private matter, so when it's used as a work support, it's not something that's looked kindly upon," says Takanishi.

Indeed, the issue affects nearly all families with children, regardless of income. The number of married mothers in the workforce with children under 6 has jumped from 11 percent in 1949 to 64 percent in 2001. Fifty-seven percent of women with infants are now in the workforce, while two-thirds of all 3- to 5-year-olds spend at least 35 hours a week being cared for by someone other than a parent, and that care is wildly expensive. Those costs put a significant dent in the average American family's finances.

People such as New York Times columnist Paul Krugman frequently note that the median household income in the United States has barely budged in the past 20 years, and that it's fallen for families in the bottom one-fifth of the income scale. What those numbers don't reflect is that most of the increases occurred not because salaries went up but because women went to work. To do so, they had to pay someone else to look after their kids. Today, the median income for a family of four—about $62,000 in 2000—may have increased 10 percent since 1979, but it doesn't account for the cost of child care, which could eat up nearly half of a second wage earner's salary. As a result, a family of four is probably getting by on far less than it did 20 years ago.

Yet advocacy groups have largely neglected these folks in their quest for more government child-care support, on the not-so-unreasonable grounds that whatever aid they can wrest from Congress—which isn't likely to be much—should go to those most in need. While the approach is well-intentioned, it neglects to enlist the critical support of the middle class, whose political heft might add some urgency to the issue. As a result, child

care is now viewed as a "poverty program," and it gets treated
as such.

In 2001, President George W. Bush actually proposed cutting   20
$200 million from the Child Care and Development Block Grant
to help pay for his massive tax cut for the rich. And [2002], the
administration advanced a version of welfare-reform reauthorization that would have forced even more mothers into the
workforce without providing any new money to care for their
children. The prospects for meaningful progress in the next
Congress are grim. "We're in a deficit and we're at war. We don't
have the money. No one is going to take money out of social
security. It's going to be a bad year for kids," says a Senate staffer
whose boss is involved in the debate.

It's not yet clear whether congressional Democrats—now in
the minority—will demand funding for such broad-based initiatives
as universal preschool and after-school programs, which would
also relieve some of the burden shouldered by middle-class parents. While Al Gore initially campaigned on the issue of universal
preschool in 2000, it has all but disappeared since September 11.
And infant care is expensive and in chronically short supply, not
to mention of extremely poor quality.

California has already demonstrated that such programs are
tremendously popular with voters who are now largely ignored by
political campaigns. The state recently passed the first paid
parental-leave law in the country—a measure that national polls
show 82 percent of women and 75 percent of men support.
California voters also overwhelmingly approved Arnold Schwarzenegger's ballot initiative to provide universal after-school care
for the state's children so they wouldn't continue to be sent home
to empty houses.

Fixing child care is likely to be expensive, but $50 billion a year
is pocket change compared with what the nation is paying to cover
last year's tax cuts, which will amount to more than $200 billion
annually. And there is little doubt that a significant government expenditure for child-care programs would actually serve the public
interest by helping to nurture and educate the future workforce—
at all income levels. Universal all-day preschool, in fact, could have
saved the life of 3-year-old Asan'te Burgess. Sadly, while Georgia is
the only state in the country that offers universal, free preschool
for 4-year-olds, the state has been unable to come up with the
money to expand the program to include 3-year-olds and to make it
all-day. If the federal government had filled in the gap, Asan'te

would likely still be alive and playing with her new public-school classmates rather than having met an untimely death in the backseat of her mother's car.

Questions for Discussion

1. Why does Mencimer open her article with stories of children whose parents have had to leave them in their cars while they worked because they were unable to find child care? Why is she critical of the media for presenting these situations as "freak events" that are uncommon? How effective is this introduction? How does Mencimer refer back to it in her conclusion?
2. In 1988 Marian Wright Edelman, founder of the Children's Defense Fund, helped to convince Congress to pass the Act for Better Child Care Services. Why did the progress made in improving child-care services begin to decline in 1996?
3. Why are the attempts to subsidize child care through welfare inadequate? Why does Mencimer think that child-care reform needs to become part of a national debate? What forces are in place that stand in opposition to such a debate?
4. Why and how does Mencimer argue that national federal child care is the only viable solution for all parents and their children? Do you agree with her implicit conclusion that the national government is responsible for Asan'te's death?

Ideas for Writing

1. Write a research argument for or against a federally supported child-care program for all parents and their children.
2. Write a research essay that supports Mencimer's claim that "there is little doubt that a significant government expenditure for child-care programs would actually serve the public interest by helping to nurture and educate the future workforce—at all income levels."

Legacy of Dreams
LISA TAKEUCHI CULLEN

Lisa Takeuchi Cullen is a reporter for Time *magazine who has written on the job market, international trends in pop music, diet pills and plastic surgery, the commercialization of the Internet, and other popular cultural issues. The essay that follows, "Legacy of Dreams," appeared originally in* Time *in 2004. In this essay*

Takeuchi Cullen explores the stories of several immigrant and minority-group family business owners that have thrived because of the creative input of educated second-generation youth, who in previous decades might have split off from the family enterprise to work as professionals and/or for large corporations.

——————————— ✦ ———————————

For Peter Kim, the call to join the family business came as a rude awakening. Snoring away a spring-break morning at the University of Southern California in 1994, Kim picked up the phone to hear his father Sang Hoon Kim shouting at him in Korean. "He goes, 'The company's got problems. Everybody's got to help out,'" recalls the younger Kim. The son did a lot more than that. At the time, office workers were no longer buying the polyester blouses the family company, Protrend, churned out. Sales were tumbling 50% every year. What's more, the father had invested in real estate during a market peak, and as a result the company shouldered $10 million in debt. Today Peter Kim, 33, is CEO of a debt-free, $15 million-a-year business. In 1999 he launched Drunknmunky, an Asian-influenced men's street-wear line that pulls in the bulk of the company's revenue. Battling low-cost production from competitors in China and elsewhere, Kim decided to pursue the higher profit margins in design and retail. "That's where I believe the industry is going: either you're a brand or you're dirt cheap," he says.

The Kims are part of a phenomenon sociologists call ethnic niche business, in which an immigrant group comes to dominate an industry, often with no discernible connection to its original culture. Think Chinese and laundry services, Arabs and gas stations, Koreans and groceries. And garments too. Experts estimate that more than half the 144,000 garment workers in Southern California are of Korean origin and up to half the companies are Korean owned. Entrepreneurs of Indian origin today own 38% of all hotels in the U.S. and more than half of budget motels. Mexican Americans whose forebears worked California's vineyards are becoming owners. Once, immigrant business owners were reluctant to pass the torch to their kids, hoping their labor would hoist the younger generation into more prestigious professions. That's changing. As the businesses grow, American-born heirs are increasingly willing to follow in their immigrant parents' footsteps. Armed with native English, advanced education and a comfort with change, the new generation is modernizing the family businesses in ways their parents never dreamed possible.

This generation's business strategies and goals far outpace their parents'. Drunknmunky, for instance, publicizes its popularity with hip-hop acts like Cypress Hill and Linkin Park and sponsors raves and rap concerts. Kim's ambitions include music and video-game production, accessories, bags and shoes. "I'd like to be more of a household brand, not just a clothing company—like [Ralph Lauren's] Polo," he says. Unlike their parents, Kim and his peers pursue deals outside their immigrant communities; Drunknmunky works with partners in FUBU, the African-American-owned clothing line. Instead of hewing to production, most Korean-owned companies are now full package, offering everything from fabric to manufacturing to export for major American labels, says Bruce Berton of Los Angeles' Fashion Institute of Design and Merchandise (where half the students are second- or third-generation Korean Americans).

Changing attitudes toward money have allowed the next generations to update and expand their companies. Early immigrants, suspicious of and unable to secure standard loans, turned to community loan clubs, in which relatives and friends put up money to help start businesses. This financing method is common but limited. What Koreans call *kye* is a *hui* for the Chinese, *ekub* for Ethiopians, *san* for Dominicans. Today, says Steven Gold, a sociologist at Michigan State University, immigrant businesses have access to loans from other ethnic sources, including banks or investors that cater to their community. The younger generation is also far savvier about landing tax-advantaged loans from the Small Business Administration and various minority-business-development funds. Some companies, including the Korean-owned clothing retailer Forever 21, are planning to go public.

5   Koreans arriving in the 1970s specialized in apparel manufacturing for some of the same reasons Indian immigrants gravitated toward the hotel industry: those businesses let them use family members as staff, conduct transactions in cash and get by with minimal English or experience. The Patel family's entry into the hotel business is exceedingly typical, right down to their surname. Natu Patel, a banana farmer in the Gujarat region of India—where most of the U.S.'s Indian hoteliers have roots and the majority of residents are named Patel—arrived in San Francisco nearly three decades ago with his family and $10. He learned the business working for motels owned by wife Hansa's relatives and then sought out affordable properties in remote

regions before settling on a small inn in Cleveland, Tenn., later adding motels in Waco, Texas, and Kennesaw, Ga.

Priti Patel, 33, hardly remembers another life. At 8, she was counting change and working the front desk. "I used to hate it," she says. "Everybody else gets to go home after school and get a snack. I had to help at the hotel. On weekends I had to cut grass." When friends drove by and saw her working, she would feel embarrassed. Still, the industry intrigued her enough to pursue a business degree at the University of Tennessee, and afterward she worked for the Small Business Administration. She returned to the family's HNP Enterprises to take over as manager of the Kennesaw motel in 1997.

Patel's management style differs from that of her parents. For one thing, she refuses to live on property, choosing instead to separate her work life from her family. Unlike her parents, who prefer to do the work themselves, she employs a housekeeping manager, a desk manager and a sales manager to oversee the property in her place. "I let go a lot more than my dad does," she says. Patel and her brother Hitesh, 25, plan to expand into restaurant franchises. Though their methods and goals may differ, says Patel, their father is proud of their achievements. "That's why he sent us to school."

Education is proving a key tool in grooming the second generation of Indian hoteliers. Unlike, say, the construction business, hospitality is an immigrant-heavy industry with a ready infrastructure of formal training. Over the past five years or so, as a new generation has come of age, students of Indian background have flooded hotel schools like the one at Cornell University. There they learn how to broker acquisitions, arrange complicated financing, set up room-booking technology and modernize marketing. Many take internships and first jobs in related fields like real estate or investment banking. The training helps "prepare them to take on an industry vastly more competitive and complex than when their parents entered it," says Cornell professor Chekitan Dev.

The new generation of Indian-American hotel owners is also learning, sometimes the hard way, how to play politics. After Sept. 11, ethnic-Indian proprietors suffered a wave of xenophobia, exhibited by signs outside competing hotels that claimed AMERICAN OWNED AND OPERATED. The bias cut into bookings, hurting business in an already devastating climate for travel. Yet while major hotel corporations lobbied for and received relief from Washington, the Asian American Hotel Owners Association had no presence or influence there to follow suit. "We learned from that," says Naresh (Nash) Patel, 38, current chairman of the association and a second-generation hotel owner. The group swiftly launched lobbying efforts and invited politicians like Newt Gingrich to speak at its gatherings. It set up a nationwide program to provide free hotel rooms for families of active military members on leave. Nash Patel called the owner of a Florida hotel with an offending sign. The owner took it down.

10   In some cases, the children of immigrants, thanks to education and experience, are leaving hard labor behind for good. Mexican workers in California's wine country have been preparing for generations to face their unique challenge: trading grape-stained work gloves for ownership papers. Since the 1940s, millions of Mexicans have traveled across the border to work the California vineyards. Those economics haven't changed in what is now the $33 billion U.S. wine capital. During harvest, Napa County is home to up to 2,700 migrant workers, most from Mexico. For as much as $15 an hour, the workers endure 18-hour days of backbreaking labor, often with no benefits or job security. "Without the Mexican labor force, there wouldn't be a wine industry," says Amelia Ceja, 48. Her children were to the vineyard born, all right—to migrant workers. Their grandparents toiled in the fields for $1 a day. Amelia met her husband Pedro while picking grapes at age 12. The family bought its first 15 acres, outside Napa, in 1983. By 1999, it owned 113 acres. Today Ceja Vineyards provides grapes for well-known brands in addition to its own labels. The company now produces 5,000 cases of wine annually, compared with just 750 in 2001. The Ceja children study at local universities and will inherit vineyards, not dreams.

Salvador Renteria traveled illegally across the border in the early 1960s to work in Napa. He moved up from driving stakes in the vineyards as a laborer for $20 a day to being a salaried foreman and supervisor. His son Oscar earned a college degree while learning all his father knew about vineyard management. In 1987 Salvador opened Renteria Vineyard Management, which oversees 1,500 acres of vineyard for 27 high-profile clients, employs 130 people and hauls in revenues of $8 million a year. Recently Oscar, 36, who took over the company in 1993, launched the company's own wine. "By growing grapes, there's not a lot of exposure," he says. "By making wine, you tell a story."

Sometimes the ambitions of business heirs fly far beyond anything the founders imagined. When he was rolling penny cigars on a sidewalk in early-1900s Cuba, Teorifio Perez-Carillo could not have dreamed that someday his handiwork would be legendary among Hollywood stars and other aficionados. Or that his son Ernesto would buy the building behind his sidewalk stake and turn it into a tobacco warehouse. Or that his grandson, also named Ernesto, would take over the operation in Miami and become a multimillionaire.

Ernesto Perez-Carillo Jr., 52, considers that improbable journey as he strolls among the dozen men and women sorting and rolling molasses-colored leaves in El Credito Cigars' pungent storefront in Miami's Little Havana. His father expanded production to 140,000 cigars a day, at one point supplying troops during World War II. They fled to Miami after Fidel Castro's takeover in 1959. In 1968, finally convinced the exile was permanent, the elder Ernesto paid $5,000 for a cigarmaking factory in Miami. To find a niche among the 30 or so other cigar factories, Ernesto Sr. began testing some signature brands. He developed a mail-order business to reach markets in Chicago and the Northeast, leafing through the Yellow Pages to find doctors, lawyers and other potential cigar smokers.

Though he had set out for New York City to make it as a jazz drummer, Ernesto Perez-Carillo Jr. returned to Miami when his father came down with Lou Gehrig's disease. In the midst of negotiations to sell the business, "something came over me," says Perez-Carillo. He persuaded his father to decline the offer and turn the business over to him. Ernesto Sr. died in 1980. El Credito's focus on premium lines paid off in the early '90s, gaining the company notice during the cigar boom. An article in *Cigar Aficionado* magazine sparked a flood of orders, causing a six-month backlog. Bill Cosby, Sharon Stone and Arnold Schwarzenegger became loyal clients, says Perez-Carillo.

The trickiest decision for immigrant business owners is often the exit strategy. Though both have worked in the business, Perez-Carillo's son Ernesto III, 22, is a recent Stanford grad and consultant, and his daughter Lissette McPhillips, 30, is a lawyer. So Perez-Carillo knew he faced a choice in 1999 when tobacco company Swedish Match offered to buy El Credito for a reported $20 million. He sold. "Most people would have thought, Millions and millions of dollars—this is my dream, my dream has come true," says McPhillips. But for her father, "there was a sadness there." Perez-Carillo now works for General Cigar, a subsidiary of Swedish Match, and still runs El Credito in Miami.

In part because of such potential rewards, these days many immigrant children no longer view following their parents' path

15

as a jail sentence. All the second-generation members of the Rama family, whose Greenville, S.C., JHM Group owns a string of more than 40 hotels, have worked in the family business since they could fold towels. Three are pursuing degrees in architecture, business or hotel management—by choice. "I knew I wanted to make the hotel business my career. My head was always in it," says D. J. Rama, 36, a Cornell M.B.A. and vice president of operations for JHM. "Work is the fabric that weaves the wealth the first generation built together with the next."

Others take more convincing. When he was called back to work for the family company, Peter Kim was less than thrilled. But one day he had an epiphany while driving down the freeway. "I was feeling sorry for myself," he says. "Then it hit me: You are such a coward. My parents and that whole generation come to this country with nothing—like, a suitcase and maybe, what, a couple hundred bucks?" His father, seated beside him, says, "Thirty-eight dollars."

"They don't know the language," Peter Kim continues. "They don't know the culture. They can't even find a bathroom. They know nothing but can build this. It was almost like somebody took a frying pan and smacked me on the head. I am born in this country. I am educated in this country. We can make a go of this." The American Dream, after all, is worth fighting for.

Questions for Discussion

1. What is an "ethnic niche business"? How do the examples in this article help to define this concept?
2. Why in the past were immigrant parents and their children reluctant to have their children work in the family's business? Why are the children of immigrants now deciding to stay and help with their family's business? What skills and valuable perspectives do these immigrant children bring to their parents' businesses?
3. What are some of the major issues that were explored in this article about the changing nature of immigrant family businesses? Compare the attitudes about family businesses in white middle-class families.
4. Which of the many examples included in this essay had the most persuasive impact on you? Was the content or the presentation of material more important? Do you think that family businesses can help a family to develop deeper relationships and to prosper?

Ideas for Writing

1. Identify a family-run and -owned business in your community. Request an interview with the owners and, if possible, their children who work in the business. Write an essay that reflects what you have learned about the family business and the positive and negative effects that a family enterprise can have on its members.
2. Do some research on the topic of immigrant family businesses using the sociological databases at your college library. Are they becoming more popular today? If so, why? Do they change the nature of relationships within the family? Conclude with your opinion on why family businesses will or will not survive and flourish in the 21st century. What impact might they have on our economy and on our approaches to parenting?

Extending the Theme

1. Select the topic that interested you most in this chapter. Refer to relevant articles in this chapter and do further research before formulating a thesis for your topic. If possible, also refer to your own experiences as a parent or child.
2. Write an essay about the role of men as nurturers and how that role exists in relationship to their work in the public sphere.
3. Write an essay or a story that shares your vision of a responsible and capable working family in the year 2010. Consider how our lifestyles will have changed; also project your own values into this new family unit.
4. Write an essay that presents an extended definition of a good working mother, a good working father, or a good working parent. Refer to your own experiences, materials that you have read about parenting, or perhaps films that explore issues related to parenting. Alternately, you might compare and contrast different perspectives about what makes a good father and a good mother.

CHAPTER 3

Working with Technology

Technology has always had a significant impact on human labor, from the invention of the earliest tools and weapons, which made it possible for our distant ancestors to kill more game and produce crops. By developing more sophisticated tools, people could store food and create enduring shelters that allowed ever larger communities, in which ever more specialized types of work and trade existed, to grow and flourish. During the Industrial Revolution, the definition of work changed as workers became extensions of machines and worked on parts of products. While the earlier conditions of work were more community- and family-based, and often more rewarding, the technology involved in creating big machines made work more efficient but also more dangerous and less satisfying.

In the late twentieth century, the Industrial Revolution gave way to the digital revolution, which has added ever greater speed and efficiency to production, eliminating many tedious jobs, while at the same time creating new positions in the emerging fields of computer and software design, and digital entertainment, as well as new opportunities for marketing and distributing products through the Internet. Digital technology has already drastically changed the workplace: Consider the skills that modern people need to work and to communicate, and the way companies are developed and run today. In fact, without technology, globalization could not have occurred so rapidly. Technology itself has unlimited potential to bring about change; however, any great force of power brings with it paradoxes and problems. Although technology itself may be neutral, neither good nor bad, the way that people and businesses design and utilize technology has been positive and also limiting to human communication and to the conditions of workers.

Each selection in this chapter raises issues about how the lives of workers are being changed by technology. One concern is that technological work can be isolating—removing the programmer from the human world and human problems; for example, computer programming can involve the creation of software that is supposed to serve consumers, yet programmers exist at such a remote distance from face-to-face interaction that they do not always design effective programs. In this chapter's first selection, "Getting Close to the Machine," Ellen Ullman writes about the creation of a program designed to help control the spread of the AIDS virus. She reveals the separate goals of the computer programmers and the social workers who need to use the program to protect human life. Ullman's essay reveals a basic paradox about technological work that must be confronted: "[H]uman needs must cross the line into code. They must pass through this semipermeable membrane where urgency, fear, and hope are filtered out, and only reason travels across. There is no other way." The alienation of the computer programmer from human problems leads to the failure of his program, revealing an inherent limitation of technological solutions.

A second issue in today's increasingly digital, technological workplace is that of those left behind. Many middle-aged workers grew up without computers and need training to operate the new technology. Often, managers are not quick to find help for the many employees who are not familiar with the numerous new programs for computers. The poor, especially, may find it difficult to afford computers and Internet access. African Americans, for instance, as historian Anthony Walton points out in "Technology Versus African Americans," have never been beneficiaries of technology and may feel resistant to its lure. However, Walton warns that blacks must change in the face of the digital revolution if they are to "ensure themselves a place at the American table." While Walton believes that technology does support elitism in the United States, he sees that black workers will have much to gain if they seize the opportunities offered by the new workplace technology.

Digital technology shapes our working lives in even more dramatic and immediate forms. In "Scripted Talk," our next selection, widely published writer Adria Scharf demonstrates how big chains like McDonald's and Starbucks have created efficiency scripts for employees, using digitalized cameras as well as secret customer auditors to check on their workers' compliance with company policy. Scharf argues that the human needs of workers and customers must be valued over machine-life efficiency.

Technology helps to get the job done, but often at the expense of the workers who are expected to keep up with the ever increasing stress of what one can accomplish through the use of computers. Professor of economics and activist Jeremy Rifkin argues in his essay "High-Tech Stress" for the importance of paying close attention to the health of computer and factory workers who are continually exposed to unrealistic amounts of pressure to work faster and more efficiently. Rifkin warns against the negative aspects of this stress, as modern workers are developing illnesses that make them physically and psychologically incapable of continuing to do their jobs.

Another recent effect of globalization and the digital revolution has been the phenomenon of "outsourcing," in which employers send jobs overseas to take advantage of the lower wage scales available abroad, leaving many American workers unemployed. This is a hotly contested political issue today. Businesses argue that outsourcing is necessary to remain competitive in the global marketplace, whereas labor groups and employees believe that the process is unfair to American workers and that companies need to provide job alternatives and support for the unemployed, just as the government needs to provide fiscal incentives to discourage companies from excessive outsourcing, especially in the case of skilled work in the technological sector. Jyoti Thottam examines this controversial issue from several different perspectives in her essay "Is Your Job Going Abroad?"

Our final selection presents a positive case in point of how technology has effectively made education available to workers through a business model. In "The Next University. Drive-Thru U" journalist James Traub traces the success of John Sperling, who designed the successful online University of Phoenix where high school students and adult learners can prepare themselves through distance learning for successful careers in the corporate economy. This new model of education based on technology affords people already in the work world with an opportunity to learn the skills needed to succeed in the business environment in the shortest time possible. In contrast, some educators think that corporate employees need to gain critical thinking and "human skills" through the interaction that takes place in the face-to-face reality of the traditional college campus and a workplace where community and interpersonal dialogue are respected and encouraged.

While digital technology could become a dominant source of management power over workers, controlling their lives and allowing jobs to be moved about the globe at the will of corporate employers. Technology itself is value-neutral. How we shape technology to serve our best interests will determine if it is beneficial or detrimental to human welfare. Our responsibility is clear: We must find ways to make technology serve all classes of people and all nations for their mutual benefit. We must work to help working-class people have more access to computers and provide training for all people who want to use computers and the Internet, including teachers, artists, business-people, and health-care workers. Finally, and most important of all, we must learn to use digital technology to help us better understand one another, our cultures, our histories, and our own psyches.

Getting Close to the Machine
ELLEN ULLMAN

Ellen Ullman was born in 1949 and raised in New York City. She moved to San Francisco in 1978 to work as a computer programmer and consultant. Her articles about her experiences in the computer industry have been published in magazines such as Harper's, Wired, The Washington Post, The New York Times Magazine, *and* Salon. *She is a regular guest commentator on NPR. Ullman's first book,* Getting Close to the Machine *(1997), is a personal reflection on the lifestyles and work habits of young people deeply involved in the world of creative programming. More recently, she published a novel,* The Bug *(2003), whose main character is an obsessive, overworked computer programmer at a Bay Area software company. In the essay that follows, which is excerpted from* Getting Close to the Machine, *Ullman examines the obsessive communication and thinking styles of those whose demanding technical work takes them "close to the machine"—but a long way from ordinary people.*

─────────── ✦ ───────────

I have no idea what time it is. There are no windows in this office and no clock, only the blinking red LED display of a microwave, which flashes 12:00, 12:00, 12:00, 12:00. Joel and I have been programming for days. We have a bug, a stubborn demon of a bug. So the red pulse no-time feels right, like a read-out of our brains, which have somehow synchronized themselves at the same blink rate.

"But what if they select all the text and—"
"—hit Delete."
"Damn! The NULL case!"
5   "And if not we're out of the text field and they hit space—"
"—yeah, like for—"
"—no parameter—"
"Hell!"
"So what if we space-pad?"
10   "I don't know".... Wait a minute!"
"Yeah, we could space-pad—"
"—and do space as numeric."
"Yes! We'll call SendKey(space) to—?"
"—the numeric object."
15   "My God! That fixes it!"
"Yeah! That'll work if—"
"—space is numeric!"
"—if space is numeric!"

We lock eyes. We barely breathe. For a slim moment, we are together in a universe where two human beings can simultaneously understand the statement "if space is numeric!"

20   Joel and I started this round of debugging on Friday morning. Sometime later, maybe Friday night, another programmer, Danny, came to work. I suppose it must be Sunday by now because it's been a while since we've seen my client's employees around the office. Along the way, at odd times of day or night that have completely escaped us, we've ordered in three meals of Chinese food, eaten six large pizzas, consumed several beers, had innumerable bottles of fizzy water, and finished two entire bottles of wine. It has occurred to me that if people really knew how software got written, I'm not sure if they'd give their money to a bank or get on an airplane ever again.

What are we working on? An artificial intelligence project to find "subversive" talk over international phone lines? Software for the second start-up of a Silicon Valley executive banished from his first company? A system to help AIDS patients get services across a city? The details escape me just now. We may be helping poor sick people or tuning a set of low-level routines to verify bits on a distributed database protocol—I don't care. I should care; in another part of my being—later, perhaps when we emerge from this room full of computers—I will care very much why and for whom and for what purpose I am writing software. But just now: no. I have passed through a membrane where the real world and its uses no longer matter. I am a software engineer, an independent contractor working for a department of a city government. I've hired Joel and three other programmers to work with me. Down the hall is Danny, a slim guy in wire-rimmed glasses who comes to work with a big, wire-haired dog. Across the bay in his converted backyard shed is Mark, who works on the database. Somewhere, probably asleep by now, is Bill the network guy. Right now, there are only two things in the universe that matter to us. One, we have some bad bugs to fix. Two, we're supposed to install the system on Monday, which I think is tomorrow.

"Oh, no, no!" moans Joel, who is slumped over his keyboard. "No-o-o-o." It comes out in a long wail. It has the sound of lost love, lifetime regret. We've both been programmers long enough to know that we are at *that place*. If we find one more serious problem we can't solve right away, we will not make it. We won't install. We'll go the terrible, familiar way of all software: we'll be late.

"No, no, no, no. What if the members of the set start with spaces. Oh, God. It won't work."

He is as near to naked despair as has ever been shown to me by anyone not in a film. Here, in *that place,* we have no shame. He has seen me sleeping on the floor, drooling. We have both seen Danny's puffy white midsection—young as he is, it's a pity—when he stripped to his underwear in the heat of the machine room. I have seen Joel's dandruff, light coating of cat fur on his clothes, noticed things about his body I should not. And I'm sure he's seen my sticky hair, noticed how dull I look without make-up, caught sight of other details too intimate to mention. Still, none of this matters anymore. Our bodies were abandoned long ago, reduced to hunger and sleeplessness and the ravages of sitting for hours at a keyboard and a mouse. Our physical selves have been battered away. Now we know each other in one way and one way only: the code.

Besides, I know I can now give him pleasure of an order   25
which is rare in my life: I am about to save him from despair.

"No problem," I say evenly. I put my hand on his shoulder, intending a gesture of reassurance. "The parameters *never* start with a space."

It is just as I hoped. His despair vanishes. He becomes electric, turns to the keyboard and begins to type at a rapid speed. Now he is gone from me. He is disappearing into the code—now that he knows it will work, now what I have reassured him that, in our universe, the one we created together, space can indeed be forever and reliably numeric.

The connection, the shared thought-stream, is cut. It has all the frustration of being abandoned by a lover just before climax. I know this is not a physical love. He is too young, he works for me; he's a man and I've been tending toward women; in any case, he's too prim and business-schooled for my tastes. I know this sensation is not *real* attraction; it is only the spillover, the excess charge, of the mind back into the abandoned body. *Only.* Ha. This is another real-world thing that does not matter. My entire self wants to melt into this brilliant, electric being who had shared his mind with me for twenty seconds.

Restless, I go into the next room where Danny is slouched at his keyboard. The big, wire-haired dog growls at me. Danny looks up, scowls like his dog, then goes back to typing. I am the designer of this system, his boss on this project. But he's not even trying to hide his contempt. Normal programmer, I think. He has fifteen windows full of code open on his desktop. He has overpopulated his eyes, thoughts, imagination. He is drowning in bugs and I know I could help him, but he wants me dead just at the moment. I am the last-straw irritant. *Talking:* Shit! What the hell is wrong with me? Why would I want to *talk* to him? Can't I see that his stack is overflowing?

30   "Joel may have the overlapping controls working" I say.

"Oh, yeah?" He doesn't look up.

"He's been using me as a programming dummy," I say. "Do you want to talk me through the navigation errors?" Navigation errors: bad. You click to go somewhere but get somewhere else. Very, very bad.

"What?" He pretends not to hear me.

"Navigation errors. How are they?"

35   "I'm working on them." Huge, hateful scowl. Contempt that one human being should not express to another under any circumstances. Hostility that should kill me, if I were not used to it, familiar with it, practiced in receiving it. Besides, we are at *that place.* I know that this hateful programmer is all I have between me and the navigation bug. "I'll come back later," I say.

Later: how much later can it get? Daylight can't be far off now. This small shoal of pre-installation madness is washing away even as I wander back down the hall to Joel.

"Yes! It's working!" says Joel, hearing my approach.

He looks up at me. "You were right," he says. The ultimate one programmer can say to another, the accolade given so rarely as to be almost unknown in our species. He looks right at me as he says it: "You were right. As always."

This is beyond rare. *Right:* the thing a programmer desires above, beyond all. *As always:* unspeakable, incalculable gift.

"I could not have been right without you," I say. This is true   40 beyond question. "I only opened the door. You figured out how to go through."

I immediately see a certain perfume advertisement: a man holding a violin embraces a woman at a piano. I want to be that ad. I want efficacies of reality to vanish, and I want to be the man with violin, my programmer to be the woman at the piano. As in the ad, I want the teacher to interrupt the lesson and embrace the student. I want the rules to be broken. Tabu. That is the name of the perfume. I want to do what is taboo. I am the boss, the senior, the employer, the person in charge. So I must not touch him. It is all taboo. Still—

Danny appears in the doorway.

"The navigation bug is fixed. I'm going home."

"I'll test it—"

"It's fixed."   45

He leaves.

It is sometime in the early morning. Joel and I are not sure if the night guard is still on duty. If we leave, we may not get back up the elevator. We leave anyway.

We find ourselves on the street in a light drizzle. He has on a raincoat, one that he usually wears over his too-prim, too-straight, good-biz-school suits. I have on a second-hand-store leather bomber jacket, black beret, boots. Someone walking by might wonder what we were doing together at this still-dark hour of the morning.

"Goodnight," I say. We're still charged with thought energy. I don't dare extend my hand to shake his.

"Goodnight," he says.   50

We stand awkwardly for two beats more. "This will sound strange," he says, "but I hope I don't see you tomorrow."

We stare at each other, still drifting in the wake of our shared mind-stream. I know exactly what he means. We will only see each other tomorrow if I find a really bad bug.

"Not strange at all," I say, "I hope I don't see you, either."

I don't see him. The next day, I find a few minor bugs, fix them, and decide the software is good enough. Mind-meld fantasies recede as the system goes live. We install the beginnings of a city-wide registration system for AIDS patients. Instead of carrying around soiled and wrinkled eligibility documents, AIDS clients only have to prove once that they are really sick and really poor. It is an odd system, if I think of it, certifying that people are truly desperate in the face of possible death.

55   Still, this time I'm working on a "good" project, I tell myself. We are *helping* people, say the programmers over and over, nearly in disbelief at their good fortune. Three programmers, the network guy, me—fifty-eight years of collective technical experience—and the idea of helping people with a computer is a first for any of us.

Yet I am continually anxious. How do we protect this database full of the names of people with AIDS? Is a million-dollar computer system the best use of continually shrinking funds? It was easier when I didn't have to think about the real-world effect of my work. It was easier—and I got paid more—when I was writing an "abstracted interface to any arbitrary input device." When I was designing a "user interface paradigm," defining a "test-bed methodology." I could disappear into weird passions of logic. I could stay in a world peopled entirely by programmers, other weird logic-dreamers like myself, all caught up in our own inner electricities. It was easier and more valued. In my profession, software engineering, there is something almost shameful in this helpful, social-services system we're building. The whole project smacks of "end users"—those contemptible, oblivious people who just want to use the stuff we write and don't care how we did it.

"What are you working on?" asked an acquaintance I ran into at a book signing. She's a woman with her own start-up company. Her offices used to be in the loft just below mine, two blocks from South Park, in San Francisco's Multimedia Gulch. She is tall and strikingly attractive; she wears hip, fashionable clothes; her company already has its first million in venture-capital funding. "What are you working on," she wanted to know, "I mean, that isn't under non-D?"

Under non-D. Nondisclosure. That's the cool thing to be doing: working on a system so new, so just started up, that you can't talk about it under pain of lawsuit.

"Oh, not much," I answered, trying to sound breezy. A citywide network for AIDS service providers: how unhip could I get? If I wanted to do something for people with AIDS, I should make my first ten million in stock options, then attend some fancy party where I wear a red ribbon on my chest. I should be a sponsor for Digital Queers. But actually working on a project for end users? Where my client is a government agency? In the libertarian world of computing, where "creating wealth" is all, I am worse than uncool: I am aiding and abetting the bureaucracy,

I am a net consumer of federal taxes—I'm what's wrong with this country.

"Oh, I'm basically just plugging in other people's software   60
these days. Not much engineering. You know," I waved vaguely,
"*plumbing* mostly."

My vagueness paid off. The woman winked at me. "Networks,"
she said.

"Yeah. Something like that," I said. I was disgusted with myself, but, when she walked away, I was relieved.

The end users I was so ashamed of came late in the system
development process. I didn't meet them until the software was
half-written. This is not how these things are supposed to go—the
system is not supposed to predate the people who will use it—but
it often goes that way anyhow.

The project was eight months old when my client-contact, a
project manager in a city department, a business-like women of
fifty, finally set up a meeting. Representatives of several social-
service agencies were invited; eight came. A printed agenda was
handed around the conference table. The first item was "Review
agenda." My programmer-mind whirred at the implication of
endless reiteration: Agenda. Review agenda. Agenda. Forever.

"Who dreamed up this stuff?" asked a woman who directed a   65
hospice and home-care agency. "This is all useless!" We had finally
come to item four on the agenda: "Review System Specifications."
The hospice director waved a big stack of paper—the specifications arrived at by a "task force"—then tossed it across the table.
A heavy-set woman apparently of Middle-Eastern descent, she
had probably smoked a very large number of cigarettes in the
course of her fifty-odd years on earth. Her laugh trailed off into a
chesty rumble, which she used as a kind of drum roll to finish off
her scorn.

The other users were no more impressed. A black woman who
ran a shelter—elegant, trailing Kente cloth. She arranged her
acres of fabric as some sort of displacement for her boredom; each
time I started talking, I seemed to have to speak over a high jangle
of her many bracelets set to play as she, ignoring me with something that was not quite hostility, arranged and rearranged herself.
A woman who ran a clinic for lesbians, a self-described "femme"
with hennaed hair and red fingernails: "Why didn't someone come
talk to us first?" she asked. A good question. My client sat shame-
faced. A young, handsome black man, assistant to the hospice
director, quick and smart: he simply shook his head and kept a

skeptical smile on his face. Finally a dentist and a doctor, two white males who looked pale and watery in this sea of diversity: they worried that the system would get in the way of giving services. And around the table they went, complaint by complaint.

I started to panic. Before this meeting, the users existed only in my mind, projections, all mine. They were abstractions, the initiators of tasks that set off remote procedure calls; triggers to a set of logical and machine events that ended in an update to a relational database on a central server. Now I was confronted with their fleshly existence. And now I had to think about the actual existence of the people who used the services delivered by the user's agencies, sick people who were no fools, who would do what they needed to do to get pills, food vouchers, a place to sleep.

I wished, earnestly, I could just replace the abstractions with the actual people. But it was already too late for that. The system pre-existed the people. Screens were prototyped. Data elements were defined. The machine events already had more reality, had been with me longer, than the human beings at the conference table. Immediately, I saw it was a problem not of replacing one reality with another but of two realities. I was there at the edge: the interface of the system, in all its existence, to the people, in all their existence.

I talked, asked questions, but I saw I was operating at a different speed from the people at the table. Notch down, I told myself. *Notch down.* The users were bright, all too sensitive to each other's feelings. Anyone who was the slightest bit cut off was gotten back to sweetly: "You were saying?" Their courtesy was structural, built into their "process." I had to keep my hand over my mouth to keep from jumping in. Notch down, I told myself again. *Slow down.* But it was not working. My brain whirred out a stream of logic-speak: "The agency sees the client records if and only if there is a relationship defined between the agency and the client," I heard myself saying. "By definition, as soon as the client receives services from the agency, the system considers the client to have a relationship with the provider. An internal index is created which represents the relationship." The hospice director closed her eyes to concentrate. She would have smoked if she could have; she looked at me as if through something she had just exhaled.

70   I took notes, pages of revisions that had to be done immediately or else doom the system to instant disuse. The system had no life without the user, I saw. I'd like to say that I was instantly converted to the notion of real human need, to the impact I would have on the working lives of these people at the table, on the

people living with AIDS; I'd like to claim a sudden sense of real-world responsibility. But that would be lying. What I really thought was this: I must save the system.

I ran off to call the programmers. Living in my hugely different world from the sick patients, the forbearing service providers, the earnest and caring users at the meeting, I didn't wait to find a regular phone. I went into the next room, took out my cell phone, began punching numbers into it, and hit the "send" button: "We have to talk," I said.

By the time I saw Joel, Danny, and Mark, I had reduced the users' objections to a set of five system changes. I would like to use the word "reduce" like a cook: something boiled down to its essence. But I was aware that the real human essence was already absent from the list I'd prepared. An item like "How will we know if the clients have TB?"—the fear of sitting in a small, poorly ventilated room with someone who has medication-resistant TB, the normal and complicated biological urgency of that question— became a list of data elements to be added to the screens and the database. I tried to communicate some of the sense of the meeting to the programmers. They were interested, but in a mild, backgrounded way. Immediately, they seized the list of changes and, as I watched, they turned them into further abstractions.

"We can add a parameter to the remote procedure call."

"We should check the referential integrity on that."

"Should the code be attached to that control or should it be in global scope?"

"Global, because this other object here needs to know about the condition."

"No! No globals. We agreed. No more globals!"

We have entered the code zone. Here thought is telegraphic and exquisitely precise. I feel no need to slow myself down. On the contrary, the faster the better. Joel runs off a stream of detail, and halfway through a sentence, Mark, the database programmer, completes the thought. I mention a screen element, and Danny, who programs the desktop software, thinks of two elements I've forgotten. Mark will later say all bugs are Danny's fault, but, for now, they work together like cheerful little parallel-processing machines, breaking the problem into pieces that they attack simultaneously. Danny will later become the angry programmer scowling at me from behind his broken code, but now he is still a jovial guy with wire-rimmed glasses and a dog that accompanies him everywhere. "Neato," he says to something Mark has proposed, grinning, patting the dog, happy as a clam.

"Should we modify the call to AddUser—"
80   "—to check for UserType—"
"Or should we add a new procedure call—"
"—something like ModifyPermissions."
"But won't that add a new set of data elements that repeat—"
"Yeah, a repeating set—"
85   "—which we'll have to—"
"—renormalize!"
Procedure calls. Relational database normalization. Objects going in and out of scope. Though my mind is racing, I feel calm. It's the spacey calm of satellites speeding over the earth at a thousand miles per second: relative to each other, we float. The images of patients with AIDS recede, the beleaguered service providers are forgotten, the whole grim reality of the epidemic fades. We give ourselves over to the sheer fun of the technical, to the nearly sexual pleasure of the clicking thought-stream.

Some part of me mourns, but I know there is no other way: human needs must cross the line into code. They must pass through the semipermeable membrane where urgency, fear, and hope are filtered out, and only reason travels across. There is no other way. Real, death-inducing viruses do not travel here. Actual human confusions cannot live here. Everything we want accomplished, everything the system is to provide, must be denatured in its crossing to the machine, or else the system will die.

Questions for Discussion

1. Why does programming require such intense concentration? Can you think of other types of work that require a similar kind of focus and concentration? What type of person is most likely to be suited to this kind of work? Why?
2. How does Ullman describe the culture of programmers? What makes her presentation engaging? Why does the programmer separate the act of programming from the purpose of the project? Why is he not interested in the content information that is being programmed?
3. Contrast the skills, culture, and values of the programmer with those of the social service worker. How does the contrast make it unlikely that they could understand one another or work together effectively?
4. How does Ullman distinguish between low code, high code, and applications? How does she contrast computer code language and everyday human language? Why does a real programmer want to stay "close to the machine"?

Ideas for Writing

1. Ullman acknowledges the two different languages involved in creating a program that has application for social services. Using her ideas in this essay as well as your own experiences, write an essay that discusses how conflicts between programmers' needs, the content of what is being programmed, and the needs of the user can be better integrated.
2. Computers have changed many of the jobs people have in today's workforce. Write a personal essay about how computers have influenced your job. In what ways does the computer make your job easier? In what ways does it make your work more difficult?

Technology Versus African Americans

ANTHONY WALTON

Anthony Walton (b. 1965) grew up in Chicago and in 1987 graduated with an MFA from Brown University. He has taught at several colleges and edited with Michael S. Harper The Vintage Book of African American Poetry *(1990). He is the author of* Mississippi: An American Journey *(1996), a collection of poems, song lyrics, short stories, memoirs, essays, and photographs about his family's history as slaves in Mississippi. In the following article, first published in the* Atlantic Monthly *in 1999, Walton explores the complex mixture of historical, social, and economic reasons why African-American youth are unlikely to develop their technological skills when the resources to do so are now available to them. Walton challenges and encourages African-American youth to train themselves for work with technology and in technological fields.*

───────────── ✦ ─────────────

A friend of mine owns a one-man computer firm specializing in the design and construction of Internet Web sites—those commercial, entertainment, and informational junctions in cyberspace that can be visited from personal computers around the world. From time to time he contracts for more work than he can handle, and then he posts an electronic want ad stating the number of lines of computer code to be written, the requisite computer language, the specific functions of the program being built, and the pay he's offering per line.

This ad is often answered by programmers from, as might be expected, Silicon Valley towns like San Jose and Palo Alto, or from Austin, Texas, or Cambridge, Massachusetts. The respondent might be someone recently laid off from Digital, a hacking grad student at Northwestern, or a precocious thirteen-year-old who learned the C++ language as an extra-credit project in middle school. The work is sent out over the Internet, and sent back ready to be incorporated into my friend's project. These programmers, whoever they are and wherever they're from, have proved reliable and punctual; their transactions, miraculous to the uninitiated, are so commonplace in the digital kingdom as to go unremarked.

Shortly after my friend began hiring extra help, he started getting responses from programmers in India. The Indians, often from the subcontinent's technological center of Bangalore, were savvy, literate, and, best of all, both fast and cheap—a contractor's dream. Accordingly, he has parceled out more and more programming to them and less and less to Americans. Not so patriotic, but isn't that what GATT and NAFTA are all about?

Stories like this are usually presented as cautionary tales about the loss of American jobs to the hungry masses of the Third World. But there is another troubling aspect to this story, one that loomed larger for me as I learned about what my friend did in his business and *how* he did it. Why weren't more African Americans involved in these developments, this business revolution? The activity was so clean, so sophisticated, and so lucrative; not least of all, it was the future.

5   I was reminded of the computer journalist Robert X. Cringely's documentary film *Triumph of the Nerds* (1996), about the creation of the current cyber-elite. Cringely spent time with young people at swap meets, watching them become entranced with electronics and the technological future, building their own machines and dreaming of starting the next Apple. There were no blacks in sight. Young black Americans, who could have been cashing in on the bonanza that was then buzzing through cyberspace, *didn't appear to be aware of it.* What kind of job could be more appropriate for a technologically literate inner-city youth than to perform this kind of service? Conceivably, it could be done without any capital outlay: one could surf the Net at school or the library, get the assignment and specs, and send the finished work back. Democratic guerrilla capitalism. A good job at a good wage, as the presidential hopeful Michael Dukakis[1] used to say.

There are high school kids working part time utilizing high-tech skills and college kids who are dropping out of school to work in the industry, if not starting their own companies. And as for the kids at Cringely's swap meet, it's not *likely* that any of them will start the next big thing, but it is at least possible. Apple, Hewlett Packard, and Oracle were all started with almost no capital by folks fooling around in their garages.

Where are the armies of ghetto youths ready to meet the innovation and programming needs of an exponentially expanding electronic frontier and get rich in the process, in what is perhaps the last gold rush in American history?

The history of African Americans during the past 400 years is traditionally narrated as an ongoing struggle against oppression and indifference on the part of the American mainstream, a struggle charted as an upward arc progressing toward ever more justice and opportunity. This description is accurate, but there is another, equally true way of narrating that history, and its implications are as frightening for the country as a whole as they are for blacks as a group. The history of African Americans since the discovery of the New World is the story of their encounter with technology, an encounter that has proved perhaps irremediably devastating to their hopes, dreams, and possibilities.

From the caravels, compasses, navigational techniques, and firearms of the first Portuguese explorers who reached the coast of West Africa in the 1440s to the never-ending expansion of microchip computing power and its implications for our society, the black community has had one negative encounter after another with the technological innovations of the mainstream. Within American history this aspect of blacks' experience is unique. One might argue that the disadvantageous situation of blacks vis-à-vis technology has as much to do with issues of class and wealth as it does with race, but such a critique verges on the disingenuous. As a group, blacks still lag well behind whites economically, and they have often suffered from the uses of technology in ways that other groups have not. In fact, they were often intentionally singled out to suffer. Poor whites, non-black Hispanics, and Asians were not dragged from their native lands to work as slaves and then buffeted for hundreds of years by the vagaries of technology and an economy they did not control. The historical experience of each ethnic group is unique and composed of its own problems and opportunities (or lack thereof).

What is intriguing, and deeply disturbing, is that blacks have participated as equals in the technological world only as consumers, otherwise existing on the margins of the ethos that   10 defines the nation, underrepresented as designers, innovators, and implementers of our systems and machines. As a group, they have suffered from something that can loosely be called technological illiteracy. Though this has not been the point of technological innovation, it has undeniably been its fallout. It is important that we understand and come to terms with this *now;* there are technological developments in the making that could permanently affect the destiny of black Americans, as Americans and as global citizens. The dark possibility presented by the end of highly paid low-skilled labor, ever more powerful information machines, and global capitalism renders current policy disagreements over welfare, affirmative action, integration versus separatism, and the like trivial by comparison.

These issues, in my view, go to the very marrow of black experience in North America. They may also become a matter of survival for blacks as a group and for the nation as a whole, since those two fates are inextricably connected. As the world gets faster and more information-centered, it also gets meaner: disparities of wealth and power strengthen; opportunities change and often fade away. How can black Americans achieve the promise of America when that promise is largely predicated on the sector of the country's economy (and history) that has proved most costly to them— when the disturbing outcome of their almost 500 years of encountering Western technology and its practitioners is that many regard them as at best the stepchild of the American experiment?

Europeans had prowled the Mediterranean for 2,000 years, sailing from Greece to Rome, from Rome to Egypt, from Spain to Morocco, and on hundreds of other routes, before any systematic sailing craft or technique was developed. In the 1400s the Portuguese prince who came to be known as Henry the Navigator (1394–1460) dispatched a series of voyages to make maps and chart data; by the mid-1440s the Portuguese, in search of new, unexploited trade routes, had reached Cape Verde and the Senegal River.

As they worked their way down the northwestern African coast, the Portuguese came up against what seemed at first an insurmountable problem: strong winds and currents from the north meant that a ship returning to Lisbon would have to travel long distances against the wind. Enter the caravel, with its three masts and large sails—a perfectly designed solution to the problem, and the machine that allowed Portugal to rule the waves from West Africa to India for a hundred years.

The Atlantic slave trade was one of the industries that emerged from this new capability. Western technology was involved with the rise of black slavery in other ways as well: Arab and African slave traders exchanged their human chattels for textiles, metals, and firearms, all products of Western technological wizardry, and those same slavers used guns, vastly superior to African weapons of the time, in wars of conquest against those tribes whose members they wished to capture.

The slave wars and trade were only the first of many encoun-   15
ters with Western technology to prove disastrous for people of African descent. In the United States, as in South America and the Caribbean, the slaves were themselves the technology that allowed Europeans to master the wilderness. Then, in 1793, as the efficiency of the slave economy on cotton plantations (where slaves cost more to maintain than they could generate in profits) was being questioned in some quarters, Eli Whitney, of Connecticut, invented a simple gin that allowed harvested cotton to be picked clean of seeds—an essential step before milling—on a far greater scale than had previously been possible.

Suddenly rendered cost-efficient, cotton farming became a way to get rich quick. Thousands of black Africans were imported to do the work; in Mississippi alone the number of slaves increased from 498 in 1784 to 195, 211 by 1840. Here were the roots of the millions of African Americans who would come to populate the industrial Midwest, from Kansas City to Chicago to Pittsburgh to Buffalo. Those blacks, in the great migrations following the world wars, would compose the urban proletariat that is both pouring forth black success stories and struggling with social pathologies so difficult as to seem unsolvable.

The largest northward migration of blacks took place during and after the Second World War. This exodus was largely a result of the invention of the mechanical cotton picker, which enabled three or four workers to perform a task that on some farms had required hundreds if not thousands of hands. Displaced by machinery and no longer needed in the underdeveloped American South, where they had been brought solely to do this kind of work, they went north to the industrial cities, where they encountered another kind of technology—the great factories of mass production. It was a violent shift for many whose families had known only agriculture for hundreds of years. And the Irish, Slavic, German, and Italian immigrants who were already there, felt they'd done their time, and were ready to move up resented the new competition that drove down wages. Many of the most vicious and enduring stereotypes about blacks were born of this resentment.

When those northern factories began closing and moving offshore, owing to the information and communications revolutions of the 1970s, 1980s, and 1990s, blacks were left behind in the inner cities of the Rust Belt, suffering from the metamorphosis of our society into a series of suburban megalopolises. Improvements in communications and transportation have struck the further blow of rendering the city irrelevant as a business and economic center, allowing mainstream money to be pulled out. The resulting isolation and deprivation, most eloquently outlined in the theories of the Harvard sociologist William Julius Wilson, account for the desolate urban landscapes we now see in parts of Detroit, Chicago, and Gary, Indiana.

Technology in and of itself is not at fault; it's much too simple to say that gunpowder or agricultural machinery or fiber optics has been the enemy of an entire group of people. A certain machine is put to work in a certain way—the purpose for which it was designed. The people who design the machines are not intent on unleashing chaos; they are usually trying to accomplish a task more quickly, cleanly, or cheaply, following the imperative of innovation and efficiency that has ruled Western civilization since the Renaissance.

20   Yet another aspect of technology's great cost to blacks should be considered: while the Gilded Age roared through the last part of the nineteenth century and Carnegie, Rockefeller, Vanderbilt, and others made the first great American fortunes as they wired, tracked, and fueled the new industrial society, blacks were mired in Reconstruction and its successor, Jim Crow. This circumscription limited their life prospects and, worse, those of their descendants. As the great American technopolis was built, with its avatars from Thomas Edison to Alfred P. Sloan to Bill Gates, blacks were locked out, politically and socially—and they have found it difficult to work their way in.

Blacks have traditionally been poorly educated—look at the crisis in urban public schools—and deprived of the sorts of opportunities that create the vision necessary for technological ambition. Black folkways in America, those unspoken, largely unconscious patterns of thought and belief about what is possible that guide aspiration and behavior, thus do not encompass physics and calculus. Becoming an engineer—unlike becoming a doctor or a lawyer or an insurance salesman—has not been seen as a way up in the segregated black community. These folkways developed in response to very real historical conditions, to the limited and at best ambivalent interactions between blacks and technology in this country. Folkways, the "consciousness of the race," change at a slower pace than societal conditions do—and so a working strategy can turn into a crippling blindness and self-limitation.

Some blacks—like my father, who worked for nearly fifty years in a factory that, ironically, recently moved from Illinois to the low-wage Mississippi he left as a boy—have been able to operate within these narrow parameters, to accept slow and steady progress while positioning their children to jump into the mainstream. But blacks are also Americans, and as such are subject not only to notions of a steady rise but also to the restless ambition that seems a peculiarly American disease. Not channeled to follow the largely technological possibilities for success in this society, black folkways have instead embraced the sort of magical thinking that is encouraged by the media and corporations whose sole interest in blacks is as consumers.

You, too, can be Michael Jordan or Coolio—just buy the shoes, just have the right look. No need to study, no need to work, the powers that be are against you anyway. Young blacks believe that they have a better chance of becoming Jordan, a combination of genes, will, talent, and family that happens every hundred years, than of becoming Steve Jobs, the builder of two billion-dollar corporations, the first one started with his best friend while tinkering in his garage. They also don't dream of becoming programmers at Cisco Systems, a low-profile computer giant that hires 5,000 new workers a year and scours the globe to find them. Blacks make up 13 percent of the population in this country, yet in 1995 they earned a shockingly low 1.8 percent of the Ph.D.s conferred in computer science, 2.1 percent of those in engineering, 1.5 percent in the physical sciences, and 0.6 percent in mathematics. As I lamented earlier, the very opportunities that would allow young blacks to vault over decades of injury and neglect into the modern world go unclaimed—even unseen.

Mastery of technology is second only to money as the true measure of accomplishment in this country, and it is very likely that by tolerating this underrepresentation in the technological realm, and by not questioning and examining the folkways that have encouraged it, blacks are allowing themselves to be kept out of the mainstream once again. This time, however, they will be excluded from the greatest cash engine of the twenty-first century. Inner-city blacks in particular are in danger, as "clean communities"—such as Du Page County, outside Chicago, and the beautiful suburbs that ring the decay of Hartford, glittering cybercities on the hill, the latest manifestation of the American Dream—shed the past and learn to exist without contemplating or encountering the tragedy of the inner city.

25   But all dreams end, and when we wake, we must face reality. Despite these trends, and the dangers they imply, not all is lost. What might be accomplished by an education system that truly tried to educate *everyone* to excellence, not just the children of elites and of the suburbs? Why not a technological Marshall Plan for the nation's schools? Even in this time of fiscal constriction and resistance to public expenditure—at least, any expenditure that does not directly benefit those doing the spending—such a plan is feasible. What if *uber* technocrats like Bill Gates and Larry Ellison (the billionaire CEO of Oracle) used their philanthropic millions to fund basic math and science education in elementary schools, to equip the future, instead of giving away merchandise that essentially serves to expand their customer base? That would be a gift worthy of their accomplishments, and one of true historical weight in the life of the nation.

And blacks must change as well. The ways that served their ancestors through captivity and coming to freedom have begun to lose their utility. If blacks are to survive as full participants in this society, they have to understand *and apply* what works *now*. Otherwise they will be unable to cross the next technological threshold that emerges in human civilization. Blacks have to imagine ways to encourage young people into the technological mainstream, because that looks like the future. In fact, it always has been the future, and blacks, playing catch-up yet again, must reach for it to ensure themselves a place at the American table.

Endnote

1. Michael Dukakis (b. 1933): 1988 Democratic presidential candidate.

Questions for Discussion

1. Walton argues that African Americans have had a particular and difficult connection to technology. In what way has technology harmfully affected the black community throughout history, according to Walton?
2. In what ways has the economic and political status of African Americans in the United States contributed to their negative relationship with technology? Why is technology inherently injurious to the black community, in Walton's view?
3. Why does Walton believe that it is important for African Americans to get involved with technology beyond the level of consumerism? Why does he think that "black folkways" and poor education are contributing to the lack of African-American interest in computer science?
4. Walton states that the "mastery of technology is second only to money as the true measure of [a person's] accomplishment in this country." Do you

agree with this statement? Why or why not? What are some other ways that a person's achievements can be measured?

Ideas for Writing

1. Do you agree with Walton's ideas on technology and its role in the lives of African-American workers? Why or why not? Write an essay supporting or arguing against Walton's opinions concerning technology and its relationship to African Americans.

2. Walton believes that the African-American connection to technology is unique and different from that of other ethnic people. Research the recent history of another ethnic group in the United States, such as Latinos. What has their relationship with technology been like? How is it different or similar to the experiences of African Americans? Write about your findings. Did your research support or differ from Walton's ideas?

Scripted Talk

ADRIA SCHARF

Sociologist Adria Scharf is a writer for and coeditor of the magazine Dollars & Sense, *which presents the ideas of economists, journalists, and activists committed to economic democracy and social justice. Prior to her job with* Dollars & Sense, *Scharf worked as a senior researcher and trainer at Ownership Associates, Inc. Her writing has also been published in* Left Business Observer, Journal of Employee Ownership Law and Finance, *and* Washington Housing Quarterly. *The selection below is taken from Scharf's article "Scripted Talk" (2002) and was originally published in* Dollars & Sense. *In this essay she explains how the food service industry forces its workers to utilize scripts and how its managers use spies as well as videotaping in order to increase profits. This article asks you to think about the negative effects of using technology to help employers control and monitor their employees and their interactions with customers.*

——————————— ✦ ———————————

Now one of the very first requirements for a man who is fit to handle pig iron as a regular occupation is that he shall be so stupid and so phlegmatic that he more nearly resembles in his mental make-up the ox than any other type. . . . He is so stupid that the word "percentage" has no meaning to him, and he must consequently be trained by a man more intelligent than

himself into the habit of working in accordance with the laws
of this science before he can be successful.
—Frederick Winslow Taylor, *The Principles of Scientific*
Management (1911)

Good evening and welcome to Cineplex Theater, Can I get you the super-combo popcorn-softdrink special this evening?

"Just a small drink," you say, your "hi, how are you" preempted by the question.

The worker at the snack counter takes your money, hands you a cup, and sends you off with a flat "thank you and enjoy the show."

The exchange may feel unnatural, even awkward. But scripted talk is more than just an annoying quirk of the modern service economy. It represents a deep form of managerial control—a regimentation of the labor process so total that it extends even to speech. Scripts are a fact of life for retail and service workers whose employers make use of a timeworn early-20th century managerial strategy: Taylorism.

5   In the 1910s and 1920s, a harsh new management system swept the nation's stockyards and factories. It called for managers to break jobs down into easily replicable, often mind-numbing, steps. The originator and foremost proponent of the system, Frederick W. Taylor, called his approach "scientific management," as it purported to apply scientific principles to the production process.

Taylor advocated strict separation between "thinking" and "doing." Managers and engineers in the central planning department were to do the "thinking"; workers, the "doing." He emptied labor of discretion and skill by reducing jobs to series of regimented tasks, eliminating all unnecessary body movements. A foreman with a stopwatch monitored and timed performance.

In the manufacturing sector, Taylorism was met with resistance from workers who saw their jobs deskilled and their control over the shop floor eroded. Over time, management developed more participatory practices like quality circles and suggestion systems that aim to elicit worker effort through overtures of collaboration. (And many manufacturing operations continue to rely primarily on Taylorist methods.)

But in large swaths of the economy—especially in the service, retail, and clerical occupations that employ up to 42% of the U.S. workforce—old-fashioned Taylorism is expanding. And in service jobs that require workers to interact with customers, Taylorist control extends to the words workers utter. From "Welcome to McDonald's" to "Paper or plastic?" scripted talk is the rule for much "interactive service work." It's found in operations where volume sales drive profit, industry competition is intense, and where management takes a uniform, cookie-cutter approach to delivering a service—for example, in chain fast-food joints, coffee houses, and restaurants, and in call centers and mass retail stores.

Corporate scripting of speech expands the deskilling of workers to personal and social terrain. Not only are workers' bodily movements broken down into standardized subtasks, monitored intensively, and clocked, but their ability to converse with consumers and sometimes with each other is also subject to company control. The surveillance once performed by a foreman takes stealthy and invasive new forms in the service economy. Retail and restaurant companies use undercover "secret shoppers" to monitor workers' adherence to company scripts, while call centers— which employ 3% of the U.S. workforce—use sophisticated new technologies to record workers' every interaction with customers.

Managers argue that Taylorism is efficient. And to many   10
time-harried consumers, it offers predictable service and reduces kinks and slowdowns produced by disorganization. But the human toll of this mode of control is steep. And it turns out that the benefits may not be as great as managers—or Taylor himself— have claimed. Indeed, the expansion of Taylorism into the service sector has replicated all the problems that it caused in mass production—profound worker alienation, physical exhaustion, and stress—which contribute to astronomical quit rates in Taylorized jobs. Moreover, research suggests that other more humane ways of organizing work can be equally effective.

REGIMENTED TALK

At Taylorized service companies, work is organized much like in mass production assembly plants. "At McDonald's, almost every decision about how to do crew people's tasks has been made in advance by the corporation," says sociologist Robin Leidner in her book *Fast Food, Fast Talk*. Counter workers at McDonald's follow the Six Steps of Window Service: greet the customer, take the order, assemble the order, present the order, receive payment, thank the customer and ask for repeat business. The specific way they speak to customers may even be subject to rules. Leidner says McDonald's workers were instructed to say "May I help you, ma'am" rather than "Can I help someone?"

At Starbucks coffee shops, workers are supposed to greet the customer within 30 seconds from the time he or she enters the store; chat with the customer before taking the order; "call out" the coffee drink to the barista according to company specs (listing the temperature, the size, the modifiers, then the name of drink, in that order); then make eye contact and say "Have a nice day."

CLOCKED TALK

Telephone operators now typically handle 1,000 calls a day, and their job-cycle time (for example, the length of time it takes to answer a directory assistance request) averages just 20 seconds, according to Cornell University economist Rosemary Batt.

In interactive service work, whether at the drive-through window of a fast-food restaurant or a call-center computer station, speed is paramount. Employers time each step of the work procedure and drive workers to complete transactions at top speed so as to maximize volume and minimize labor costs. Scripting of speech is essential to this end.

15   Fast-food drive-through window workers must greet customers almost instantly—often within three seconds from the time the car reaches the menu board. Digital timers—visible to the worker, manager, and sometimes the customer—are wired to sensors buried underneath the drive-through lane. They measure how long it takes the worker to issue the greeting, take the order, and process the payment. When a worker falls behind the "targeted time goal" for a particular subtask, timers spur her on with chimes, sirens, or recorded messages. Sales of timers have doubled each year since 1994, according to the *Wall Street Journal*.

Former McDonald's CEO Jack Greenberg claimed that unit sales increase 1% for every six seconds saved at the drive-through. Because restaurant profits lie in shaving seconds off of "window time," store managers strive for drive-through times of 90 seconds (the industry average is 204 seconds).

SLICK TALK

Many consumers have come to expect national fast-food corporations to require their workers to follow standardized scripts. A new generation of corporate scripts, though, has taken more insidious forms.

Chains like Starbucks write employee scripts to sound not merely polite, but chatty and sincere. "We're effectively required to make small talk," says James Boone, who works the register at a Starbucks in southern Louisiana. "The company provides a list of questions it suggests we use to start the small talk, like 'How's that weather?' 'How's the family?' We're not supposed to talk about politics. And we have to close with 'Have a nice day.'" Should the customer actually be an undercover secret shopper sent by management to evaluate workers. Boone knows he'll get points docked for not saying "Have a nice day."

Mass retail stores, restaurants, and call centers also require their workers to participate in subtle or overt sales work. Besides simply ringing up purchases, taking a menu order, or answering consumer questions, workers are directed to hawk products, services, gimmicks, or expensive menu items in every service encounter. Because many workers find this task manipulative, awkward and alienating, employers enforce their compliance through covert surveillance.

SECRET SHOPPERS AND DIGITAL RECORDING TECHNOLOGY

Fekkak Mamdouh, Director of the Restaurant Opportunities   20
Center of New York (ROC-NY), a worker center, has a term for secret or mystery shoppers. "We call them 'busters.' Few of them will tell the boss that everything is perfect." Mamdouh knows of workers who were fired based on mystery shoppers' allegations.

Companies like Starbucks, the Olive Garden, and Marriott Hotels contract with mystery shopper companies to dispatch "service quality auditors"—secret shoppers—who, disguised as regular customers, monitor worker performance. Most national restaurant chains and hotels, and many mass retailers, now contract with mystery shopper companies. Virtually all of Taco Bell's 5,300 restaurants receive at least one visit from a clandestine auditor each month.

Rochelle Thomas has worked for five years at the Seattle franchise of a national Italian restaurant chain. Headquarters makes sure that Thomas' store is "secret shopped" every two weeks. "When we take the dinner order, we have to suggestively sell five things: a drink, a side dish, a dessert, specials, and a special offer. You have to mention all five." Suggestive selling means naming specific high-price menu items. "We can't say, 'Would you like something to drink?' We have to say, 'Can I start you off with a glass of chianti?' If they have kids, we suggest sparkling water." At any one of her tables, an undercover monitor may be checking to make sure she complies with the suggestive selling requirements. "If you get a 'bad shopper' [meaning a bad report], the restaurant gives you terrible shifts for a week as punishment, and fewer tables. And they say if you get a couple of bad ones, they'll fire you."

The uncertainty makes secret shoppers an economical way for companies to control workers. Because workers don't know when they are actually being secret shopped, they modify their behavior as if they were always being watched.

At call centers, workers simultaneously talk on the telephone and navigate through computer screens. As in restaurants and chain stores, adherence to scripts is monitored and enforced. A 2002 survey of 735 North American call centers shows that 93% monitor customer service agent calls, an increase over the past two years, according to the book *Call Center Operation: Design, Operation, and Maintenance*. Forty percent monitor both workers' voices and their computer screens. And modern monitoring techniques go beyond supervisors' occasionally listening in for "quality assurance purposes." Sophisticated new digital tapping technologies ensure that every transaction is either heard or recorded. Furthermore, supervisors may convert a voice transaction to text, do word searches, and even e-mail the interaction transcript to higher-ups in the company for disciplinary action or "training opportunities." And they can alternate among multiple workers' screens to monitor an entire group. Secret monitoring modes enable supervisors to observe workers undetected. Finally, some "quality monitoring systems" claim to measure customer service representatives' stress levels and other emotional indices. Sales of call recording software reached $323 million last year, up $45 million since 2001, and the market analysis firm Datamonitor predicts sales will hit $538 million a year by 2007, according to the *New York Times*.

25 Call center workers are required to sell corporate products, services, and special offers—not just in "outbound" centers like telemarketing firms, but in "inbound" centers that answer toll-free calls as well. "There's an attempt to convert any service into a sales call," says Batt. And workers know that if they deviate from the script, they may face disciplinary action.

The convert monitoring exacerbates stress and physical exhaustion. Rochelle Thomas explains, "We have to greet the table within 30 seconds of sit-down—to at least welcome the customer and say 'I'll be right with you.' We take their drink order within three minutes. After food hits the table, within three minutes we check back to make sure everything is OK. If I'm working a whole section, I have to push myself all night because the 30-second rule doesn't change, even if I'm juggling 10 tables. There's just no slack." It's not surprising that chain restaurants have a median worker turnover rate of 125% per year. In the call center industry, turnover rates are typically 35% to 50% per year, and far higher in some companies.

In the capitalist employment relationship, employers by definition have the right to direct the work of employees. But Taylorism takes the logic of managerial authority to an extreme. It applies intensive managerial control to the bodily movements and behavior of working people. In requiring workers to perform scripted talk, it produces alienation from one's own words and from one another. As Robin Leidner puts it, the "standardization of human interactions does encroach on social space not previously dominated by economic rationality. It shifts the meanings of such fundamental values as individuality and authenticity, raising troubling issues of identity for workers and customers."

ANOTHER WAY IS POSSIBLE

There are other, better, ways to organize service work. The Communication Workers of America has developed contract language on working procedures in call centers. The language prevents managers from using monitoring to discipline workers. Recordings are to be used for training purposes only. The union is also developing new formulas for sales quotas and call handling time.

Economist Rosemary Batt found that call center jobs organized as self-managed teams were far more productive in terms of sales volume and customer service than Taylorized call center jobs within the same company. The self-managed teams could decide how to conduct their work and interact with customers, and they set group goals and regulated themselves.

Finally, in the United States there are an estimated 1,000 to 5,000 worker cooperatives, or businesses owned by worker-members, and many more collectives—nonhierarchial organizations that are not cooperatives but do make decisions democratically. In worker cooperatives and collectives, authority resides in the workforce as a whole. For instance, at the Seward Cafe, a collectively owned and managed restaurant in Minneapolis, there is no manager. A set of job descriptions defines the basic work procedures but allows flexibility within those descriptions. Speech is not scripted. "As a consensus organization, we value a whole variety of different ways of communicating and interpreting what's happening. We value the fact that workers aren't censored," says Tom Pierson, a counter worker at the cafe. He says that speed is not compromised. But even if it were, the tradeoff would certainly be worth it.

Questions for Discussion

1. Scharf says that "corporate scripting of speech expands the de-skilling of workers to personal and social terrain." How does she support her thesis? Do you agree with her? Why or why not? Do you think that there is any way a person who works in the service industry could practice personal and social skills outside of "scripted" interactions?

2. Saving time is one of the major goals of corporations in the service industry. What are some of the ways that the industry utilizes language in order to make employees perform more efficiently? After reading this article, do you think that "scripted talk" helps these businesses realize their goal? Why or why not?

3. How are "secret" or "mystery shoppers" employed to make sure that service workers are using scripted speech? Why does this covert monitoring lead to high stress among these employees? Can you think of alternative ways that employers could supervise their personnel?

4. What are some of the suggestions that Scharf provides for "better ways to organize service work"? Do you agree with her ideas? Why or why not? Can you suggest some alternative ways to manage businesses in the service industry?

Ideas for Writing

1. Write an essay about "Taylorism" and its connection to scripted talk. Who was Frederick W. Taylor and what was his approach to scientific management? How does the use of scripted talk fit into this type of management? Why do so many businesses organize their companies in this fashion, making their service workers use scripted talk? Do you think "Taylorism" and scripted talk make companies run more efficiently? Why or why not?

2. Take a few trips to local service industry stores like Starbucks and McDonald's and listen to the language that the employees use. Take notes on the phrases that they use and see if they seem to be utilizing a script. Write an essay about your findings. Did you find this type of speech to be helpful or alienating, neither, or both? What other reactions did you have to the scripted talk? Why? After studying your experience of interacting with a worker employing scripted talk, do you think these scripts should be used? Why or why not? Write an essay that presents your point of view. Do research on this topic and also use your personal experiences to support your perspective.

High-Tech Stress

JEREMY RIFKIN

Jeremy Rifkin has a degree in international affairs from Tufts University and an economics degree from the University of Pennsylvania's Wharton School of Business. His lectures, articles, and books have had a great influence on public perception and international policy in areas such as environmentalism, bioethics, globalization, and the modern high-tech workplace. He is founder and president of the activist organization, Foundation on Economic Trends (at http://www.foet.org), located in Washington, D.C. Rifkin also writes for journals and newspapers, such as the Los Angeles Times, The Guardian, Frankfurter Allgemeine, *and* Le Monde, *and has made numerous television appearances. Rifkin's books include* The Biotech Century *(1998),* The Age of Access: The New Culture of Hypercapitalism *(2000), and* The Hydrogen Economy *(2002). In the following chapter from his book* The End of Work *(1995) Rifkin argues that the stress and anxiety of the high-tech workplace can do damage to one's physical and mental health.*

————————— ✦ —————————

Much has been said and written about quality-control circles, teamwork, and greater participation by employees at the worksite. Little, however, has been said or written about the de-skilling of work, the accelerating pace of production, the increased workloads, and the new forms of coercion and subtle intimidation that are used to force worker compliance with the requirements of post-Fordist production practices.

The new information technologies are designed to remove whatever vestigial control workers still exercise over the production process by programming detailed instructions directly into the machine, which then carries them out verbatim. The worker is rendered powerless to exercise independent judgment either on the factory floor or in the office, and has little or no control over outcomes dictated in advance by expert programmers. Before the computer, management laid out detailed instructions in the form of "schedules," which workers were then expected to follow. Because the execution of the task lay in the hands of the workers, it was possible to introduce a subjective element into the process. In implementing the work schedule, each employee placed his or her unique stamp on the production process. The shift from scheduling production to programming production has profoundly altered the relationship of workers to work. Now, an increasing number of workers act solely as observers, unable to participate or intervene in the production process. What unfolds in the plant or office has already been pre-programmed by another person who may never personally participate in the automated future as it unfolds.

When numerically controlled equipment was first introduced in the late 1950s, management was quick to appreciate the increased element of control it provided over work on the factory floor. In an address before the Electronic Industries Association in 1957, Air Force Lieutenant General C. S. Irvine, Deputy Chief of Staff for Materiel, noted that "heretofore, regardless of how carefully drawn and specified on paper, a finished piece [of machinery] could not be any better than the machinist's interpretations." The advantage of numerical control, argued Irvine, is that "since specifications are converted to objective digital codes of electronic impulses, the element of judgment is limited to that of the design engineer alone. Only his interpretations are directed from the tool to the workplace." Others shared Irvine's enthusiasm for numerical control. In the late 1950s. Nils Olesten, general supervisor of Rohr Aircraft, stated publicly at the time what was privately on every manager's mind. "Numerical control," said Olesten, "gives maximum control of the machine to management. . . . since decision making at the machine tool has been removed from the operator and is now in the form of pulses on the control media." The quick adoption of numerical control was inspired as much by management's desire to consolidate greater control over decision making on the shop floor as to boost productivity.

A machinist at a Boeing plant in Seattle at the time numerical controls were first introduced voiced the frustration and anger of many semiskilled and skilled workers whose expertise was being transferred onto a magnetic tape: "I felt so stifled, my brain wasn't needed any more. You just sit there like a dummy and stare at the damn thing [a four-axis N/C milling machine]. I'm used to being in control, doing my own planning. Now, I feel like someone else has made all the decisions for me."

5   Of course, it is true that re-engineering and the new information technologies allow companies to collapse layers of management and place more control in the hands of work teams at the point of production. The intent, however, is to increase management's ultimate control over production. Even the effort to solicit the ideas of workers on how to improve performance is designed

to increase both the pace and productivity of the plant or office and more fully exploit the full potential of the employees. Some critics, like German social scientist Knuth Dohse, contend that Japanese lean production "is simply the practice of the organizational principles of Fordism under conditions in which management prerogatives are largely unlimited."

A wealth of statistics collected over the past half decade bring into serious question the merits of many of the "new" management techniques being introduced into factories and offices around the world. In Japanese factories, for example, where working hours are 200 to 500 hours longer each year than in the United States, life on the assembly line is so fast-paced and stressful that most workers experience significant fatigue. According to a 1986 survey by the All Toyota Union, more than 124,000 of the company's 200,000 member workers suffered from chronic fatigue.

It should be pointed out that the principles of scientific management have long been known in Japan. Japanese automakers began using them in earnest in the late 1940s. By the mid-1950s, Japanese companies had created a hybrid form of Taylorism uniquely suited to their own circumstances and production goals. ... In post-Fordist production, work teams made up of staff and line employees participate in planning decisions in order to improve productivity. Once a consensus has been reached, however, the plan of action is automated into the production process and carried out unflaggingly by everyone on the line. Workers are also encouraged to stop the production line and make on-the-spot quality control decisions, again with the intent of increasing the pace and predictability of operations.

Unlike traditional scientific management practiced in the United States, which denied workers any say in how the work is to be done, Japanese management decided early on to engage its workers in order to more fully exploit both their mental and physical labor, using a combination of motivational techniques and old-fashioned coercion. On the one hand, workers are encouraged to identify with the company, to think of it as their home and security. As noted earlier, much of their life outside of work is involved with company-related programs, including quality circles and social outings and trips. The companies become "total institutions," say Kenney and Florida, "exerting influence over many aspects of social life." In this regard, "they bear some resemblance to other forms of total institutions such as religious orders or the military." On the other hand, in return for their loyalty, workers are guaranteed lifetime employment.

Japanese workers often remain with the same company for their entire career.

Management often relies on its work teams to discipline members. Peer-review committees continually pressure recalcitrant or slow workers to perform up to par. Because the work teams are not supplied with additional help to make up for absentee workers, the remaining members must work even harder to catch up. As a result, tremendous peer pressure is exerted on employees to be at work on time. Japanese management is unyielding on the issue of absenteeism. In many plants all absences, even documented illnesses, are put on the employee's record. If a worker at Toyota misses five days of work a year, he or she is subject to dismissal.

10 Authors Mike Parker and Jane Slaughter, who studied the Toyota-GM joint venture in California to make Toyota Corollas and Chevrolet Novas, characterize Japanese lean-production practices as "management by stress." The Toyota-GM plant has succeeded in greatly improving productivity, reducing the work time required to assemble a Nova from twenty-two hours to fourteen. They have accomplished this by introducing an overhead visual display, called an Andon board. Each worker's station is represented by a rectangular box. If a worker falls behind or needs help, he pulls a cord and his rectangular area lights up. If the light remains on for one minute or more, the line stops. In a traditional plant the desired goal would be to keep the light off and production running smoothly. In management by stress, however, unlit warning lights signal inefficiency. The idea is to continually speed up and stress the system to find out where the weaknesses and soft spots are, so that the new designs and procedures can be implemented to increase the pace and performance.

According to Parker and Slaughter, "stressing the system can be accomplished by increasing the line speed, cutting the number of people or machines, or giving workers more tasks. Similarly, a line can be 'balanced' by decreasing resources or increasing the work load at positions that always run smoothly. Once problems have been corrected, the system can be further stressed and then balanced again. . . . The ideal is for the system to run with all stations oscillating between lights on and lights off."

Parker and Slaughter believe that the team concept of lean production is as far removed from enlightened management practices as is possible to conceive and that from the workers' perspective is merely a new, more sophisticated way to exploit them. While the authors acknowledge the limited participation of workers in planning and problem solving, they say it serves only to make workers willing accomplices in their own exploitation. Under management by stress, when the workers are able to identify weak points on the line and make recommendations or take remedial action, management simply increases the pace of production and further stresses the system. The key is to continually locate weak spots in a never-ending process of continuous improvement or *kaizin*. The effect on the workers of this Draconian method of management is devastating: "As the line goes faster and the whole system is stressed, it becomes harder and harder to keep up. Since tasks have been so painstakingly charted, refined, and recharted, management assumes any glitch is the workers' fault, chimes and lights of the Andon board immediately identify the person who is not keeping up."

The pace of production in Japanese-managed plants often results in increased injuries. Mazda reported three times the number of injuries per hundred than in comparable General Motors, Chrysler, and Ford auto plants.

Worker stress under lean-production practices has reached near-epidemic proportions in Japan. The problem has become so acute that the Japanese government has even coined a term, *karoshi*, to explain the pathology of the new production-related illness. A spokesperson for Japan's National Institute of Public Health defines *karoshi* as "a condition in which psychologically unsound work practices are allowed to continue in such a way that disrupts the worker's normal work and life rhythms, leading to a buildup of fatigue in the body and a chronic condition of overwork accompanied by a worsening of preexisting high blood pressure and finally resulting in a fatal breakdown."

Karoshi is becoming a worldwide phenomenon. The introduction of computerized technology has greatly accelerated the pace and flow of activity at the workplace, forcing millions of workers to adapt to the rhythms of a nanosecond culture.

BIORHYTHMS AND BURNOUT

The human species, like every other species, is made up of myriad biological clocks that have been entrained, through the long period of evolution, to the rhythms and rotation of the earth: Our bodily functions and processes are timed to the larger forces of nature—the circadian day, lunar and seasonal cycles. Until the modern industrial ear, bodily rhythms and economic rhythms were largely compatible. Craft production was conditioned by the speed of the human hand and body and constrained by the power that could be generated by harnessing animals, wind, and water. The introduction of steam power and later electrical power vastly increased the pace of transforming, processing, and producing goods and services, creating an economic grid whose operating speed was increasingly at odds with the slower biological rhythms of the human body. Today's computer culture operates on a nanosecond time gradient—a unit of duration that is so small that it cannot even be experienced by the human senses. In a snap of the fingers more than 500 million nanoseconds have elapsed. Author Geoff Simons draws an analogy that captures the awesome speed of computer time: "Imagine . . . two computers conversing with each other over a period. They are then asked by a human being what they are talking about, and in the time he takes to pose the question, the two computers have exchanged more words than the sum total of all the words exchanged by human beings since Homo sapiens first appeared on earth 2 or 3 million years ago."

In the industrial era, workers became so enmeshed in the rhythms of mechanical machinery that they often described their own fatigue in machine terms—complaining of being "worn-out" or experiencing a "breakdown." Now, a growing number of workers are becoming so integrated with the rhythms of the new computer culture that when they become stressed, they experience "overload" and when they feel unable to cope they "burn out" and "shut down," euphemisms that reflect how closely workers have come to identify with the pace set by computer technology.

Psychologist Craig Brod, who has written extensively on stress induced by the high-tech computer culture, says that the increased pace of the workplace has only increased the impatience of workers, resulting in unprecedented levels of stress. In office situations, clerical and service workers become accustomed to "interfacing" with computers and "accessing" information at lighting speeds. In contrast, slower forms of human interaction become increasingly intolerable and a source of growing stress. Brod cites the example of the office worker who "becomes impatient with phone callers who take too long to get to the point." Even the computer itself is becoming a source of stress as a growing number of impatient users demand faster and faster responses. One study found that a computer response time of more then 1.5 seconds in duration was likely to trigger impatience and stress on the part of the user.

Computer monitoring of employee performance is also causing high levels of stress. Brod recounts the experience of one of his patients, a supermarket cashier. When Alice's employer installed electronic cash registers, built into the computer-run machines was a counter that "transmits to a central terminal a running amount of how many items each cashier has run up that day." Alice no longer takes the time to talk with customers, as it slows down the number of items she can scan across the electronic grid and might jeopardize her job.

A repair service company in Kansas keeps a running computer tally of the number of calls its employees process and the amount of information collected with each telephone call. One stressed employee explains that "if you get a call from a friendly person who wants to chat, you have to hurry the caller off because it would count against you. It makes my job very unpleasant."

According to a 1987 report published by the Office of Technology Assessment, entitled *The Electronic Supervisor,* between 20 and 35 percent of all clerical workers in the United States are now monitored by sophisticated computer systems. The OTA report warns of an Orwellian future of "electronic sweatshops" with employees doing "boring, repetitive, fast paced work that requires constant alertness and attention to detail, where the supervisor isn't even human" but an "unwinking computer taskmaster."

The critical factor in productivity has shifted from physical to mental response and from brawn to brain. Companies are continually experimenting with new methods to optimize the "interface" between employees and their computers. For example, in an effort to speed up the processing of information, some visual display units are now being programmed so that if the operator does not respond to the data on the screen within seventeen seconds it disappears. Researchers report that operators experience increasing stress as the time approaches for the image to disappear on the screen. "From the eleventh second they begin to perspire, then the heart rate goes up. Consequently, they experience enormous fatigue."

Even small, subtle changes in office routine have increased the stress level of workers. Brod recalls the experience of Karen, a typist. Before the shift from typewriters to word processors Karen would "use the physical cue of removing the paper from her typewriter to remind her to take a break." Now, sitting in front of the computer display terminal, Karen processes an unending stream of information. There is never a natural point to signal an end and a break. According to Brod, Karen "no longer takes time to chat with the other secretaries in the office pool," because they are

20

similarly glued to their screens, processing their own incessant flow of information. "At the end of the morning," says Brod, "she is exhausted, and wonders how she'll find the energy to complete the day's work."

The new computer-based technologies have so quickened the volume, flow, and pace of information that millions of workers are experiencing mental "overload" and "burnout." The physical fatigue generated by the fast pace of the older industrial economy is being eclipsed by the mental fatigue generated by the nanosecond pace of the new information economy. According to a study conducted by the National Institute of Occupational Safety and Health (NIOSH), clerical workers who use computers suffer inordinately high levels of stress.

25   The hyperefficient high-tech economy is undermining the mental and physical well-being of millions of workers around the world. The International Labor Organization says that "stress has become one of the most serious health issues of the 20th century." In the United States alone, job stress costs employers in excess of $200 billion a year in absenteeism, reduced productivity, medical expenses, and compensation claims. In the United Kingdom, job stress costs up to 10 percent of the annual gross national product. According to an ILO report, published in 1993, the increased levels of stress are a result of the fast pace set by new automated machinery both on the factory floor and in the front offices. Of particular concern, says the ILO, is computer surveillance of workers. The UN agency cites a University of Wisconsin study that found that "electronically monitored workers were 10 to 15 percent more likely to suffer depression, tension and extreme anxiety."

High stress levels often lead to health-related problems, including ulcers, high blood pressure, heart attacks, and strokes. Increased stress also results in alcohol and drug abuse. The Metropolitan Life Insurance Company estimated that an average of one million workers missed work on any given day because of stress-related disorders. Another study commissioned by the National Life Insurance Company found that 14 percent of the workers sampled had quit or changed jobs in the previous two years because of workplace stress. In recent surveys, more than 75 percent of American workers "describe their jobs as stressful and believe that the pressure is steadily increasing."

More than 14,000 workers die from accidents on the job each year and another 2.2 million suffer disabling injuries. Although the ostensible cause of the accidents can vary from faulty equipment to the pace of production, investigators say that stress is most often the trigger that precipitates the errors. Says one ILO investigator, "of all the personal factors related to the causation of accidents, only one emerged as a common denominator, a high level of stress at the time the accident occurred. . . . A person under stress is an accident about to happen."

Questions for Discussion

1. How do computer-automated machines take all of the power away from skilled workers and contribute to job stress and frustration, according to Rifkin?

2. How does Rifkin respond to the argument that the "Japanese lean production" approach puts more power in the hands of work teams than the older "Fordist," hierarchical production structure? Is his use of surveys, personal testimony, and quotations from "authorities" on this issue convincing? If you were not convinced, what was missing in Rifkin's rhetorical approach?

3. How effective is Rifkin's presentation of the metaphors that workers use to describe their job stress in the modern computer culture workplace? Can you think of other expressions that use machine imagery to describe their physical or mental health issues? How effective are these images?

4. How well does Rifkin make his point that the computer-oriented and -monitored workplace is causing employees' "mental and physical well-being" to suffer? What hard facts and statistics does he provide to support his causal argument here?

Ideas for Writing

1. Rifkin's book was written over ten years ago. Do some contemporary research on workers' compensation claims and related statistics; then write an essay in which you demonstrate whether workplace stress has increased or decreased over the past decade. Is it possible that the stress Rifkin describes could be due in part to workers being unaccustomed to using high-tech machines in the workplace, and that younger workers today who have grown up in high-tech environments have fewer stress-related problems than workers from the previous generation?

2. Write an essay in which you suggest some alternatives to the feeling of "powerlessness" that many workers experience in a highly controlled technological workplace. Do some research on this issue before writing your essay. Include any personal experiences that are relevant.

Is Your Job Going Abroad?
JYOTI THOTTAM

Raised in Queens, New York, and Houston, Texas, Jyoti Thottam is a graduate of Yale and Columbia Universities. She has worked as a journalist in India and Thailand, and has published articles in the Wall Street Journal, *the* Village Voice, *and the* Christian Science Monitor. *Currently, she is a reporter for* Time *magazine. Her articles help to explain complex technology and workplace issues to audiences lacking advanced knowledge on her topic. In the article below, "Is Your Job Going Abroad?" (2004), Thottam examines the nature and consequences of "outsourcing," a strategy whereby U.S. companies hire workers overseas to do manufacturing and technology jobs at lower costs, a practice that can lead to a loss of jobs for American employees.*

✦

Rosen Sharma is sure about one thing. His nine-month-old company, Solidcore, a start-up that makes backup security systems for computers, could not survive without outsourcing. By lowering his development costs, the 18 engineers who work for him in India for as little as one-fourth the salary of their American counterparts allow him to spend money on 13 senior managers, engineers and marketing people in Silicon Valley. If he doesn't outsource, in fact, the venture capitalists who fund start-ups like his won't give him a nickel. Sharma's Indian-American team, tethered by a broadband connection, gets his product in front of customers faster and cheaper. "As a business, you have to stay competitive," he says. "If we don't do it, our competitors will, and they're going to blow us away."

But Sharma's sharp analysis loses its edge when he thinks about what decisions like his will mean someday for his children, a 2-year-old daughter and another on the way. "As a father, my reaction is different than my reaction as a CEO," he says. He believes that companies like his will always need senior people in the U.S., like the systems architects who design new products and the experienced salespeople who close deals. "But if you're graduating from college today, where are the entry level jobs?" Sharma asks quietly. How do you get to that secure, skilled job when the path that leads you there has disappeared?

That's an issue that economists, politicians and workers are struggling with as the U.S. finds itself in the middle of a structural shift in the economy that no one quite expected. There must be a mix-up here. We ordered a recovery, heavy on the jobs, please. What we're getting is a new kind of homeland insecurity powered by the rise of outsourcing, a bland yet ominous piece of business jargon that seems to imply that every call center, insurance-claims processor, programming department and Wall Street back office is being moved to India, Ireland or some other place thousands of miles away.

To be sure, public anxiety and election-year finger pointing have blurred some important distinctions. To set them straight: most of the jobs that have shifted to places like Mexico and China in the past several decades have been in manufacturing, which is being done with ever increasing sophistication in low-wage countries. Some have also blamed trade-liberalization deals like the North American Free Trade Agreement (NAFTA), which the Labor Department estimates was responsible for the loss of more than 500,000 U.S. jobs between 1994 and 2002. That's a significant number but modest in comparison with the millions of jobs that are created and lost annually in the constant churn of the U.S. economy. Indeed, much of the job loss during the recent U.S. recession was cyclical in nature. But in recent years, one noteworthy segment of the economy began suffering from the permanent change of outsourcing (or off-shoring), particularly the movement of service-industry, technology-oriented jobs to overseas locations with lower salaries. What puts teeth into the buzz word is the sense that getting outsourced could happen to almost anyone.

Outsourcing, primarily to India, accounts for less than 10% 5 of the 2.3 million jobs lost in the U.S. over the past three years. But the trend is speeding up, and it is quickly becoming the defining economic issue of the election campaign. The administration learned that the hard way a few weeks ago, when President Bush's chief economic adviser suddenly found himself on the wrong side of the issue. In a casually imperious tone worthy of Martha Stewart, Gregory Mankiw declared, "Outsourcing is just a new way of doing international trade.... More things are tradable than were tradable in the past, and that's a good thing."

Many economists agree with him. Anything that makes an economy more efficient tends to help in the long run. . . .

Unfortunately for Bush, outsourcing has become Exhibit A in any gripe session about why the economic recovery has been weak in creating new jobs. To some extent, he succeeded in making a plausible connection between his tax cuts and the robust pace of economic growth. "People have more money in their pocket to spend, to save, to invest," he has said. "[Tax relief] is helping the economy recover from tough times." But his efforts to sell a pastiche of programs to help the unemployed have had a tougher time punching through. When it comes to jobs, the numbers fail him. On the basis of previous recoveries, Bush was promising to add 2.6 million new jobs [in 2004]. That pledge is starting to look like fantasy, and the Administration has distanced itself from its own predictions.

In crafting an effective response to outsourcing, all the candidates face the same challenge: dealing with a relatively new phenomenon. Their responses are a work in progress, ranging from mild proposals of dubious effectiveness to ideas that sound vaguely like protectionism. In the meantime, voters are left to separate the myths from the realities. Some answers:

FROM MEXICO TO INDIA: HOW DID WE GET THERE?

Before acquiring its current incendiary meaning, outsourcing referred to the practice of turning over noncritical parts of a business to a company that specialized in that activity. At first it was ancillary functions like running the cafeteria or cleaning the offices. Then it started moving up to corporate-service functions. Why operate a call center if what you really do, your core competence, is running a credit-card business? So credit-card companies hired independent call centers to take over the phones, and that industry put down roots in places like Omaha, Neb., which early on had a fiber-optic hub. But as the price of information technology fell and the Internet exploded, capacity began popping up around the world. Which meant that all you needed to run a call center, or a customer-service center, was information technology (IT) and employees who spoke English. Hello, India.

10   From there, multinational companies began moving up the food chain. Silicon Valley, which for years had been importing highly educated Indian code writers—driving up wage and real estate costs—discovered it was a lot cheaper to export the work to the same highly educated folks over there. So did Wall Street, which employs an army of accountants, analysts and bankers to pore over documents, do deal analysis and maintain databases. The potential list gets longer: medical technicians to read your X-rays, accountants to prepare your taxes, even business journalists to interpret companies' financial statements.

Jared Bernstein, senior economist at the Economic Policy Institute, says the frustration of these educated workers is what gives the debate over outsourcing such intensity. "There is no safety net for $80,000-a-year programmers," he says, and perhaps there shouldn't be. Their education is supposed to provide that. Bernstein says that after the factory closings of the 1980s and the emergence of the "knowledge economy," many liberals and conservatives alike had reached a consensus that manufacturing jobs could not be saved but the "lab coat" jobs would always stay here. "Now that vision is under siege," Bernstein says. And the white-collar middle class is feeling the sting of insecurity that manufacturing workers know so well.

WHY SO FAST?

It's doubly difficult for people to watch outsourcing accelerate as the economy improves. The stock market had a strong 2003, and corporate profits in many industries exceeded expectations, so why haven't companies that started outsourcing as a way to cut costs reversed course and brought the jobs back home? That might have happened after other recessions, but this shift is different. To some extent, companies are gun-shy about committing to full-time workers and the attendant fringe benefits. Instead of rushing to expand their computer systems and hiring people to maintain them, firms are keeping their outsourcing companies on speed dial.

That's why outsourcing to India has exploded during the recovery. It jumped 60% in 2003 compared with the year before, according to the research magazine *Dataquest,* as corporations used some of their profits (not to mention tax breaks) to expand overseas hiring. That translates to 140,000 jobs outsourced to India last year. Vivek Paul, president of Wipro, one of India's leading outsourcing companies (it handles voice and data processing for Delta Airlines, for instance), says its service business grew 50% in the last quarter of 2003. "Companies that are emerging from the slowdown are beginning to invest some of that in India," he says. John McCarthy, author of the Forrester Research landmark study that predicted 3.3 million jobs would move overseas by 2015 (there are about 130 million jobs in the U.S. today), says last year's gains in outsourcing didn't come from new companies jumping on the bandwagon. The most dramatic changes came from outsourcing dabblers who finally made a commitment and now allocate as much as 30% of their IT budgets offshore.

Another factor speeding things up is the development of an industry devoted to making outsourcing happen, thanks to entrepreneurs like Randy Altschuler and Joe Sigelman. Just five years ago, they were junior investment bankers at the Blackstone Group and Goldman Sachs, one in New York City, the other in London. During one particularly long night of proofreading Power Point slides and commiserating by phone about finding yet another error courtesy of their companies' in-house document service, they had an epiphany. They would find a better way of doing that work. This was at the height of the dotcom boom, and everyone they knew was trying to figure out a way to Silicon Valley. These two had a different idea. They would go to India, set up a team of accountants and desktop-publishing experts and persuade investment banks in New York to outsource their confidential financial documents and client presentations halfway around the world.

15   The entrepreneurs' families, not to mention Silicon Valley's venture capitalists, "were looking at us in a crazy way," Sigelman says, especially when he relocated to Madras. Five years later, as it moves into more complex work, OfficeTiger, with $18 million from British investors, plans to increase the number of its employees in India [in 2002] from 1,500 to 2,500 and more than triple its U.S. work force, from 30 to 100.

GETTING LEFT BEHIND

Billy Johnson of Altamonte Springs, Fla., is convinced that one of the tens of thousands of new jobs in India should be his. Johnson, 41, was a programmer for World-Com when the company imploded in the wake of a massive accounting scandal. After six months of looking for a programming job, Johnson realized that the work he knows is exactly what outsourcing companies do best. "I spent $5,000 of my own money to become an Oracle [enterprise software] developer," he says. "Nobody's hiring Oracle developers." For a while, he believed it was just the economy. A lifelong Republican, he believed that when the Bush tax cuts kicked in, the jobs would follow. "I feel like I've been betrayed," he says. "I keep hearing about jobs being created, but I don't see them."

Vince Kosmac of Orlando, Fla., has lived both sad chapters of outsourcing—the blue-collar and white-collar versions. He was a trucker in the 1970s and '80s, delivering steel to plants in Johnstown, Pa. When steel melted down to lower-cost competitors in Brazil and China, he used the G.I. Bill to get a degree in computer science. "The conventional wisdom was, 'Nobody can take your education away from you,'" he says bitterly. "Guess what? They took my education away." For nearly 20 years, he worked as a programmer and saved enough for a comfortable life. But programming jobs went missing two years ago, and he is impatient with anyone who suggests that he "retrain" again. "Here I am, 47 years old. I've got a house, I've got a child with cerebral palsy. I've got two cars. What do I do—push the pause button on my life? I'm not a statistic."

Neither is Scott Kirwin, 37, of Wilmington, Del., who represents another trend. A career contract worker, he is under constant threat from outsourcing. He is the breadwinner in his family—his wife is a medical student, and they have a 7-year-old son—and he has twice lost his job to outsourcing. In both cases, he had been hired as a contractor, and he sees little opportunity for anything else. "It's really nasty if you're looking for stability," he says. During unemployment spells, his family accumulates debt and reverts to making minimum credit-card payments. Vague talk about retraining leaves Kirwin cold. "Tell me which other industry I should train for," he says. A few people have suggested his father's trade, plumbing. His father had an eighth-grade education and expected better options for his college-educated son. "My father would be outraged," Kirwin says.

WHOM WILL OUTSOURCING AFFECT NEXT

As it proves its value to more companies, outsourcing will change the way they hire. San Francisco-based DFS Group, a division of luxury-goods maker LVMH that runs duty-free shops in airports around the world, reduced operating expenses about 40% after hiring the outsourcing firm Cognizant, based in Teaneck, N.J., to take most of its 265-person internal IT operations in 2002. Today those jobs are being done in India. DFS reinvested the savings primarily in better software. "They can add more stores efficiently. They know more about the products in the store," says Ron Glickman, DFS's former chief information officer. DFS continues to hire in the U.S. but only for certain key functions. When it needs more IT support at peak times or for special projects, DFS is more likely to turn to Cognizant. "We're going to go to them first," Glickman says.

That shift marks another fundamental change in the way companies do business. "Intrinsic to outsourcing is the replacement of the employer-employee function with a third party," says Gregg Kirchhoefer, a partner with the law firm Kirkland & Ellis in Chicago. Kirchhoefer, who has been handling outsourcing transactions with   20

Indian companies since the early 1990s, sees outsourcing as the logical extension of the evolutionary process that began with contract manufacturing and continued into corporate services. Thanks to technology, more kinds of work can now be spun off into contracts rather than tied to employees. Once a person's labor can be reduced to a contract, it matters little whether the contract is filled in India or Indiana; the only relevant issue is cost. And the speed of technological change accelerates the process. As soon as a job becomes routine enough to describe in a spec sheet, it becomes vulnerable to outsourcing. Jobs like data entry, which are routine by nature, were the first among obvious candidates for outsourcing. But with today's advanced engineering, design and financial-analysis skills can, with time, become well-enough understood to be spelled out in a contract and signed away.

Without a "social contract" binding employer and employee, long-term jobs are an illusion. For the past two years, the Department of Labor has reported that household employment is much stronger than payroll numbers—indicating that workers are getting by with freelance or contract work, whether or not they want to. In January [2004], for example, there were 2.8 million more people employed than in January 2002, according to the household survey, while the payroll numbers were almost flat at 130 million.

CAN AMERICANS LEARN TO LOVE OUTSOURCING?

While it's small consolation to workers who lose their jobs, outsourcing has become an essential element of corporate strategy, even for small companies. "Any start-up today, particularly a software company, that does not have an outsourcing strategy is at a competitive disadvantage," says Robin Vasan, managing director of Mayfield, a venture-capital firm based in Menlo Park, Calif. He felt so strongly about "global sourcing" that Mayfield organized a daylong session for the firms it invests in to meet with outsourcing companies and experts. About 60% of them now have an outsourcing plan. "That's a good start," Yasan says.

The move to outsourcing forces a company to use its resources where they count most, like product development. "For some of them, it's almost a question of survival. If they don't develop new products, they'll fail," says Laxmi Narayanan, CEO of Cognizant. Nielsen Media Research, which rates television shows, used Cognizant's programmers in India to develop NetRatings for websites. That new line of business allowed the company to hire sales staff and analysts in the U.S. to interpret the ratings for clients and eventually to start selling the product in Asia. Lightpointe, an optical-networking firm based in San Diego, will add about 10 people to its 75-person staff this year thanks to an arrangement with a company in China. That firm will handle Lightpointe's sales and marketing there as the company expands into a huge new market. Without the local help, says Lightpointe CEO John Griffin, he could not have entered the Chinese market and would have been limited to the flailing U.S. telecom market. "Some of my competitors were not as flexible," Griffin says. "They're dead. All those employees are gone."

SHOULD OUTSOURCING BE CONTROLLED?

As the rhetoric of the campaign heats up, so does populist sentiment that there ought to be a law against outsourcing—or at least something to slow it down. Various schemes have been proposed, such as tax initiatives or trade barriers to keep jobs from moving. Some companies may feel political pressure. Dell has moved some call-center support for business-enterprise customers back to the U.S., but the company cited poor service as the reason.

Analysts doubt that any protectionist strategy will slow what   25
appears to be a permanent shift in the way the U.S. does business. As Mankiw tried to explain before he was shouted down by fellow Republicans, structural change like this is inevitable and recurring. It's just that the transition can be ugly. New England was a textile center until that business went south, to the Carolinas, then east, to China. Software supplanted steel in Pittsburgh, Pa. In both places, high-tech companies later occupied some of the old mill buildings. Now some of those companies' programmers have gone the way of loom operators and steel rollers.

The Economic Policy Institute's Bernstein says businesses ought to find a way to "share some winnings with those who lose" by creating funds for wage insurance or retraining. Otherwise there is a risk that the benefits of outsourcing will widen the gap between the rich and everyone else. The McKinsey Global Institute, a think tank run by McKinsey & Co., recommends that companies sending jobs abroad contribute about 5% of their savings to an insurance fund that would compensate displaced workers for part of the difference in wages paid by their old and new jobs. During the 1980s and '90s, most workers displaced by trade found only lower-paying jobs. Those displaced by outsourcing are likely to share the same fate.

As demand for Indian workers increases, their prices are rising, just like anything else. Wipro's Paul says that even though his sales soared 50% last fall, his margins are shrinking, mostly because of rising labor costs. "India has been discovered," he says. "It's something that is as susceptible to global competition as anything else." Wipro, in an effort to rein in expenses, is pushing workers to be more productive. But at some point in the future, the trend that is putting jobs out of America will catch up with India. Somewhere a lower-wage alternative will develop—Central Asia, the Philippines or Thailand—and Indian politicians and workers will be clamoring about foreigners taking their jobs. It's not pretty wherever it happens, but it's just the way the business world turns.

Questions for Discussion

1. Why does Rosen Sharma, the owner of a start-up company, say that from a business point of view he must outsource? How does Sharma's perspective change when he thinks about the future of his two-year-old daughter? In what ways may outsourcing affect the job outlook for upcoming college graduates?

2. What did the term "outsourcing" formerly refer to? What does it mean today? How do you think that outsourcing will affect your own employment in the future?

3. What is the lesson of Billy Johnson's story in relation to jobs going abroad? Whom else does outsourcing potentially threaten? Which jobs do you think will be moving out of the country next?

4. What do the analysts in this article say in regard to overcoming the negative effects of outsourcing? Why do they doubt that a "protectionist strategy" designed to stop companies from taking jobs abroad will work? Do you agree with them? Do you believe their suggestions to businesses will ever be utilized? Why or why not?

Ideas for Writing

1. Write an essay about the impact of outsourcing on the future of work in America. Why has outsourcing been so widely utilized by American businesses? What types of jobs do you think will be safe from outsourcing? Is it possible to stop this trend? Do some research on this topic before writing your paper.

2. After doing some research, write a paper that reports on the effects of outsourcing on people in your state or community. Discuss what has been and what can be done to create employment for workers who have lost their jobs.

The Next University
Drive-Thru U.: Higher Education
for People Who Mean Business

JAMES TRAUB

James Traub is a contributing writer for The New York Times Magazine *who also has served as a staff writer for* The New Yorker. *He has written on a wide variety of subjects including foreign affairs, national politics, education, and urban policy. He is the author of two books:* Too Good to Be True: The Outlandish Story of Wedtech *(1990) and* City on a Hill: Testing the American Dream at City College *(1994). His article "The Next University. Drive-Thru U," which first appeared in the* The New Yorker, *has been widely read and discussed at universities as it presents an innovative model of higher education through online instruction. In this essay Traub profiles the University of Phoenix, a business-model distance learning enterprise, which has grown into our nation's largest university, with learning sites all around the country.*

✦

At the University of Phoenix, which describes itself as the second-largest private university in the United States, terms that normally have a clear and literal meaning are used in an oddly evanescent way; this seems especially true of the language that evokes our most romantic feelings about higher education. The university has, for example, a "bookstore" on the ground floor of its central administration building. The store is a boutique offering backpacks, T-shirts, coffee mugs, beer glasses, and ties, all bearing the school logo; the only books are textbooks, which you have to order from someone standing behind a counter. The U. of P.'s "library" can be found, as Kurt Slobodzian, the librarian, likes to say, "wherever there's a computer"; students can access thousands of journals via the On-line Collection. And the word "campus" is understood, at the University of Phoenix, to mean "site," or even "outlet." The university is a franchise operation, with forty-seven sites all over the West and in Michigan, Florida, and Louisiana; most of them consist of an office building, or merely a few floors of a building, just off a highway exit ramp. When I was talking to the director of the university's "distance learning" program I noticed that he was using the word "campus" to apply to himself and three other people, who ran the program from a suite of offices. The University of Phoenix is, in fact, a para-university. It has the operational core of higher education—students, teachers, classrooms, exams, degree-granting programs—without a campus life, or even an intellectual life. There are no tenured professors, and the most recent issue of the university's only academic journal contained but a single academic article, about copyright law.

You cannot get a rise out of the university's top officials by pointing any of this out. William Gibbs, a former Price Waterhouse manager, who is the president of the U. of P., said to me, "The people who are our students don't really want the education. They want what the education provides for them—better jobs, moving up in their career, the ability to speak up in meetings, that kind of stuff. They want it to *do* something for them."

Apparently, it does. Enrollment may be flat at élite institutions, but the U. of P. has grown from three thousand students to forty thousand over the last decade. It offers accredited bachelor's-degree programs in business, nursing, and education, and an M.B.A. as well. The university is also the principal subsidiary of a profit-making company called the Apollo Group. Since late 1994, when the company first offered shares on the NASDAQ exchange, Apollo stock has increased in value from two dollars to thirty-five dollars, on a split-adjusted basis. One broker I spoke to said that most of his customers were professors at Arizona State, who had concluded that the U. of P. delivered pretty much the same product they did, only more efficiently. The University of Phoenix is competing not with the Ivy League but with the big state schools and the small, unheralded private colleges, where most students enroll. It's a Darwinian world out there: some two hundred colleges have closed during the last ten years.

College, for most of us, means greenswards, dreamy spires, professors with elbow patches, old volumes in the stacks; but no more than several dozen colleges answer to this description. Higher education in America is now a vast industry that accommodates two thirds of America's high school graduates, or more than fourteen million people. Most of the nation's thirty-seven hundred colleges see themselves as market-driven institutions trying to satisfy customer demand. As I drove around Phoenix, I kept hearing ads on the radio for Ottawa University, a Kansas institution that has three campuses in Arizona and others in Singapore, Malaysia, and Hong Kong. "Ottawa," the announcer said, "majors in *you*."

Almost half of America's freshmen attend community col-   5
leges, institutions with no residential facilities and, often, no
campus. According to a study conducted by Arthur Levine, the
president of Teachers College, at Columbia University, only a
sixth of America's college students fit the stereotype: full-time students, living on campus. Levine says that a survey of the five-
sixths who do not has found that "they wanted the kind of relationship with a college that they had with their bank, their
supermarket, and their gas company. They say, 'I want terrific
service, I want convenience, I want quality control. Give me
classes twenty-four hours a day, and give me in-class parking, if
possible.' These are students who want stripped-down classes.
They don't want to buy anything they're not using." Such students
understand clearly that higher education has become an indis-
pensable passport to a better life.

In a 1994 book entitled "Dogmatic Wisdom," a history professor named Russell Jacoby faults critics on both the left and the
right for focussing on the intellectual melodramas that agitate a
tiny number of institutions—"canon wars" and battles over
"speech codes"—while ignoring the "narrow practicality" that
dominates educational practice at almost all the others. Jacoby
quotes a Department of Education study showing that of a million bachelor's degrees awarded in 1991 seven thousand three
hundred were in philosophy and religion, twelve thousand in foreign languages, and about two hundred and fifty thousand in
business. The institution that sees itself as a steward of intellectual culture is becoming increasingly marginal; the others are
racing to accommodate the new student. And the University of
Phoenix, according to Arthur Levine, "is the first of the new
breed."

John Sperling, the founder of the University of Phoenix and
the chairman of the Apollo Group, is a blunt, ornery seventy-six-
year-old from the Ozarks. In the company's bland and studiously
polite environment, he stands out for his willingness to call an
idiot an idiot. Sperling is an economic historian by profession,
and, like many economists, he considers himself one of the few
rational people on earth. Among the people he counts as idiots
are those who believe that market forces can be ignored; during
one of several conversations, he observed that the principal
effect of the war on drugs was that it forced users to commit
crimes. Along with George Soros and Peter Lewis, Sperling

helped finance the Arizona referendum to permit the medical use of marijuana.

Sperling himself had a classical education—a B.A. in history at Reed, a master's in history at Berkeley, and a D. Phil. in economic history at Cambridge. He recalls his time at Berkeley as among the happiest years of his life. He was, however, far too restless to stick with the academic routine. In the early seventies, while teaching courses in the humanities at San Jose State, Sperling won a government contract to offer a variety of classes to teachers and police officers, and that was the beginning of what he considers his real education. "They were the best students I ever had," he told me. "They really fell in love with education. It wasn't long before they said, 'We'd like to get a degree.' So I went to the administration, and they said, 'No way.' I said, 'I'm bringing you students.' And they said, "We don't need no stinking students.' "

Sperling developed a program with twenty-five hundred teachers and police at the University of San Francisco and two other colleges in California, but he claims that the regional accrediting body said, "Either get rid of these programs or we'll pull your accreditation for the whole university." Sperling came to see higher education as a closed system whose gates were manned by the accrediting agencies—a racket designed to squelch the forms of individual choice.

10   Sperling reached the Wild West of the free-market system in 1976, when he went to Phoenix, visited a local low firm, and drew up a charter for a new university and, just like that, the University of Phoenix opened for business. He targeted the niche market that he had already begun serving—the adult learner. The University of Phoenix would accept anybody who was twenty-three or older and was working. Students had to have sixty college credits when they arrived, so the need for general education, liberal arts, and all the other stuff that takes up so much time and money at college could be dispensed with. Sperling wanted to provide a useful and profitable service, not replicate higher education. What interested him was not so much what to teach this population as *how* to deliver it. "Higher education is one of the most inefficient mechanisms for the transfer of knowledge that have ever been invented," Sperling said. "I decided to go back to my economics and conceive of education as a production function, in which you specify the learning outcomes that you want—they're your product—and then do a regression and figure out the most efficient way of producing them."

Just as the Ivy league model was developed two centuries ago to accommodate aspiring clerics, so the University of Phoenix is shaped by the needs of working adults in the corporate economy. And because it was created all at once it's a highly rational institution. Classes are held at night, from six to ten. Courses consist of five or six weekly sessions, taken one at a time and one right after another. Each degree program is identical from one campus to the next. Laura Palmer Noone, whose title is vice-president for academic affairs—elsewhere she would be called "provost"—says, "What we have found is that adults don't want all that much flexibility; they want it to be simple."

One of Sperling's early insights was that adults also put very little stock in academic opinion. He concluded, "You were going to have to draw your faculty from the world they were familiar with—the world of work. If you had a Ph.D. that didn't mean shit." Marketing would be taught by a marketing executive, and accounting by an accountant. In a vocational setting, these teachers had the credentials that mattered. The "practitioner" system also, and not incidentally, allowed the university to deliver coursework far more cheaply than its competitors, since it paid its instructors an average of about a thousand dollars for each five-week course. Many of the teachers, and especially the businessmen, say they do their nighttime job for the sheer satisfaction of it. Hugh McBride, the executive director and chair of the graduate business programs, told me, "It's really a joy to have someone say, 'You know, Hugh, I used that last week in the company.'". . .

The University of Phoenix is still one of the few for-profit academic institutions established to date; but the distinction between profit-making companies and educational institutions is becoming increasingly moot. Several education experts I spoke to volunteered the idea that a new kind of institution would come into being as the result of an alliance between a state-university system, a "content provider," like Disney, and a technology firm, like Motorola. The fastest-growing sector of higher education is, in fact, the "corporate university," which typically provides training for middle and upper management. A 1994 book by Stan Davis and Jim Botkin entitled "The Monster Under the Bed" observes that the increase in "classroom contact hours" for corporate employees in one year, 1992, exceeded the enrollment growth at all the colleges built between 1960 and 1990. The authors foresee the business model, with its focus on "competition, service, and standards," supplanting the current educational model.

This may be a bit premature, but the line between corporate training and academic education has clearly blurred. One day, I drove into Tempe, a suburb just beyond Phoenix (itself a sprawling suburb), to visit Motorola University, a gleaming facility on landscaped grounds that looks more like a university than the University of Phoenix does. Motorolans, as they are known, were taking courses in Behavioral Interviewing and Developing Your Human Potential, along with some in recondite aspects of computer-chip design. The curriculum sounded a lot like the one at the University of Phoenix, and, in fact, the U. of P. offers several of its courses on the campus. Motorola does not provide an academic degree, as some corporate universities do, but Arizona State offers a master's in Management of Technology on the Motorola campus, using teachers from both institutions. In Phoenix, if not yet in Boston or New York, the corporate university is part of a web, not of a pecking order—one of several kinds of "providers" filling in different aspects of a "learner's" needs. Arthur Levine, of Teacher's College, predicts that several generations from now "we'll still have some number of residential colleges and some number of research universities, but most of the rest will disappear." Corporations may simply make postsecondary education an in-house function. Non-élite institutions, Levine suggests, will be reduced largely to examining and certifying students for workplace readiness.

15   Like any successful business, the University of Phoenix is oriented toward growth, and in recent years it has begun to expand into the realm of the conventional university. The number of credits required for admission has dropped from sixty to zero. The U. of P. has created a General Studies department, which offers courses not only in Oral Communications but in Philosophy and Religion. (Bill Gibbs, though, says that he would like to see the Religion course focus on such practical advice as how to do business among different bodies of believers.) In effect, it is now taking responsibility for the entire undergraduate education of many of its students. The administration hired William Pepicello, who has a Ph.D in linguistics from Brown and a manner that is identifiably academic, to establish a Gen. Ed. Curriculum and embody the school's new identity. Last year, the U. of P. sought permission from accreditors to offer undergraduate degrees in whatever subjects it wished, and to establish a doctoral program. Both of these proposals were rejected—a decision that infuriated many at the school. The general view in Phoenix is that the forces

of convention which have been trying to throttle John Sperling for a quarter of a century still have the upper hand in academe. An alternative point of view is that there are still standards for an academic education, and the university may have been threatening to transgress them. Stephen Spangehl, an official of the North Central Association, which is the regional accrediting body, declines to give specific reasons for the decision but says that the group was concerned about, among other things, the university's lack of rigorous academic assessment. "They seem more concerned about customer satisfaction." Spangehl says. "Our focus has always been on learning."

It's that sort of curt dismissal that makes John Sperling furious. "Jesus, they're disgusting," he said when I asked him about the decision. But he was moving ahead, looking for new markets. He had recently returned from a trip to the Far East. There were, he said, a million potential customers for information-systems training in Malaysia alone, and the China market was incalculable. The Apollo Group was making a big push into distance learning, and that may well be the growth market for postsecondary education. Moreover, the whole public-school market was opening up. Jorge Klor de Alva, a former anthropology professor at Berkeley, who is now the chair of the U. of P.'s academic cabinet, told me that the advent of school vouchers "will create huge opportunities for private, for-profit schools." Apollo could own a chain of schools, provide management services, and market curricular material. Once you conceive of education as a product, and regress from the needs of the consumer, a whole world of possibilities presents itself.

Sperling himself seems unable to decide whether he has created a superior model for higher education or a viable alternative to the existing one. As we were having dinner one evening, he started going on about the uselessness of classical education. "One of my favorite books is 'Tom Jones,'" he said. "I read 'Tom Jones' for the sheer pleasure, but I didn't go out and rut with some maid in the canebreakes. It's all part of what happens up here." He pointed to his head, but he sounded so thoroughly exasperated that he might as well have been talking about his appendix. "The University of Phoenix causes you to *apply* what you've learned *the next day at work.*" Then, lest I get the wrong idea, he reminded me of how deeply he had loved Berkeley.

"Why don't you want all your students to have the experience you had?" I asked.

"Because they can't afford to."

20   "Wouldn't it be good if they could?"
         Sperling gave me a weary look, and said, "I'm not involved in social reform." He had once tried to build a chain of technical schools for inner-city youth, he told me, and when that failed he had vowed never again to create something there wasn't a demand for. "Microsoft is a much more powerful force shaping the world than Harvard or Yale or Princeton," he said. "So if you can't beat 'em join 'em."

Questions for Discussion

1. How do online universities like the University of Phoenix transform the meaning of the word "campus"? How do they make education more accessible for working persons?
2. What is a "para-university"? How do these schools make more profits than regular schools? In what ways are they more efficient?
3. Why did John Sperling create the University of Phoenix? Who initially opposed this new means of course presentation and why? In what way is Traub's presentation of "Drive-Thru U" sympathetic and persuasive? Why is he critical of the new way of educating people?
4. In what educational direction is the University of Phoenix moving? How will these changes reshape the future of education? Do you think this type of education will help or hurt the public school system and more traditional private colleges? Explain.

Ideas for Writing

1. Write an essay that explores the benefits of and the problems with online university education. What is missing from this type of education? Do you think it is necessary to one's learning process to attend classes in person and interact with other students and a teacher? Why or why not? Do you think people can obtain as good an education online as they do in traditional classrooms?
2. Write an essay that speculates about the role that online education will take on in the future. You can shape the focus of your essay in relationship to your interests on this topic. Consider how the shift to online learning, especially for employed persons and those pursuing higher job status and career changes, will influence the workforce mentality of future generations.

Extending the Theme

1. Write an essay that discusses the impact that computers have had and will continue to have on a specific type of workplace. How will the skills and resources necessary to be a successful worker change? Ideas for workplaces to study might include a public school, a small business, a big department store, a fast-food chain, emergency nursing and rescue care, surgery—be imaginative in selecting your workplace and be thorough and thoughtful in your response to the prompt.
2. How have computers defined, and will they continue to define, the culture of work? Do you think that computers will make people feel more isolated or more connected to those with whom they work? Do you think that computers will make learning and community more or less playful, creative, and intuitive? Or will they make learning and communicating more routine and distant?
3. Write an essay in which you discuss the way that your education has been changed by the use of computers. First think back to the first time computers were used in your classroom and compare that to how computers are used in classrooms today. Have computers made learning more imaginative and fun? Do computers make learning feel more lonely and isolated?
4. Although the United States remains a leader in technological innovation, more and more jobs in technology, some increasingly creative, are being outsourced to foreign countries. Do some research into recent trends in high-tech outsourcing to establish which jobs are most at risk in this area. How can workers on the innovative side of U.S. technology work to maintain their job security and respect in the marketplace of ideas, or is the idea of such job security just a thing of the past?

CHAPTER 4

The Working Poor

Although we are consistently reminded of the lives of the rich and the middle class, we rarely hear about the working experiences of the poor. In 2002, statistics showed that, based on a statistical formula reflecting the cost of living, 12.1 percent of the population was below the federal poverty line—a figure that is no doubt much higher considering what it actually costs to live in the United States. Aside from such formulas, we need to find a suitable, more complex definition for what it means to be poor, as poverty not only concerns one's financial situation; it also has to do with one's psychological state of being, with one's desire to succeed, and with having the will to do so. In this chapter the readings will help you to understand who these poor workers are and what their lives are like. If we are not aware of the working situation of these individuals, then we will be unable to create humane solutions to the issues that arise for the working poor.

A central concept that relates to the working poor is that of the American dream of success through hard work. In this chapter we will read selections that show how this ideal can be both harmful to the poor and unrealistic times, although at times it can still be a powerful force for personal motivation. This chapter raises the point: How does the American dream relate to the lives of the chronically poor? Do we have a moral obligation to change the system so that no person has to suffer in a country with an abundance of wealth? Why do we blame the poor for the living conditions they must endure?

Another theme that our readings uncover is the difficult working situations of the poor. From the high stress of young service workers to the backbreaking conditions of migrant farm workers, we can see how essential it is for us as a society to help create better wages and work environments for these individuals. For instance, in our first selection, from the book *The Working Poor,* David K. Shipler examines the problems experienced by what he perceives to be forty million poor people in the United States. He describes a whole class of people barely surviving from paycheck to paycheck. These individuals constantly live in debt and in fear of any small disaster—such as an automobile accident that could potentially lead them into destitution. Shipler argues that we must create an awareness of the working poor for society at large in order to change their situations.

In "Evaluation," a selection from Barbara Ehrenreich's best-selling book *Nickel and Dimed,* we also learn in more detail about the lives of the underclass who subsist in fear of emergency situations such as Shipler describes. Ehrenreich, a prominent sociologist, spent a year working alongside and living with waitresses, house cleaners, and department store clerks. In her excerpt "Evaluation," she explains why these employees are trapped at the poverty level, even though they work long hours. Knowing no other life and feeling intimidated by their bosses subjecting them to constant drug testing and surveillance, they are barely surviving and can easily lose their jobs and rented rooms or apartments through minor setbacks such as a temporary lay-off, or illness.

In our next selection, "The Just-Add-Water Kennedys and Barbecue Bread Violence" by writer and rock musician Polyestra, we also encounter the issue of the reality and difficulty of making the American dream come true. She uses the rhetorical device of black humor to capture social realities. Through her dark satirical autobiography, Polyestra shows us how it is almost impossible to live the American dream or to "jump class." She reveals that because of this difficulty the working poor should not necessarily be accused of being moral failures.

In this chapter's first three selection, we see how the American dream may be inspirational, but that it also has the reverse effect of blaming those who cannot succeed in a system that seems rigged against them. Next we look at an excerpt from Stuart Tannock's *Youth at Work,* a study of young people who work in the service industry, particularly in fast-food outlets and grocery stores. Tannock reveals the stress involved in these workplaces, stress created by both customers and managers who consistently make difficult demands on young workers who are unprotected because they have no status and no job security, and are considered to be easily expendable. These workers also suffer from very low self-esteem—although in reality Tannock shows that they do have many useful skills. He demonstrates why these workers deserve better pay, the right to unionize, and greater respect from managers and customers.

Eric Schlosser's selection from *In the Strawberry Fields* helps to illustrate an even more difficult type of job: agricultural work performed by impoverished immigrant farmworkers. He describes life and work in California's strawberry fields, where most workers are Mexican immigrants who are paid very little. These workers are exploited by farmers, yet they are also a vital part of the farming community because no one else wants to do this extremely strenuous and unrewarding work.

Our final selection points to one of the key reasons why society at large is not even aware of the huge numbers of the working poor. In "Media Magic: Making Class Invisible" by Gregory Mantsios, we learn about how little media coverage is given to the poor and their problems. Stories about sports, the stock market, and the scandals of the upper and middle class are more "exciting" than showing what is happening in this country to the working or chronically underemployed class. When newspapers, magazines, and television report on the lives of the poor, they focus too often on blaming the poor for their financial problems, claiming that some of the poor are criminals and drug abusers, and that they will get out of poverty as soon as our cyclical economy moves out of a temporary recession. The sheer statistics—that there are some 40 million poor people living in this country—are seldom mentioned.

At the Edge of Poverty
DAVID K. SHIPLER

David K. Shipler worked for The New York Times *from 1966 to 1988 before serving as its chief diplomatic correspondent in Washington, D.C. He has also written for* The New Yorker, The Washington Post, *and the* Los Angeles Times. *Shipler is the author of* Solemn Dreams *(1983),* Arab and Jew: Wounded Spirits in a Promised Land *(1986), and* A Country of Strangers: Blacks and Whites in America *(1999). He has been a guest scholar at the Brookings Institution and a senior associate at the Carnegie Endowment for International Peace, and has taught at Princeton*

*University and Dartmouth College. The selection that follows is ex-
cerpted from Shipler's most recent book,* The Working Poor *(2004);
it encourages readers to rethink our social myth of poverty and to
consider what it means to be poor in an affluent society like ours.*

——————— ✦ ———————

*Tired of wishes,
Empty of dreams*

—CARL SANDBURG

The man who washes cars does not own one. The clerk who files
cancelled checks at the bank has $2.02 in her own account.
The woman who copyedits medical textbooks has not been to a
dentist in a decade.

This is the forgotten America. At the bottom of its working
world, millions live in the shadow of prosperity, in the twilight
between poverty and well-being. Whether you're rich, poor, or
middle-class, you encounter them every day. They serve you Big
Macs and help you find merchandise at Wal-Mart. They harvest
your food, clean your offices, and sew your clothes. In a
California factory, they package lights for your kids' bikes. In a
New Hampshire plant, they assemble books of wallpaper samples
to help you redecorate.

They are shaped by their invisible hardships. Some are climb-
ing out of welfare, drug addiction, or homelessness. Others have
been trapped for life in a perilous zone of low-wage work. Some
of their children are malnourished. Some have been sexually
abused. Some live in crumbling housing that contributes to their
children's asthma, which means days absent from school. Some
of their youngsters do not even have the eyeglasses they need to
see the chalkboard clearly.

This book is about a few of these people, their families, their
dreams, their personal failings, and the larger failings of their
country. While the United States has enjoyed unprecedented affluence, low-wage employees have been testing the American doctrine that hard work cures poverty. Some have found that work
works. Others have learned that it doesn't. Moving in and out of
jobs that demand much and pay little, many people tread just
above the official poverty line, dangerously close to the edge of
destitution. An inconvenience to an affluent family—minor car
trouble, a brief illness, disrupted child care—is a crisis to them,
for it can threaten their ability to stay employed. They spend

everything and save nothing. They are always behind on their bills. They have minuscule bank accounts or none at all, and so pay more fees and higher interest rates than more secure Americans. Even when the economy is robust, many wander through a borderland of struggle, never getting very far from where they started. When the economy weakens, they slip back toward the precipice.

5   Millions have been pushed into a region of adversity by federal welfare reform's time limits and work mandates. Enacted in 1996 during an economic boom, the reform is credited by many welfare recipients for inducing them to travel beyond the stifling world of dependence into the active, challenging, hopeful culture of the workplace. They have gained self-confidence, some say, and have acquired new respect from their children. Those with luck or talent step onto career ladders toward better and better positions at higher and higher pay. Many more, however, are stuck at such low wages that their living standards are unchanged. They still cannot save, cannot get decent health care, cannot move to better neighborhoods, and cannot send their children to schools that offer a promise for a successful future. These are the forgotten Americans, who are noticed and counted as they leave welfare, but who disappear from the nation's radar as they struggle in their working lives.

      Breaking away and moving a comfortable distance from poverty seems to require a perfect lineup of favorable conditions. A set of skills, a good starting wage, and a job with the likelihood of promotion are prerequisites. But so are clarity of purpose, courageous self-esteem, a lack of substantial debt, the freedom from illness or addiction, a functional family, a network of upstanding friends, and the right help from private or governmental agencies. Any gap in that array is an entry point for trouble, because being poor means being unprotected. You might as well try playing quarterback with no helmet, no padding, no training, and no experience, behind a line of hundred-pound weaklings. With no cushion of money, no training in the ways of the wider world, and too little defense against the threats and temptations of decaying communities, a poor man or woman gets sacked again and again—buffeted and bruised and defeated. When an exception breaks this cycle of failure, it is called the fulfillment of the American Dream.

      As a culture, the United States is not quite sure about the causes of poverty, and is therefore uncertain about the solutions. The American Myth still supposes that any individual from the humblest origins can climb to well-being. We wish that to be true, and we delight in examples that make it seem so, whether fictional or real. The name of Horatio Alger, the nineteenth-century writer we no longer read, is embedded in our language as a synonym for the rise from rags to riches that his characters achieve through virtuous hard work. The classic immigrant story still stirs the American heart, despite the country's longstanding aversion to the arrival of "the wretched refuse" at "the golden door," in the words etched on the Statue of Liberty. Even while resenting the influx of immigrants, we revel in the nobility of tireless labor and scrupulous thrift that can transform a destitute refugee into a successful entrepreneur. George W. Bush gave voice to the myth when he was asked whether he meant to send a message with the inclusion of two blacks, a Hispanic, and two women in the first senior appointments to his incoming administration. "You bet," the president-elect replied: "that people who work hard and make the right decisions in life can achieve anything they want in America."

The myth has its value. It sets a demanding standard, both for the nation and for every resident. The nation has to strive to make itself the fabled land of opportunity; the resident must strive to use that opportunity. The ideal has inspired a Civil Rights Movement, a War on Poverty, and a continuing search for ways to ease the distress that persists in the midst of plenty.

But the American Myth also provides a means of laying blame. In the Puritan legacy, hard work is not merely practical but also moral; its absence suggests an ethical lapse. A harsh logic dictates a hard judgment: If a person's diligent work leads to prosperity, if work is a moral virtue, and if anyone in the society can attain prosperity through work, then the failure to do so is a fall from righteousness. The marketplace is the fair and final judge; a low wage is somehow the worker's fault, for it simply reflects the low value of his labor. In the American atmosphere, poverty has always carried a whiff of sinfulness. Thus, when Judy Woodruff of CNN moderated a debate among Republican presidential candidates in March 2000, she asked Alan Keyes why he thought morality was worsening when certain indicators of morality were improving: Crime was down, out-of-wedlock births were down, and welfare was down, she noted. Evidently, welfare was an index of immorality.

There is an opposite extreme, the American Anti-Myth, which 10 holds the society largely responsible for the individual's poverty. The hierarchy of racial discrimination and economic power creates a syndrome of impoverished communities with bad schools and closed options. The children of the poor are funneled into delinquency, drugs, or jobs with meager pay and little future. The individual is a victim of great forces beyond his control, including profit-hungry corporations that exploit his labor.

In 1962, Michael Harrington's eloquent articulation of the Anti-Myth in his book *The Other America* heightened awareness; to a nation blinded by affluence at the time, the portrait of a vast "invisible land" of the poor came as a staggering revelation. It helped generate Lyndon B. Johnson's War on Poverty. But Johnson's war never truly mobilized the country, nor was it ever fought to victory.

Forty years later, after all our economic achievements, the gap between rich and poor has only widened, with a median net worth of $833,600 among the top 10 percent and just $7,900 for the bottom 20 percent. Life expectancy in the United States is lower, and infant mortality higher, than in Japan, Hong Kong, Israel, Canada, and all the major nations of Western Europe. Yet after all that has been written, discussed, and left unresolved, it is harder to surprise and shock and outrage. So it is harder to generate action.

In reality, people do not fit easily into myths or anti-myths, of course. The working individuals in this book are neither helpless nor omnipotent, but stand on various points along the spectrum between the polar opposites of personal and societal responsibility. Each person's life is the mixed product of bad choices and bad fortune, of roads not taken and roads cut off by the accident of birth or circumstance. It is difficult to find someone whose poverty is not somehow related to his or her unwise behavior—to drop out of school, to have a baby out of wedlock, to do drugs, to be chronically late to work. And it is difficult to find behavior that is not somehow related to the inherited conditions of being poorly parented, poorly educated, poorly housed in neighborhoods from which no distant horizon of possibility can be seen.

How to define the individual's role in her own poverty is a question that has shaped the debate about welfare and other social policies, but it can rarely be answered with certainty, even in a specific case. The poor have less control than the affluent over their private decisions, less insulation from the cold machinery of government, less agility to navigate around the pitfalls of a frenetic world driven by technology and competition. Their personal mistakes have larger consequences, and their personal achievements yield smaller returns. The interaction between the personal and the public is so intricate that for assistance such as job training to make a difference, for example, it has to be tailored to each individual's needs, which include not only such "hard skills" as using a computer or running a lathe, but also "soft skills" such as interacting with peers, following orders willingly, and managing the deep anger that may have developed during years of adversity. Job trainers are discovering that people who have repeatedly failed—in school, in love, in work—cannot succeed until they learn that they are capable of success. To get out of poverty, they have to acquire dexterity with their emotions as well as their hands.

An exit from poverty is not like showing your passport and crossing a frontier. There is a broad strip of contested territory between destitution and comfort, and the passage is not the same distance for everyone. "Comfortable is when I can pay my rent with one paycheck—I don't have to save for two weeks to pay one month's rent," said Tyrone Pixley, a slender man of fifty in Washington, D.C. He was especially undemanding, having emerged from a tough life as a day laborer and a heroin user. "I don't want to have to scuffle," he said simply. "I want to be able to live comfortable, even if it's in a ten-by-ten room. And in the course of a month I can pay all my bills out of my pay. I don't have to have anything saved. For me to be comfortable, I don't have to have a savings account." 15

In such a rich country, most people have more appetite than Tyrone Pixley. Surrounded by constant advertising from television sets that are almost always turned on, many Americans acquire wants that turn into needs. "You're living in the projects, your mom's on welfare, so if you got six kids or five or seven, eight kids growing up, you be wantin' things all your life, and you can't have," explained Frank Dickerson, a janitor who dealt drugs in Washington to get things he didn't have. "You got kids want to have the nice tennis shoes, the jackets; they can't get that with a mom with six, seven kids on welfare. How they gonna get it? They may be getting older, growing up, they want to have nice stuff, so the only way to get that is turn to drugs. That's right. You go out there, you deal, and you get the things that you need. Car, apartments, clothes." Frank Dickerson spent three years in prison, but he and his wife also bought a house in the Maryland suburbs with the money he made from drugs.

Poverty, then, does not lend itself to easy definition. It may be absolute—an inability to buy basic necessities. It may be relative—an inability to buy the lifestyle that prevails at a certain time and place. It can be measured by a universal yardstick or by an index of disparity. Even dictionaries cannot agree. "Want or scarcity of means of subsistence," one says categorically. "Lack of the means of providing material needs *or comforts,*" says another. "The state of one who lacks *a usual or socially acceptable* amount of money or material possessions," says a third (emphases added).

By global or historical standards, much of what Americans consider poverty is luxury. A rural Russian is not considered poor if he cannot afford a car and his home has no central heating; a rural American is. A Vietnamese farmer is not seen as poor because he plows with water buffalo, irrigates by hand, and lives in a thatched house; a North Carolina farmworker is, because he picks cucumbers by hand, gets paid a dollar a box, and lives in a run-down trailer. Most impoverished people in the world would be dazzled by the apartments, telephones, television sets, running water, clothing, and other amenities that surround the poor in America. But that does not mean that the poor are not poor, or that those on the edge of poverty are not truly on the edge of a cliff.

"The American poor are not poor in Hong Kong or in the sixteenth century; they are poor here and now, in the United States," Michael Harrington wrote before Hong Kong's prosperity soared. "They are dispossessed in terms of what the rest of the nation enjoys, in terms of what the society could provide if it had the will. They live on the fringe, the margin. They watch the movies and read the magazines of affluent America, and these tell them that they are internal exiles. . . . To have one bowl of rice in a society where all other people have half a bowl may well be a sign of achievement and intelligence; it may spur a person to act and to fulfill his human potential. To have five bowls of rice in a society where the majority have a decent, balanced diet is a tragedy.

20   Indeed, being poor in a rich country may be more difficult to endure than being poor in a poor country, for the skills of surviving in poverty have largely been lost in America. Visit a slum in Hanoi and you will find children inventing games with bottles and sticks and the rusty rims of bicycle wheels. Go to a slum in Los Angeles and you will find children dependent on plastic toys and video games. Living in Cambodia, my son Michael marveled at the ingenuity bred by necessity, the capacity to repair what would be thrown away at home; when his television remote stopped working in Phnom Penh, he got it fixed at the corner for a dollar.

In the United States, the federal government defines poverty very simply: an annual income, for a family with one adult and three children, of less than $18,392 in the year 2003. That works out to $8.89 an hour, or $3.74 above the federal minimum wage, assuming that someone can get a full forty hours of work a week for all fifty-two weeks of the year, or 2,080 working hours annually. With incomes rising through the economic expansion of the 1990s, the incidence of official poverty declined, beginning the new decade at 11.3 percent of the population, down from 15.1 percent in 1993. Then it rose slightly in the ensuing recession, to 12.1 percent by 2002.

But the figures are misleading. The federal poverty line cuts far below the amount needed for a decent living, because the Census Bureau still uses the basic formula designed in 1964 by the Social Security Administration, with four modest revisions in subsequent years. That sets the poverty level at approximately three times the cost of a "thrifty food basket." The calculation was derived from spending patterns in 1955, when the average family used about one-third of its income for food. It is no longer valid today, when the average family spends only about one-sixth of its budget for food, but the government continues to multiply the cost of a "thrifty food basket" by three, adjusting for inflation only and over-looking nearly half a century of dramatically changing lifestyles.

The result burnishes reality by underestimating the numbers whose lives can reasonably be considered impoverished. More ac-curate formulas, being tested by the Census Bureau and the National Academy of Sciences, would rely on actual costs of food, clothing, shelter, utilities, and the like. Under those calculations, income would include benefits not currently counted, such as food stamps, subsidized housing, fuel assistance, and school lunches; living costs would include expenditures now ignored, such as child care, doctor's bills, health insurance premiums, and Social Security payroll taxes. When the various formulas were run in 1998, they increased by about three percentage points the proportion of the population in poverty, from the official 34.5 mil-lion to a high of 42.4 million people. A later variation raised the poverty rate in 2001 by 0.6 percent. Such a change would pre-sumably make more families eligible for benefits that are linked to the poverty level; some programs, including children's health insurance, already cover households with incomes up to 150 or 200 percent of the poverty threshold, depending on the state.

Even if revised methods of figuring poverty were adopted, however, they would provide only a still photograph of a family's momentary situation. In that snapshot, the ebb and flow of the moving picture is lost. By measuring only income and expenses during a current year and not assets and debts, the formulas ig-nore the past, and the past is frequently an overwhelming burden on the present. Plenty of people have moved into jobs that put them above the threshold of poverty, only to discover that their student loans, their car payments, and the exorbitant interest charged on old credit card balances consume so much of their cash that they live no better than before.

25   When the poor or the nearly poor are asked to define poverty, however, they talk not only about what's in the wallet but what's in the mind or the heart. "Hopelessness," said a fifteen-year-old girl in New Hampshire.

"Not hopelessness—helplessness," said a man in Los Angeles. "Why should I get up? Nobody's gonna ever hire me because look at the way I'm dressed, and look at the fact that I never finished high school, look at the fact that I'm black, I'm brown, I'm yellow, or I grew up in the trailer."

"The state of mind," said a man in Washington, D.C. "I believe that spirituality is way more important than physical."

"I am so rich," said a woman whose new job running Xerox machines was lifting her out of poverty, "because—not only material things—because I know who I am, I know where I'm going now."

Another woman, who fell into poverty after growing up middle class, celebrated her "cultural capital," which meant her love of books, music, ideas, and her close relationships with her children. "In some senses, we are not at all poor; we have a great richness," she said. "We don't feel very poor. We feel poor when we can't go to the doctor or fix the car."

30   For practically every family, then, the ingredients of poverty are part financial and part psychological, part personal and part societal, part past and part present. Every problem magnifies the impact of the others, and all are so tightly interlocked that one reversal can produce a chain reaction with results far distant from the original cause. A run-down apartment can exacerbate a child's asthma, which leads to a call for an ambulance, which generates a medical bill that cannot be paid, which ruins a credit record, which hikes the interest rate on the auto loan, which forces the purchase of an unreliable used car, which jeopardizes a mother's punctuality at work, which limits her promotions and earning capacity, which confines her to poor housing. . . . If she or any other impoverished working parent added up all of her individual problems, the whole would be equal to more than the sum of its parts. . . . Isolating the individual problems, as a laboratory would extract specific toxins, would be artificial and pointless. They exist largely because of one another, and the chemical reaction among them worsens the overall effect.

If problems are interlocking, then so must solutions be. A job alone is not enough. Medical insurance alone is not enough.

Good housing alone is not enough. Reliable transportation, careful family budgeting, effective parenting, effective schooling are not enough when each is achieved in isolation from the rest. There is no single variable that can be altered to help working people move away from the edge of poverty. Only where the full array of factors is attacked can America fulfill its promise.

The first step is to see the problems, and the first problem is the failure to see the people. Those who work but live impoverished lives blend into familiar landscapes and are therefore overlooked. They make up the invisible, silent America that analysts casually ignore. "We all live in the suburbs now, not in the inner cities," proclaimed Professor Michael Goldstein of the University of Colorado, explaining on PBS why Woolworth's had been replaced by Wal-Mart in the Dow Jones Industrial Average.

Tim Brookes, a commentator on National Public Radio, once did a witty screed against overpriced popcorn in movie theaters. Indignant at having been charged $5 for a small bag, he conducted research on the actual expenses. He calculated that the $5\frac{1}{4}$ ounces of popcorn he received cost 23.71875 cents in a supermarket but only 16.5 cents at prices theater managers paid for fifty-pound sacks. He generously figured 5 cents in electricity to cook the popcorn and 1 cent for the bag. Total cost: 22.5 cents. Subtracting the sales tax, that left a profit of $4.075, or 1,811 percent.

Evidently, the theater had the remarkable sense not to hire   35
any workers, for Brookes gave no hint of having noticed any people behind the counter. Their paltry wages, which wouldn't have undermined the excessive profits, were absent from his calculation. The folks who popped the corn, filled the bag, handed the bag to him, and took his money must have been shrouded in an invisibility cloak. No NPR editor seemed to notice.

I hope that this book will help them to be seen.

Questions for Discussion

1. According to Shipler, why do Americans still pay homage to the myth of tireless labor and thrift transforming a poor immigrant into a successful business person? What example does he use to illustrate the validity of his claim? Is it effective? In what ways does this myth have both a positive and negative impact on Americans and our culture?

2. Despite a national War on Poverty that began in 1962, why does Shipler argue that the current gap between the rich and the poor is now wider than it was 40 years ago?

3. Why does Shipler argue that poverty in America is not easy to define? What factors influence people's being poor and their resulting psychological state of mind? Why is it hard for people in the United States to break out of their cycle of poverty? Why does Shipler believe it is harder to be poor in America than in a developing nation? Do you agree? Explain.

4. Why does Shipler think that the national government and all citizens—rich and poor—need to start thinking differently about the meaning of poverty in America? How does he believe we can begin to find solutions to the cycle of poverty, and its human and social consequences that are growing more serious every day?

Ideas for Writing

1. Write a research paper that supports or refutes Shipler's claim that "low-wage employees have been testing the American doctrine that hard work cures poverty."

2. Write a definition of poverty that captures the unique and very real circumstances that make poverty a heavy burden on the spirits of poor individuals, their families, and the nation as a whole. Focus your definition within the context of a particular class or group of workers.

Evaluation
BARBARA EHRENREICH

Activist writer Barbara Ehrenreich (b. 1951) holds a Ph.D. from Rockefeller University (1968) and has taught at the University of California at Berkeley in the School of Journalism. She has been the recipient of a Guggenheim Fellowship and of a prestigious MacArthur grant. Her essays and reviews have appeared in many national newspapers and magazines, including Harpers, The Atlantic Monthly, The Nation, *and* Time. *Ehrenreich's most recent books include* Blood Rites: Origins and History of the Passions of War *(1997),* Nickel and Dimed: On (Not) Getting by in America *(2001), and* Global Woman: Nannies, Maids, and Sex Workers in the New Economy *(2003). The following selection from* Nickel and Dimed, *an evaluation of her experiences working with the underclass in various underpaid jobs in America for a year, draws provocative conclusions about the underlying causes of this kind of exploitation.*

✦

. . . There is a way that low-income workers differ from "economic man." For the laws of economics to work, the "players" need to be well informed about their options. The ideal case—and I've read that the technology for this is just around the corner—would be the consumer whose Palm Pilot displays the menu and prices for every restaurant or store he or she passes. Even without such technological assistance, affluent job hunters expect to study the salary-benefit packages offered by their potential employers, watch the financial news to find out if these packages are in line with those being offered in other regions or fields, and probably do a little bargaining before taking a job.

But there are no Palm Pilots, cable channels, or Web sites to advise the low-wage job seeker. She has only the help-wanted signs and the want ads to go on, and most of these coyly refrain from mentioning numbers. So information about who earns what and where has to travel by work of mouth, and for inexplicable cultural reasons, this is a very slow and unreliable route. Twin Cities job market analyst Kristine Jacobs pinpoints what she calls the "money taboo" as a major factor preventing workers from optimizing their earnings. "There's a code of silence surrounding issues related to individuals' earnings," she told me. "We confess everything else in our society—sex, crime, illness. But no one wants to reveal what they earn or how they got it. The money taboo is the one thing that employers can always count on."[1] I suspect that this "taboo" operates most effectively among the lowest-paid people, because, in a society that endlessly celebrates its dot-com billionaires and centimillionaire athletes, $7 or even $10 an hour can feel like a mark of innate inferiority. So you may or may not find out that, say, the Target down the road is paying better than Wal-Mart, even if you have a sister-in-law working there.

Employers, of course, do little to encourage the economic literacy of their workers. They may exhort potential customers to "Compare Our Prices!" but they're not eager to have workers do the same with wages. I have mentioned the way the hiring process seems designed, in some cases, to prevent any discussion or even disclosure of wages—whisking the applicant from interview to orientation before the crass subject of money can be raised. Some employers go further; instead of relying on the informal "money taboo" to keep workers from discussing and comparing wages, they specifically enjoin workers from doing so. The *New York Times* recently reported on several lawsuits brought by employees who had allegedly been fired for breaking this rule—a woman, for example, who asked for higher pay after learning from her male coworkers that she was being paid considerably less than they were for the very same work. The National Labor Relations Act of 1935 makes it illegal to punish people for revealing their wages to one another, but the practice is likely to persist until rooted out by lawsuits, company by company.[2]

But if it's hard for workers to obey the laws of economics by examining their options and moving on to better jobs, why don't more of them take a stand where they are—demanding better wages and work conditions, either individually or as a group? This is a huge question, probably the subject of many a dissertation in the field of industrial psychology, and here I can only comment on the things I observed. One of these was the co-optative power of management, illustrated by such euphemisms as *associate* and *team member*. At The Maids, the boss—who, as the only male in our midst, exerted a creepy, paternalistic kind of power—had managed to convince some of my coworkers that he was struggling against difficult odds and deserving of their unstinting forbearance. Wal-Mart has a number of more impersonal and probably more effective ways of getting its workers to feel like "associates." There was the profit-sharing plan, with Wal-Mart's stock price posted daily in a prominent spot near the break room. There was the company's much-heralded patriotism, evidenced in the banners over the shopping floor urging workers and customers to contribute to the construction of a World War II veterans' memorial (Sam Walton having been one of them). There were "associate" meetings that served as pep rallies, completed with the Wal-Mart cheer: "Gimme a 'W,'" etc.

5   The chance to identify with a powerful and wealthy entity—the company or the boss—is only the carrot. There is also a stick. What surprised and offended me most about the low-wage workplace (and yes, here all my middle-class privilege is on full display) was the extent to which one is required to surrender one's basic civil rights and—what boils down to the same thing—self-respect. I learned this at the very beginning of my stint as a waitress, when I was warned that my purse could be searched by management at any time. I wasn't carrying stolen salt shakers or anything else of a compromising nature, but still, there's something about the prospect of a purse search that makes a woman feel a few buttons short of fully dressed. After work, I called around and found that this practice is entirely legal; if the purse is on the boss's property—which of course it was—the boss has the right to examine its contents.

Drug testing is another routine indignity. Civil libertarians see it as a violation of our Fourth Amendment freedom from "unreasonable search"; most jobholders and applicants find it simply embarrassing. In some testing protocols, the employee has to strip to her underwear and pee into a cup in the presence of an aide or technician. Mercifully, I got to keep my clothes on and shut the toilet stall door behind me, but even so, urination is a private act and it is degrading to have to perform it at the command of some powerful other. I would add preemployment personality tests to the list of demeaning intrusions, or at least much of their usual content. Maybe the hypothetical types of questions can be justified—whether you would steal if an opportunity arose or turn in a thieving coworker and so on—but not questions about your "moods of self-pity," whether you are a loner or believe you are usually misunderstood. It is unsettling, at the very least, to give a stranger access to things, like your self-doubts and your urine, that are otherwise shared only in medical or therapeutic situations.

There are other, more direct ways of keeping low-wage employees in their place. Rules against "gossip," or even "talking," make it hard to air your grievances to peers or—should you be so daring—to enlist other workers in a group effort to bring about change, through a union organizing drive, for example. Those who do step out of line often face little unexplained punishments, such as having their schedules or their work assignments unilaterally changed. Or you may be fired; those low-wage workers who work without union contracts, which is the great majority of them, work "at will," meaning at the will of the employer, and are subject to dismissal without explanation. The AFL-CIO estimates that ten thousand workers a year are fired for participating in union organizing drives, and since it is illegal to fire people for union activity, I suspect that these firings are usually justified in terms of unrelated minor infractions. Wal-Mart employees who have bucked the company—by getting involved in a unionization drive or by suing the company for failing to pay overtime—have been fired for breaking the company rule against using profanity.[3]

So if low-wage workers do not always behave in an economically rational way, that is, as free agents within a capitalist democracy, it is because they dwell in a place that is neither free nor in any way democratic. When you enter the low-wage workplace—and many of the medium-wage workplaces as well—you check your civil liberties at the door, leave America and all it supposedly stands for behind, and learn to zip your lips for the

duration of the shift. The consequences of this routine surrender
go beyond the issues of wages and poverty. We can hardly pride
ourselves on being the world's preeminent democracy, after all, if
large numbers of citizens spend half their waking hours in what
amounts, in plain terms, to a dictatorship.

Any dictatorship takes a psychological toll on its subjects. If
you are treated as an untrustworthy person—a potential slacker,
drug addict, or thief—you may begin to feel less trustworthy yourself. If you are constantly reminded of your lowly position in the
social hierarchy, whether by individual managers or by a plethora
of impersonal rules, you begin to accept that unfortunate status.
To draw for a moment from an entirely different corner of my life,
that part of me still attached to the biological sciences, there is
ample evidence that animals—rats and monkeys, for example—
that are forced into a subordinate status within their social systems
adapt their brain chemistry accordingly, becoming "depressed" in
humanlike ways. Their behavior is anxious and withdrawn; the
level of serotonin (the neurotransmitter boosted by some antidepressants) declines in their brains. And—what is especially relevant here—they avoid fighting even in self-defense.[4]

10   Humans are, of course, vastly more complicated; even in situations of extreme subordination, we can pump up our self-esteem
with thoughts of our families, our religion, our hopes for the future. But as much as any other social animal, and more so than
many, we depend for our self-image on the humans immediately
around us—to the point of altering our perceptions of the world so
as to fit in with theirs.[5] My guess is that the indignities imposed on
so many low-wage workers—the drug tests, the constant surveillance, being "reamed out" by managers—are part of what keeps
wages low. If you're made to feel unworthy enough, you may come
to think that what you're paid is what you are actually worth.

It is hard to imagine any other function for workplace au-
thoritarianism. Managers may truly believe that, without their
unremitting efforts, all work would quickly grind to a halt. That is
not my impression. While I encountered some cynics and plenty
of people who had learned to budget their energy, I never met an
actual slacker or, for that matter, a drug addict or thief. On the
contrary, I was amazed and sometimes saddened by the pride
people took in jobs that rewarded them so meagerly, either in
wages or in recognition. Often, in fact, these people experienced
management as an obstacle to getting the job done as it should
be done. Waitresses chafed at managers' stinginess toward the
customers; housecleaners resented the time constraints that

sometimes made them cut corners; retail workers wanted the floor to be beautiful, not cluttered with excess stock as management required. Left to themselves, they devised systems of cooperation and work sharing; when there was a crisis, they rose to it. In fact, it was often hard to see what the function of management was, other than to exact obeisance.

There seems to be a vicious cycle at work here, making ours not just an economy but a culture of extreme inequality. Corporate decision makers, and even some two-bit entrepreneurs like my boss at The Maids, occupy an economic position miles above that of the underpaid people whose labor they depend on. For reasons that have more to do with class—and often racial—prejudice than with actual experience, they tend to fear and distrust the category of people from which they recruit their workers. Hence the perceived need for repressive management and intrusive measures like drug and personality testing. But these things cost money—$20,000 or more a year for a manager, $100 a pop for a drug test, and so on—and the high cost of repression results in ever more pressure to hold wages down. The larger society seems to be caught up in a similar cycle: cutting public services for the poor, which are sometimes referred to collectively as the "social wage," while investing even more heavily in prisons and cops. And in the larger society, too, the cost of repression becomes another factor weighing against the expansion or restoration of needed services. It is a tragic cycle, condemning us to ever deeper inequality, and in the long run, almost no one benefits but the agents of repression themselves.

But whatever keeps wages low—and I'm sure my comments have barely scratched the surface—the result is that many people earn far less than they need to live on. How much is that? The Economic Policy Institute recently reviewed dozens of studies of what constitutes a "living wage" and came up with an average figure of $30,000 a year for a family of one adult and two children, which amounts to a wage of $14 an hour. This is not the very minimum such a family could live on; the budget includes health insurance, a telephone, and child care at a licensed center, for example, which are well beyond the reach of millions. But it does not include restaurant meals, video rentals, Internet access, wine and liquor, cigarettes and lottery tickets, or even very much meat. The shocking thing is that the majority of American workers, about 60 percent, earn less than $14 an hour. Many of them get by by teaming up with another wage earner, a spouse or grown child. Some draw on government help in the form of food stamps, housing vouchers, the earned income tax credit, or—for those coming off welfare in relatively generous states—subsidized child care. But others—single mothers for example—have nothing but their own wages to live on, no matter how many mouths there are to feed.

Employers will look at that $30,000 figure, which is over twice what they currently pay entry-level workers, and see nothing but bankruptcy ahead. Indeed, it is probably impossible for the private sector to provide everyone with an adequate standard of living through wages, or even wages plus benefits, alone: too much of what we need, such as reliable child care, is just too expensive, even for middle-class families. Most civilized nations compensate for the inadequacy of wages by providing relatively generous public services such as health insurance, free or subsidized child care, subsidized housing, and effective public transportation. But the United States, for all its wealth, leaves its citizens to fend for themselves—facing market-based rents, for example, on their wages alone. For millions of Americans, that $10—or even $8 or $6—hourly wage is all there is.

15   It is common, among the nonpoor, to think of poverty as a sustainable condition—austere, perhaps, but they get by somehow, don't they? They are "always with us." What is harder for the nonpoor to see is poverty as acute distress: The lunch that consists of Doritos or hot dog rolls, leading to faintness before the end of the shift. The "home" that is also a car or a van. The illness or injury that must be "worked through," with gritted teeth, because there's no sick pay or health insurance and the loss of one day's pay will mean no groceries for the next. These experiences are not part of a sustainable lifestyle, even a lifestyle of chronic deprivation and relentless low-level punishment. They are, by almost any standard of subsistence, emergency situations. And that is how we should see the poverty of so many millions of low-wage Americans—as a state of emergency.

In the summer of 2000 I returned—permanently, I have every reason to hope—to my customary place in the socioeconomic spectrum. I go to restaurants, often far finer ones than the places where I worked, and sit down at a table. I sleep in hotel rooms that someone else has cleaned and shop in stores that others will tidy when I leave. To go from the bottom 20 percent to the top 20 percent is to enter a magical world where needs are met, problems are solved, almost without any intermediate effort. If you want to get somewhere fast, you hail a cab. If your aged parents have grown tiresome or incontinent, you put them away where others will deal with their dirty diapers and dementia. If you are part of the upper-middle-class majority that employs a maid or maid service, you return from work to find the house miraculously restored to order—the toilet bowls gleaming, the socks that you left on the floor levitated back to their normal dwelling place. Here, sweat is a metaphor for hard work, but seldom its consequence. Hundreds of little things get done, reliably and routinely every day, without anyone's seeming to do them.

The top 20 percent routinely exercises other, far more consequential forms of power in the world. This stratum, which contains what I have termed in an earlier book the "professional-managerial class," is the home of our decision makers, opinion shapers, culture creators—our professors, lawyers, executives, entertainers, politicians, judges, writers, producers, and editors.[6] When they speak, they are listened to. When they complain, someone usually scurries to correct the problem and apologize for it. If they complain often enough, someone far below them in wealth and influence may be chastised or even fired. Political power, too, is concentrated within the top 20 percent, since its members are far more likely than the poor—or even the middle class—to discern the all-too-tiny distinctions between candidates that can make it seem worthwhile to contribute, participate, and vote. In all these ways, the affluent exert inordinate power over the lives of the less affluent, and especially over the lives of the poor, determining what public services will be available, if any, what minimum wage, what laws governing the treatment of labor.

. . . In a 2000 article on the "disappearing poor," journalist James Fallows reports that, from the vantage point of the Internet's nouveaux riches, it is "hard to understand people for whom a million dollars would be a fortune . . . not to mention those for whom $246 is a full week's earnings."[7] Among the reasons he and others have cited for the blindness of the affluent is the fact that they are less and less likely to share spaces and services with the poor. As public schools and other public services deteriorate, those who can afford to do so send their children to private schools and spend their off-hours in private spaces— health clubs, for example, instead of the local park. They don't ride on public buses and subways. They withdraw from mixed neighborhoods into distant suburbs, gated communities, or guarded apartment towers; they shop in stores that, in line with the prevailing "market segmentation," are designed to appeal to the affluent alone. Even the affluent young are increasingly unlikely to spend their summers learning how the "other half" lives, as lifeguards, waitresses, or housekeepers at resort hotels. The *New York Times* reports that they now prefer career-relevant activities like summer school or interning in an appropriate professional setting to the "sweaty, low-paid and mind-numbing slots that have long been their lot."[8]

Then, too, the particular political moment favors what almost looks like a "conspiracy of silence" on the subject of poverty and the poor. The Democrats are not eager to find flaws in the period of "unprecedented prosperity" they take credit for; the Republicans have lost interest in the poor now that "welfare-as-we-know-it" has ended. Welfare reform itself is a factor weighing against any close investigation of the conditions of the poor. Both parties heartily endorsed it, and to acknowledge that low-wage work doesn't lift people out of poverty would be to admit that it may have been, in human terms, a catastrophic mistake. In fact, very little is known about the fate of former welfare recipients because the 1996 welfare reform legislation blithely failed to include any provision for monitoring their postwelfare economic condition. Media accounts persistently bright-side the situation, highlighting the occasional success stories and downplaying the acknowledged increase in hunger.[9] And sometimes there seems to be almost deliberate deception. In June 2000, the press rushed to hail a study supposedly showing that Minnesota's welfare-to-work program had sharply reduced poverty and was, as *Time* magazine put it, a "winner."[10] Overlooked in these reports was the fact that the program in question was a pilot project that offered far more generous child care and other subsidies than Minnesota's actual welfare reform program. Perhaps the error can be forgiven—the pilot project, which ended in 1997, had the same name, Minnesota Family Investment Program, as Minnesota's much larger, ongoing welfare reform program.[11]

20   You would have to read a great many newspapers very carefully, cover to cover, to see the signs of distress. You would find, for example, that in 1999 Massachusetts food pantries reported a 72 percent increase in the demand for their services over the previous year, that Texas food banks were "scrounging" for food, despite donations at or above 1998 levels, as were those in Atlanta.[12] You might learn that in San Diego the Catholic Church could no longer, as of January 2000, accept homeless families at its shelter, which happens to be the city's largest, because it was already operating at twice its normal capacity.[13] You would come across news of a study showing that the percentage of Wisconsin food-stamp families in "extreme poverty"—defined as less than 50 percent of

the federal poverty line—has tripled in the last decade to more than 30 percent.[14] You might discover that, nationwide, America's food banks are experiencing "a torrent of need which [they] cannot meet" and that, according to a survey conducted by the U.S. Conference of Mayors, 67 percent of the adults requesting emergency food aid are people with jobs.[15]

One reason nobody bothers to pull all these stories together and announce a widespread state of emergency may be that Americans of the newspaper-reading professional middle class are used to thinking of poverty as a consequence of unemployment. During the heyday of downsizing in the Reagan years, it very often was, and it still is for many inner-city residents who have no way of getting to the proliferating entry-level jobs on urban peripheries. When unemployment causes poverty, we know how to state the problem—typically, "the economy isn't growing fast enough"—and we know what the traditional liberal solution is—"full employment." But when we have full or nearly full employment, when jobs are available to any job seeker who can get to them, then the problem goes deeper and begins to cut into that web of expectations that make up the "social contract." According to a recent poll conducted by Jobs for the Future, a Boston-based employment research firm, 94 percent of Americans agree that "people who work full-time should be able to earn enough to keep their families out of poverty."[16] I grew up hearing over and over, to the point of tedium, that "hard work" was the secret of success: "Work hard and you'll get ahead" or "It's hard work that got us where we are." No one said that you could work hard—harder even than you ever thought possible—and still find yourself sinking ever deeper into poverty and debt.

When poor single mothers had the option of remaining out of the labor force on welfare, the middle and upper middle class tended to view them with a certain impatience, if not disgust. The welfare poor were excoriated for their laziness, their persistence in reproducing in unfavorable circumstances, their presumed addictions, and above all for their "dependency." Here they were, content to live off "government handouts" instead of seeking "self-sufficiency," like everyone else, through a job. They needed to get their act together, learn how to wind an alarm clock, get out there and get to work. But now that government has largely withdrawn its "handouts," now that the overwhelming majority of the poor are out there toiling in Wal-Mart or Wendy's—well, what are we to think of them? Disapproval and condescension no longer apply, so what outlook makes sense?

Guilt, you may be thinking warily. Isn't that what we're supposed to feel? But guilt doesn't go anywhere near far enough; the
appropriate emotion is shame—shame at our *own* dependency, in
this case, on the underpaid labor of others. When someone works
for less pay than she can live on—when, for example, she goes
hungry so that you can eat more cheaply and conveniently—then
she has made a great sacrifice for you, she has made you a gift of
some part of her abilities, her health, and her life. The "working
poor," as they are approvingly termed, are in fact the major philanthropists of our society. They neglect their own children so that
the children of others will be cared for; they live in substandard
housing so that other homes will be shiny and perfect; they endure privation so that inflation will be low and stock prices high.
To be a member of the working poor is to be an anonymous
donor, a nameless benefactor, to everyone else. As Gail, one of my
restaurant coworkers put it, "you give and you give."

Someday, of course—and I will make no predictions as to exactly when—they are bound to tire of getting so little in return
and demand to be paid what they're worth. There'll be a lot of
anger when that day comes, and strikes and disruption. But the
sky will not fall, and we will all be better off for it in the end.

Endnotes

1. Personal communication, July 24, 2000.
2. "The Biggest Company Secret: Workers Challenge Employer Practices
   on Pay Confidentiality," *New York Times*, July 28, 2000.
3. Bob Ortega, *In Sam We Trust*, p. 356; "Former Wal-Mart Workers File
   Overtime Suit in Harrison County," *Charleston Gazette*, January 24,
   1999.
4. See, for example, C. A. Shively, K. Laber-Laird, and R. F. Anton,
   "Behavior and Physiology of Social Stress and Depression in Female
   Cynomolgus Monkeys," *Biological Psychiatry* 41:8 (1997), pp.
   871–882, and D. C. Blanchard et al., "Visible Burrow System as a
   Model of Chronic Social Stress: Behavioral and Neuroendocrine
   Correlates," *Psychoneuroendocrinology* 20:2 (1995), pp. 117–134.
5. See, for example, Chapter 7, "Conformity," in David G. Myers, *Social
   Psychology* (New York: McGraw-Hill, 1987).
6. *Fear of Falling: The Inner Life of the Middle Class* (New York:
   Pantheon, 1989).
7. "The Invisible Poor," *New York Times Magazine*, March 19, 2000.
8. "Summer Work Is Out of Favor with the Young," *New York Times*,
   June 18, 2000.

9. The *National Journal* reports that the "good news" is that almost six million people have left the welfare rolls since 1996, while the "rest of the story" includes the problem that "these people sometimes don't have enough to eat" ("Welfare Reform, Act 2," June 24, 2000, pp. 1,978–93).

10. "Minnesota's Welfare Reform Proves a Winner," *Time*, June 12, 2000.

11. Center for Law and Social Policy, "Update," Washington, D.C., June 2000.

12. "Study: More Go Hungry since Welfare Reform," *Boston Herald*, January 21, 2000; "Charity Can't Feed All while Welfare Reforms Implemented," *Houston Chronicle*, January 10, 2000; "Hunger Grows as Food Banks Try to Keep Pace," *Atlanta Journal and Constitution*, November 26, 1999.

13. "Rise in Homeless Families Strains San Diego Aid," *Los Angeles Times*, January 24, 2000.

14. "Hunger Problems Said to Be Getting Worse," *Milwaukee Journal Sentinel*, December 15, 1999.

15. Deborah Leff, the president and CEO of the hunger-relief organization America's Second Harvest, quoted in the *National Journal*, op. cit.; "Hunger Persists in U.S. despite the Good Times," *Detroit News*, June 15, 2000.

16. "A National Survey of American Attitudes toward Low-Wage Workers and Welfare Reform," Jobs for the Future, Boston, May 24, 2000.

Questions for Discussion

1. How is Ehrenreich's real job different from that of a low-wage worker? Why did her professional studies lead her to conduct the experiment she describes in this selection? In what ways is her work at various low-paying corporations an example of field research?

2. Why do you think that *Nickel and Dimed* became an instant national bestseller and continues to be read widely? What types of readers do you think that Ehrenreich wanted to reach? How do her profiles and the issues she identifies, her style of writing and the types of information she includes help you to answer this question?

3. Why does Ehrenreich believe that the poor remain invisible to the upper middle class? What does she believe can be done to change this situation? What do you think the government needs to do to improve this situation?

4. Why does Ehrenreich argue that the economic status of the poor has declined since welfare reform? Why does she believe that the working poor are the major philanthropists of our society? Do you agree with her position on both of these intertwined issues? Explain your point of view.

Ideas for Writing

1. Do some more research on the working poor. Write an essay that provides solutions to their problems. For example, what types of legislation could be passed to protect workers from being exploited by large corporations?
2. Focusing on a particular major corporation or franchise business, write a research paper that discusses some of the ways that a change in corporate policy could make worker's environment safer, more humane, and more rewarding.

The Just-Add-Water Kennedys and Barbecue Bread Violence

POLYESTRA

Polyestra is a painter, poet, rock singer, and filmmaker. She is currently working on her second novel and a collection of short stories. Her band, also called Polyestra, is recording an album in Montana, where she lives with her husband and children. Polyestra's work has been published in several anthologies; she has also self-published over a dozen poetry books. In the following reading, "Just-Add-Water Kennedys and Barbecue Bread Violence," Polyestra describes how she was raised by a family whose primary goal was to "get rich" and "jump class," but never quite made it.

──────────── ✦ ────────────

Fewer than one percent of Americans break out of the class they are born into. Despite these grim odds, people like my parents still base their entire lives on the dream of class jumping. The television gospel told them it was not only possible, but normal. To not increase your wealth was more shameful, to my family, than a brown lawn, unusual offspring, and unemployment combined. They considered that every day that went by without a yacht and a swimming pool embarrassing. And everyone else in the neighborhood who didn't miraculously obtain a new Cadillac or a vacation home at the beach, or who was still working construction or driving a cab, was equally shameful. To my parents, every day in this working-class neighborhood was temporary. It was just a matter of working hard enough.

My parents didn't think of "class" as an ingrained culture, as a part of who they were. They had no pride in where they came from, only in where they dreamed of going. They were two out of millions

who erased themselves for the homogeneity of TV-inspired bland-
ness, smiling into cereal commercials like adoring fans. The
American Dream. Television was a sick ritual for people like my
parents. After dinner my father would peel down to his undershirt
and light up a cigar, clenching it between his lead- and mercury-
filled molars (some strange side effect of serving in the military).
He reclined in his personal chair, his oiled black pompadour shin-
ing in the TV's light. My mother perched posture-perfectly on the
sinking couch. They pored over images of gluttonous mansions
and commented on how they would arrange the furniture in such a
place, what color scheme they would apply to each room, where to
put the remote control, rotating fireplace, and wishing fountain.
They wanted every car in every car ad, every diamond ring, dinette
set, wide-screen television. Their idea of "rich" wasn't being able to
afford furniture from somewhere other than Sears, but being able
to afford the most expensive furniture, and a lot of it, from Sears.

Every weekend we went to my grandparents' house, no skip-
ping allowed. If we were all dying of pneumonia, we were still required to go, or suffer the wrath of Thelma and Johnny. My father's
parents were hard-core about their son becoming a millionaire.
They had been through the Depression. Their lives reeked of financial failure and poverty—one big drag for all the world to know
about—and now it was up to my father to save them from dying in
shame. These were bitter people. The old man chain-smoked and
drank canned beer while the woman actually wept over "the mixing of the races." They had been robbed or hurt themselves so
many times they had developed a fear of hordes of non-Caucasians
entering their row house at night to kill them and make off with
their nicotine-stained divan, their silver utensils (which were hidden in the wall of the cellar), their rechargeable electric grass clip-
pers, their monogrammed pen and notepad set from 1939. Even in
the worst dry spell of generic-cigarette half-price sales, their son
would surely save them. Even if they ran out of green olives for
their "special occasion" martinis, even if the TV went on the fritz
during *The Lawrence Welk Show,* my father would save them. Even
if my grandfather slipped away into an alternate plane, humming
songs of Austria while belching up bile and swallowing it again,
which he did, my father would take care of them. And so he did.

My parents had two kids, both of whose purpose in life was to
become rich. The torch had been passed. It was now my parents'
goal to mold us into something "rich," to strategically insert us
into the upper crust, thus ensuring a wealthy retirement. Their
first attempt at this was to enroll my sister and me in private

school (from which we were rapidly ejected, since they couldn't pay for it). They insisted this would give my sister and me a much better chance of marrying some sweaty-palmed old-money boy when the time came. Unfortunately, they overlooked the fact that these rich children wanted nothing to do with us. The rich, like those mysterious Masons and the CIA, have seriously tight-ass circles that not just anyone can penetrate. This really messed with my sister's mind; she was in a constant state of agony. All the other girls in her classes had designer jeans, and my sister was the only one in the whole school suffering without. My mother sewed fake patches onto generic jeans, but this only made the whole thing worse when a classmate ratted her out.

5   Next they enrolled my sister and me in ballroom-dancing classes at the country club, where we were nearly guaranteed to become "cultured" and "civilized." This move was in part a response to my natural attraction to vandalism and dirt-bike ganging, which severely infringed upon my parents' princess dreams. At the country club, they thought, we would learn how to charm the hell out of the rich, play their games, rub elbows with the next generation of money people. Membership was by invitation only. We were the only kids in the classes whose parents weren't members. These kids came from well-known, old-money families. For them, the waltz and the fox trot were some sort of perverse "fun," where they got dressed up and twirled around a ballroom like royalty. To me, it was horror.

Everything about me showed I didn't belong, from my inappropriate, not-quite-formal tube dresses to my macramé jewelry. (Our clothing arrived in the mail from our Canadian cousins—hand-me-downs from the hinterland—and was better suited to square dancing and getting beat up in a big city.) My mother tried to compensate by hand-sewing me the gaudiest satin and lace dresses. She went for the latest fad: low-waisted, poofed-out dresses that made me look like my torso was twice as long as my legs, like some shapeless, disproportionate mutant. She even bought me little white gloves—like the JonBenet freakazoids wear on the creepy children's talent shows in Atlantic City—and patent-leather Mary Janes.

Once a week, my mother, in her beige polyester London Fog–style overcoat and metallic-blue eye shadow, her helmet perm and beige secretary pumps, drove me up the winding road of manicured grounds in our clunking Toronado station wagon. At the top of the hill sat the Colonial castle within which waited the liverwurst-scented old ladies with castanets and the teeming brood of the stinking rich of Delaware, all prissied up like miniature millionaires. There I slouched in a "period" chair against the wall while all the little boys in suits and gloves chose all the little girls in velvet and lace, leaving me to sit there for the entire time. One of the deeply creased, too-much-sun-in-a-lifetime old ladies sometimes forced one of the boys to dance with me—more as a punishment to some lazy boy than to help me. Their parents were Du Ponts and oil tycoons, and one boy, his rubbery hand like a hoof on my hip, said to me, "You'll never marry one of us."

"I know," I said, and I wasn't offended. I had gone to private school with this arrogant little boy, who was commonly known as "Booger" for his eversunken finger in his ape-shaped right nostril. I just wanted to go ride my bike down a steep, rocky embankment, give someone a black eye. Instead I found myself seated at a very long table, my eyes full of what seemed like hundreds of sparkling utensils. We were "quizzed" during each course of a sickeningly massive meal as to which utensil to use. My hand trembled over the fourth fork from the left, the knife located beside the smallest plate, expecting a slap on the wrist from one of the wrinkled mummies. Each item presented by some annoyed waiter was smothered in hollandaise. Boiled meat and hollandaise. String beans and hollandaise. All this in preparation for a final banquet and ball, to which the parents were invited to get loaded and watch their kids do the bunny hop. I was thankful to find out we weren't invited, but my sister wept bitter tears for days. Her sorrow worsened when we found out we were the only ones enrolled in the classes who weren't invited. My parents complained that they hadn't gotten their money's worth for the classes. They couldn't understand what had gone wrong.

My mother worked at a bank with Bruce Willis's mom. Every day, sucking up minimum wage, my mom told Bruce Willis's mom about how she would be rich someday. My father worked at Sears with Elvis Presley's drummer. He did the same. He asked a customer, "You want us to rotate the tires while we're at it?" and then told Elvis Presley's drummer how he would be rich someday. Elvis Presley's drummer rotated the tires, smiled slowly at my dad, and went to the bar after work like everyone else. The reality of working shit jobs somehow didn't sway them from their delusion. Instead of resenting the rich, who would never let them into their club, they talked about them as if they were family: "George Wellingham III got a new Porsche!" "Ivana Porkroll is divorcing Richard—it will split the families for sure." "Little Rutherford Hoggerton has been chosen to go to the military academy—did you hear, girls? He's your age!"

10   Every day when I walked to school I walked past the private school, where my friends and I were harassed by a bunch of horse-faced blondes in team shorts, holding on to lacrosse sticks. It just so happened that the school had constructed a pedestrian tunnel under the road, and a few kids from our school had been killed crossing the street there, so we opted to walk through the tunnel. "No white trash allowed!" they would bellow, threatening to call the cops. The property between the private school and the public school was all Du Pont estates. One day an old lady in the back of a limo pulled up next to us on the street and told us she didn't want us walking past her driveway—on the public street. She wrote down our names and said she would notify the authorities of our intentions to rob the Du Ponts. My associates and I decorated the walls of the tunnel with slogans, such as, Rich Fucks, Fucking Snobs, Eat Shit Moneybags.

      My father quit Sears and plunged headlong into sales. Real estate. He worked seven-day weeks for the same or less pay than the Sears job. It seemed like a turn for the worse, but then, rather suddenly, my father started making money. A lot of money. They went on vacations to the Caribbean (a perk from the company for high sales), from which they returned with rolls of photos of dangerously sunburned, severely inebriated Realtors and their spouses, their heads wrapped in wet towels, their swollen faces sucking on mixed drinks; dance floors full of drunken, Delawarean Realtors screaming into the dirt under a limbo bar; Realtor wives shielding their eyes from the camera while Realtor husbands bend them over folding chairs for a mimicked spanking.

      My parents gave in to the reality of their long-awaited fantasy. They bought stuff like crazy. They bought rental properties and a beach house, new cars, an antique car. They hired a maid. They bought my sister and me jewelry and clothing, furniture and toys, new everything they could get their hands on. The hand-me-down hoe-down clothes were quickly replaced by rich-kid fashion, which sent me into a junior-high identity crisis. For the first time I realized I was trapped between classes—considered too uppity by the poorer kids, and having nothing in common, except the same uniform, with the richer kids. I sat alone in my suddenly made-over bedroom, stripped of its chaotic wall of Scratch-n-Sniff stickers, Scott Baio and *Dukes of Hazzard* posters, and giant carnival-prize stuffed animals. My completely whitewashed new room, with custom-designed cabinets, framed fine art posters, and a vanity full of gold jewelry and make-up, was completely foreign and frightening. I hid the jewelry, afraid it would be stolen and my parents would never forgive me.

Now we were going to lunch at ritzy hotels, driving to Pennsylvania to try the latest new fancy restaurant. It was all an abrupt turn from my mother's infamous boiled-chicken dinner. It seemed like one night we were carefully removing the nearly liquid white skin from a boiled chicken leg, swallowing half a softer-than-butter boiled onion—and the next night our dinner was being served on fire. My father, who was almost always embarrassingly drunk and loud at such occasions, was glaringly out of place in his red suit and American flag/bald eagle tie, using a long umbrella with the head of a duck as a cane, his lips pulled back in a huge, unconvincing smile, framing half an unlit cigar in his teeth. Yet there I sat, in some hideous pastel dress and flats, watching the waiter's mouth as he asked us to quiet down/put out that cigar/pay the tab and leave.

At home in our big house flanked by new cars and gaudy decoration, our better-than-thou neighbors' posturing was scandalously tarnished by barbecue bread violence. My father insisted on a loaf of bread being present at meals, to save him from choking (some weird thing from my grandmother). During the summer we usually ate outside on our deck, which was highly visible to the entire neighborhood. By the end of the meal, my drunk-ass dad would almost always be ready for a fight—any fight—and he usually let loose on the bag of bread first. Neighbors would stare shamelessly as my father pitched the loaf into the chain-link fence, where it would explode into a tragedy of misshapen slices while he bellowed, "I bring home the bread!" This popular exclamation was heard by all on many occasions from my father: from the second-floor balcony in his underwear, from the lawn with shotguns in each hand, from his car wrestling with my mother for the keys.

Their dream for us hadn't died. Higher education, to my par-   15
ents, was still a way for their children to jump class. And so, when the time came, they insisted we go to college, though both of us protested. We would be the first in both of their families to go. They were sure that with our first step on campus we would meet scads of tall, block-jawed future doctors and lawyers who would fall in love with our cultured, high-class charm as soon as they laid eyes on us. My sister's Mohawk and chain-smoking of menthol 100s, and my common pastime of watching TV flat on my back with a bowl of cereal propped between my breasts, somehow didn't dissolve their mirage. These were just phases that would end with high school, they assured us. Apparently they looked at me and saw a potential cheerleading sorority girl in the raw, ready to be polished for action at any moment, unleashing those two years of private school and dance-class etiquette.

No matter how hard they tried to turn us into just-add-water Kennedys, all of this posturing failed, and so did college. The bottom line was that we were lower class, and there was no way we could be any different. As we were dragged nearly screaming off to college, the late-eighties economy steadily sank into the toilet. Their rental properties remained vacant, the beach house unrented; the cars wouldn't sell, and the real-estate market floundered. Their debt grew so out of control they were faced with declaring bankruptcy. All of the Realtors from the tropical vacation photos were declaring bankruptcy like dominoes, but my father couldn't deal with the shame. His suicide note was addressed mostly to his parents, and said how he had failed them by not being rich. He also declared his right, in the freest nation in the world, to choose death.

Our family was left in a sinkhole of debt. People came to the house during the funeral to claim cars and to try and buy the house. Everything was liquidated, and we all went our separate ways.

Despite my parents' arduous attempts at my reconstruction, I have retained bits of my native culture that will now be offered up to my daughter whether she likes it or not. Like eating green olives and watching *Lawrence Welk*, dirt-bike ganging and the art of survival in a classist nation, flamboyant American-flag apparel preferably worn in conjunction with a Mohawk or similar angst hairdo, and, most important, keeping a bag of bread on the table—not for fear of choking, or as a festering analogy to money, but to eat.

Questions for Discussion

1. Polyestra begins her essay with the following statement: "Fewer than one percent of Americans break out of the class they are born into." Were you surprised by this statement? How does this information relate to the American dream and one's ability to achieve it?

2. What was the life purpose of Polyestra's grandparents and parents? How did their unrealized goals contribute to their anger and frustrations? How did her parents and grandparent's dream "to become rich" manifest itself in their behaviors?

3. What is "barbecue bread violence" in the context of this essay? What does it represent to Polyestra? How does she now relate to "a bag of bread on the table"? What is she rejecting by taking this action with a loaf of bread?

4. How did you feel when you read that Polyestra's father had committed suicide? Why did her father take his own life? How did his unfulfilled dreams relate to his death? Do you think she lacked sympathy for him?

Ideas for Writing

1. A great deal of humor is employed throughout this essay. Do you think it helped to get the author's message across? How did you respond to Polyestra's wit? Did you find it funny or upsetting? Do you consider the use of humor to be appropriate when writing about dark subjects like suicide and family abuse? Write an essay about the use of dark comedy when writing about status- or work-related topics, giving examples from your own observations and experiences if possible.

2. Write an essay about the American dream and "class jumping." How are the two interrelated? What is class jumping, according to Polyestra? Do you agree with Polyestra that this strategy for success is seldom successful in America? If you know of a family or person who has "jumped class" or obtained the American dream, discuss the strategies that were helpful in the "ascent."

On the Front Lines of the Service Sector

STUART TANNOCK

Stuart Tannock (b. 1969) is a lecturer in the social and cultural studies program in the Graduate School of Education at the University of California, Berkeley. He has written extensively on the subject of young workers, who often take the lowest-paying, lowest-status jobs available in the retail, food, and entertainment service sectors, sometimes called "McJobs." He has written several articles, including "Why Do Working Youth Work Where They Do?" (in Youth at Work in the Post-Industrial Cities of North America and Europe, *2002) and "I Know What It's Like to Struggle: The Working Lives of Young Students in an Urban Community College" (Labor Studies Journal 2003). The selection below is taken from Tannock's acclaimed book* Youth at Work: The Unionized Fast-food and Grocery Workplace *(2001), which is based on a study of 95 interviews of young fast-food and grocery workers, many of whom attest to the stress of their jobs and the abusive nature of their on-the-job interactions. As you read the selection that follows, consider your perceptions of the status of service workers and the author's point of view.*

✦

In the 1994 film *Reality Bites*, high-flying Lelaina Pierce—college graduate, class valedictorian, aspiring documentary filmmaker— loses her job as a production assistant on a TV talk show, and, after a series of futile attempts to find a replacement job within the media industry, is driven in desperation to apply for work at a fast-food company called "Wienerschnitzel." Lelaina is interviewed for the fast-food job by a cashier in a "Wienerdude" cap, who—while in constant motion preparing food, serving customers, and barking out orders to subordinates—asks: "Miss Pierce, do you have any idea what it means to be a cashier at Wienerschnitzel?" When Lelaina suggests that being a cashier might involve taking orders and handling cash, the Wienerdude laughs:

> *Wienerdude:* No, it's a juggling act. . . . I mean, you got people coming at you from the front, coming at you from the back, from the side, people at the condiment exchange, people at the drive-through, kids on bikes, and all depending on who?
> *Lelaina:* Me?
> *Wienerdude:* Yeah. . . . You got to be 150 percent on your toes 150 percent of the time.

The Wienerdude then gives Lelaina a math quiz, asking her to add 85 and 45 in her head as quickly as she can. After Lelaina three times comes up with the wrong number—"140? 150? 160?"—the Wienerdude shakes his head and scoffs, "It's not an auction, Miss Pierce. There's a reason I've been here six months." Lelaina, needless to say, is not offered the job at Wienerschnitzel. She does, however, eventually manage to get her life back on track, enjoys some success as a filmmaker, and, by the end of the film, is even able to find true love in an old college friend. Meanwhile, the Wienerdude, after his brief but action-packed cameo, is never heard from again.

This [article] . . . is about the Wienerdudes of the world. It is about the young workers in those low-end service and retail jobs that are the butt of countless jokes—jobs that, as many would say, "any trained monkey could do." Stereotypes of fast-food and other low-end service jobs (including grocery) typically trade on these jobs' simplicity and simple-mindedness. Indeed, *Reality Bites* finds humor in parodying the Wienerdude's apparently ludicrous and self-important inflating of the complex and demanding nature of his work at Wienerschnitzel. What this chapter seeks to show is that the Wienerdude is, in many ways, absolutely right: Work in fast-food, grocery, and other low-end service jobs is, or can be, difficult, demanding, and unrewarding. Fast-food and grocery work is high-stress, low-status, and low-wage work. It is work that, on the one hand, is subject to routinization, close surveillance, and management control but, on the other, calls for high levels of self-motivation and investment from workers. It can also be physically dangerous: Grocery and restaurant workers throughout North America face some of the highest risks of all occupational groups of being injured, attacked, or even killed on the job.

HIGH STRESS, LOW STATUS, LOW WAGES

"I would say the stress is the worst thing about it," a young Fry House cashier says of her fast-food job. "Sometimes I get so stressed out, 'cause some days you're in a bad mood yourself, you know, having to deal with people, you just don't want to, you'd rather be somewhere else, anywhere except work." High stress levels are the most widespread complaint young workers in Box Hill and Glenwood have about their grocery and fast-food employment. Stress can be caused by many aspects of grocery and fast-food work: difficult relations with customers and managers; repetitive work tasks; low occupational status and small pay-checks; continual workplace surveillance; and hot, greasy, and often dangerous work environments. But the number-one factor young workers point to as the cause of workplace stress is the lack of time to do the work they are expected to do. Either there are not enough workers on shift to cover customer rushes and necessary preparation and cleaning work, or workers are not given long enough shifts to get their work stations ready for lunch and evening rushes and clean up after such rushes are through.

Lack of time lies behind almost all other causes of workplace stress. Young workers regularly endure abuse from their customers. Workers are yelled at, sworn at, and insulted by customers; they are frowned at, glared at, and sneered at; they are ignored, treated as social inferiors, and assumed to be servants whose role in life is to cater to and anticipate a customer's every whim and fancy. There are different reasons for such abusiveness. Young grocery and fast-food workers make easy targets for the displacement of hostility. "Often people come into Fry House," a cashier in Glenwood says, "because they've been yelled at by their bosses, they don't have anybody they can yell at, so they yell at us 'cause they think they can." "Customers go off on some grocery employee," says a stocker in Box Hill, " 'cause it makes 'em feel powerful."

Grocery and fast-food workers also incite abuse when their job responsibilities put them in conflict with customers' interests.   5

Checkers in Box Hill, for example, become the target of customers' anger when they are put in the position of having to police
company rules on accepting checks or enforce government laws
for using food stamps or selling alcohol. In one supermarket, I
witnessed a checker politely decline to sell alcohol to a young couple who were clearly intoxicated—as she was required to do by
law, under penalty of losing her job. The couple stalked out of the
store, and on their way out turned to yell at the checker, "Fuck
you! Fuck you, you fucking bitch!" while giving her the finger.

Beyond these various motivations, however, many young
workers feel that grocery and fast-food customers are abusive primarily because they fail to appreciate the time pressure under
which workers labor:

> That's the worst aspect of it for me, having to explain to people
> [customers] that, well, this is how it works, because they don't
> know. . . . I've said, you're welcome to come back here, take a
> tour, sit here for an hour, watch us when it's busy, please.
> Actually, a lady who worked here for about a month, and then
> she got another job . . . she said, "You know, I used to get really
> mad when I had to wait for stuff, but I have a total new respect
> for people that work in fast-food. I know what you have to do. I
> know what it's like. I feel so bad for any time I ever blew up at
> anybody." She says, "I don't know how you guys do it; how you
> can handle it. I really, really, really admire you guys for that, for
> keeping your cool the way you do, 'cause it's hard to do."

"They think we're dumb and slow," a Fry House cashier complains of his customers, "but they don't understand. If they came
in here and tried to do what we're doing, they'll be about three
times as slow as we are." Young workers are often caught in difficult situations in their relations with customers: On the one hand,
they are not given enough time or staff support by their employers
to perform at the speed and quality levels their customers would
prefer; on the other, they lack the status to be able to persuade
customers to respect them for the work that they do manage to do
under what are often difficult and stressful working conditions.

Managers are another primary source of workplace stress. Like
customers, some managers yell and swear at their young employees,
talk down to them, and call them "stupid," "incompetent," and
"lazy." Many workers believe that the younger the worker, the more
latitude managers feel they have in verbally attacking and belittling
that worker. Managers in fast-food and grocery, young workers say,
often "go on power trips," order workers around, and "tell you every

little thing you do wrong"—all the while, failing to provide encouragement or acknowledgment of jobs well done. Managers criticize workers behind their backs; worse, they dress employees down to their faces, in front of coworkers and customers. Young workers in both Box Hill and Glenwood complain widely of the stress caused by managerial favoritism—by managers picking on workers they dislike and conferring favors on workers they prefer. Many feel that managers will abuse their power by trying to get rid of employees they don't want working in their stores. "When a manager doesn't want you to work there," explains a cook in Glenwood, "they look for things, they kinda set you up so they can give you something bad."

As it does with customer-caused stress, time pressure often stands behind manager-caused workplace stress. Workers, for example, sometimes encounter what they refer to as "office managers"— managers who hide in their offices (claiming to be doing needed paperwork) and avoid helping with rushes. Because stores' labor budgets generally assume that managers will work on the floor when needed, "office managers" put increased stress on already overloaded workers. Workers have to deal with "cheap" managers—managers who (in efforts to keep costs low and earn year-end bonuses) skimp on allocating labor hours. Workers have to deal with managerial error—with managers who regularly screw up when submitting hours to company payroll, so that workers' checks are late or incorrect, or with managers who screw up scheduling, ordering, or inventory tasks. "I notice our managers forget a lot," one Fry House worker complained, "so we have to explain to our customers, 'We have no fried chicken tonight.' 'How can you have no fried chicken when it's Fry House?' 'Well, our manager forgot to order chicken.' It's crazy!"

Managers in the grocery and (especially) fast-food industries come and go with great frequency. Fry House store managers change over about every six months, while area managers change over every couple of years. Store managers in Box Hill chain supermarkets change over less frequently, but assistant managers come and go every few months. Workers find that they can develop a relationship and system of doing things with one manager, then that manager will quit or be fired, transferred, or promoted. They will then have to start over, building up a new relationship and new system with a new manager. Over time, management instability can be as stressful and wearing as bad or abusive management. "Every time a new manager comes in, they change everything," complains a Fry House cashier. "It's just like being hired. They have to retrain you on everything. It's pretty hard, because once you get into something, you just keep with it. Then somebody else comes in, and they're like, 'No, no! You're doing it wrong; you have to do it this way.' "

10   Grocery and fast-food work is low-status work. Fast-food work especially carries a stigma, and fast-food workers are stereotyped as being stupid, lazy, slow, and lacking in life goals and initiative. . . . Fast-food and grocery "youth" jobs (baggers, stockers) are also low in status simply because they are seen as typically being held by young workers. "What's the image of a fast-food job?" a Fry House cashier asks rhetorically. "You get the image of some kid with about a hundred pimples on his face trying to take an order for somebody, and he doesn't understand what to do." Young workers in Box Hill and Glenwood are well aware that if the work they perform were considered glamorous and important, it would be adults and not youths who would be taking on these jobs.

For many young workers, grocery and fast-food work lacks real or intrinsic meaning, interest, and value. "You can't be very proud of yourself as a grocery worker," says a young stocker in Box Hill. "What is your gift to the world [if] you work at Good Grocers your whole life?" The problem with grocery and fast-food work, for many young workers, is that it is difficult to feel a sense of accomplishment or progress. A grocery bagger, for example, explains why she would never want a grocery career:

> It's tough to have a job where it's just a constant flow of people and nothing ever ends or begins, where you're always just providing a service, the same service over and over again. . . . It seems like, to be a checker, to always be saying hello, how are you, have a good day, to always be doing the same thing, I would like a job better where I started and finished something.

In grocery and fast-food work, tasks tend to repeat themselves almost without end. The work is repetitive, mundane, and often boring. Workers may find getting up to and maintaining speed in what are very fast-paced workplaces initially challenging, but once the basic set of tasks has been mastered, workplace learning plateaus, and workers are left with the drudgery of simply executing tasks that long ago became second nature.

Grocery and fast-food work is often said to be "low-skill" work—and, indeed, many young workers in Box Hill and Glenwood slam their jobs by saying that anyone "with half a brain" could do the work they do. Attributions of skill are notoriously tricky, however: They tend to involve assessments of the social standing of a particular job and the kinds of people who hold that job as much as they refer to any absolute and objective measurement of cognitive demands inherent in a given set of work tasks. Young grocery and fast-food workers develop considerable local expertise in their jobs: knowledge of how best to handle individual customers and managers; of how to bend official work rules to get work done effectively and efficiently on the ground; how to make ad hoc repairs and improvisations in the workplace when machines break down, work tools go missing, or the maddening rush of customer demand overwhelms normal working procedures. What can be said of grocery and fast-food work is that such local expertise emerges within jobs that are seen overall—by workers, customers, and managers—as repetitive and low in status, meaning, challenge, and value.

The low status of grocery and fast-food work feeds into general workplace stress. Young grocery and fast-food workers lack a "status shield" to protect them from customer and manager abuse. . . . As Robin Leidner . . . writes, "Customers who might have managed to be polite to higher-status workers [have] no compunction about taking their anger out on [low-status service-sector] employees." The low status of grocery and fast-food work also feeds into low industry wages: Because this work is not considered particularly valuable or important, and because workers in these jobs are considered unskilled and easily replaceable, pay levels in Box Hill grocery and Glenwood fast-food outlets remain depressed. Rabid employer determination to keep labor costs at a minimum, of course, further reinforces and institutionalizes downward pressures on wages.

Unionization has had some impact in Box Hill and Glenwood in raising wages and securing benefits that are unusual in North America's low-end service sector. Wages for some job classifications in the Box Hill grocery stores are relatively high compared with wages in the area's other low-end service industries, and wages in the Glenwood Fry Houses are high compared with those of other fast-food companies in town. Overall, however, wages in these two industries remain low. Even full-time workers earning top dollar in the Box Hill grocery industry stand to make only about the average yearly wage in the United States. The vast majority of grocery workers in Box Hill do not work anywhere near full-time hours—as the grocery industry (like the fast-food industry) mostly provides only part-time work. Grocery wages in Box Hill, furthermore, are divided into three tiers. Only checkers and grocery and produce clerks are paid on the top wage scale. Workers in side deli and bakery departments (who are predominantly women) are paid on a lower, second-tier wage scale, and baggers and stockers (who are predominantly youths) are not on scale, and are paid on a third wage tier, which starts only slightly above the minimum wage. . . .

Questions for Discussion

1. According to Tannock, what factors contribute to high levels of stress in the service sector workplace? Are these factors unique to service work?
2. In what ways are the service workers in this article abused by their customers and their managers? How do they respond to such abuse?
3. Why do service workers lack a "status shield"? What is this "shield" and how does it protect other types of workers? How does not having this protection affect the way service workers view themselves and how they are treated?
4. The service workers in this article claim that "anyone with half a brain" could do their jobs. What are some of the necessary skills and disciplines required to do their type of work? How does the essay attempt to convince the reader that these jobs and the young workers doing them are worthy of dignity and respect?

Ideas for Writing

1. Write an essay discussing the high levels of stress involved in working in the service sector, providing some examples from experience and research. What factors contribute to this stress, and how could they be alleviated to some degree by employers?
2. Write an essay about your own experiences in service work. Did you experience a great deal of stress or abuse from your customers or managers? What did you learn from the job? Alternatively, if you have not worked in a service position, write about your observations of people who do. Have you ever witnessed service employees being mistreated by either their customers or managers? Are you more empathetic toward them after reading this essay and observing them? Why?

In the Strawberry Fields
ERIC SCHLOSSER

Eric Schlosser (b. 1941) is an investigative journalist who won the National Magazine Award for reporting in 1994 for a series of articles in the Atlantic *about the marijuana enforcement laws. He also received the Sidney Hillman Foundation award in 1995 for his reportage on California's strawberry industry. His first book,* Fast Food

Nation *(2000), is an exposé on the impact of the fast-food industry on public health in the United States and abroad. The following selection, "In the Strawberry Fields," from his latest book,* Reefer Madness: Sex, Drugs and Cheap Labor in the American Black Market *(2003), discusses the history and negative impact of the attempt to regulate the temporary employment of Mexican nationals (many of them illegal immigrants) on large farms in the United States.*

---- ◆ ----

. . . One morning in San Diego county, I met a strawberry grower named Doug. We sat and talked in a trailer on the edge of his field. Doug's father and his grandfather had both been sent to an internment camp for Japanese Americans during World War II. Upon their release, the grandfather bought a used truck. At first he worked for other farms, then he leased some land. He spoke no English and so Doug's father, still a teenager, assumed an important role in the business. The two grew vegetables with success and eventually shifted to strawberries, shipping and processing the fruit as well. On the land where their original farm once stood, there are now condominiums, a park, and a school. Doug grows strawberries a few miles inland. His field are surrounded by chain-link fences topped with barbed wire. An enormous real estate development, with hundreds of Spanish-style condo units, is creeping up the hills toward his farm. Many of the farmers nearby have already sold their land. Doug has spent most of his life in strawberry fields, learning every aspect of the business firsthand, but now isn't sure he wants his children to do the same.

"Farming's not a glamorous business," Doug said. "Farmers don't have a high status in this community. In fact, we're resented by most people." With all the hassles today from the state and from his neighbors, he sometimes asks himself, "Hey, why do this?" Selling the land would make him instantly rich. Instead, he worries about water costs, about theft, about the strawberries from New Zealand he saw in the market the other day. Rain had wiped out a quarter of his early-season berries, just when the market price was at its peak. Doug cannot understand the hostility toward growers in California. After all, agriculture preserves open land. He thinks Americans don't appreciate how lucky they are to have cheap food. He doesn't understand why anyone would impede strawberry production by limiting his access to migrants. "My workers are helping themselves," he said. "I've picked strawberries, and let me tell you, there is no harder work. I respect these people. They work damn hard. And my jobs are open to anyone who wants to apply." Every so often college kids visit the ranch, convinced that picking strawberries would be a nice way to earn some extra money. Doug laughed. "They don't last an hour out here."

We stepped from the trailer into bright sunshine. Workers moved down the furrows under close supervision. Doug takes great pride in being a third-generation grower. He is smart, well educated, meticulous, and it showed in his field. But I wondered if Doug and his workers would still be there in a few years.

Doug picked a berry and handed it to me, a large Chandler that was brilliantly red. I took a bite. The strawberry was warm and sweet and fragrant, with a slightly bitter aftertaste from the soil.

5   That evening I inadvertently met some of Doug's workers. Ricardo Soto, a young lawyer at CRLA, had brought me to the edge of an avocado orchard to visit a hidden encampment of migrant workers. Perhaps one-third of the farmworkers in northern San Diego County—about 7,000 people—are now homeless. An additional 9,000 of their family members are homeless, too. Many are living outdoors. The shortage of low-income housing became acute in the early 1980s, and large shantytowns began to appear, some containing hundreds of crude shacks. As suburbs encroached on agricultural land in northern San Diego County, wealthy commuters and strawberry pickers became neighbors. At one large shantytown I visited, women were doing their laundry in a stream not far from a walled compound with tennis courts, a pool, and a sign promising country club living. The suburbanites do not like living beside Mexican farmworkers. Instead of providing low-income housing, local authorities have declared states of emergency, passed laws to forbid curbside hiring, and bulldozed many of the large encampments. San Diego growers appalled by the living conditions of their migrants have tried to build farmworker housing near the fields—only to encounter fierce resistance from neighboring homeowners. Although the shantytowns lower nearby property values, permanent farmworker housing might reduce property values even more. "When people find out you want to build housing for your migrants," one grower told me, "they just go ballistic."

The new encampments are smaller and built to avoid detection. At the end of a driveway, near a chain-link fence, I met a young Mixtec who lived in such an encampment. His name was Francisco, and he was eighteen years old. He looked deeply exhausted. He had just picked strawberries for twelve hours at Doug's farm. I asked what he thought of Doug as a boss. "Not bad," he said politely.

The previous year Francisco had picked strawberries from April until July. He had saved $800 during that period and had wired all of it to his mother and father in the village of San Sebastian Tecomaxtlahuaca. This was Francisco's second season in the fields, but he had not seen much of San Diego County. He was too afraid of getting caught. His days were spent at the farm, his nights at the encampment. He picked strawberries six days a week, sometimes seven, for ten or twelve hours a day. "When there's work," Francisco said, "you have to work." Each morning he woke up around four-thirty and walked for half an hour to reach Doug's field.

At dusk, thirteen tired men in dirty clothes approached us. They were all from Francisco's village. They worked together at Doug's farm and stayed at the same encampment. They knew one another's families back home and looked after one another here. The oldest was forty-three and the youngest looked about fifteen. All the men were illegals. All were sick with coughs, but none dared to see a doctor. As the sun dropped behind the hills, clouds of mosquitoes descended, and yet the migrants seemed too tired to notice. They lay on their backs, on their sides, resting on the hard ground as though it were a sofa.

Francisco offered to show me their encampment. We squeezed through a hole in the chain-link fence and through gaps in rusting barbed wire, and climbed a winding path enclosed by tall bushes. It felt like a medieval maze. As we neared the camp, I noticed beer cans and food wrappers littering the ground. We came upon the first shack—short and low, more like a tent, just silver trash bags draped over a wooden frame. A little farther up the path stood three more shacks in a small clearing. They were built of plywood and camouflaged. Branches and leaves had been piled on their roofs. The landowner did not know the migrants lived here, and the encampment would be difficult to find. These migrants were hiding out, like criminals or Viet Cong. Garbage was everywhere. Francisco pointed to his shack, which was about five feet high, five feet wide, and seven feet long. He shared it with two other men. He had a good blanket. But when it rained at night the roof leaked, and the men would go to work soaking wet the next day and dry off in the sun. Francisco had never lived this way before coming to San Diego. At home he always slept in a bed.

Beyond the sheds, bushes crowded the path again, and then it reached another clearing, where two battered lawn chairs had been placed at the edge of the hill. There was a wonderful view of strawberry fields, new houses, and the lights of the freeway in the distance.

Driving back to my motel that night, I thought about the people of Orange County, one of the richest counties in the nation—

10

big on family values, yet bankrupt from financial speculation, unwilling to raise taxes to pay for their own children's education, unwilling to pay off their debts, whining about the injustice of it, and blaming all their problems on illegal immigrants. And I thought about Francisco, their bogeyman, their scapegoat, working ten hours a day at one of the hardest jobs imaginable, and sleeping on the ground every night, for months, so that he could save money and send it home to his parents.

We have been told for years to bow down before "the market." We have placed our faith in the laws of supply and demand. What has been forgotten, or ignored, is that the market rewards only efficiency. Every other human value gets in its way. The market will drive wages down like water, until they reach the lowest possible level. Today that level is being set not in Washington or New York or Sacramento but in the fields of Baja California and the mountain villages of Oaxaca. That level is about five dollars a day. No deity that men have ever worshiped is more ruthless and more hollow than the free market unchecked; there is no reason why shantytowns should not appear on the outskirts of every American city. All those who now consider themselves devotees of the market should take a good look at what is happening in California. Left to its own devices, the free market always seeks a work force that is hungry, desperate, and cheap—a work force that is anything but free.

Questions for Discussion

1. What incentives does Doug have to sell his land? Why doesn't Doug want to sell it?
2. Contrast Doug's life and his worker Francisco's. Why does Francisco continue to work in the strawberry fields instead of returning to Mexico?
3. How does Schlosser reveal the hypocrisy of the entrepreneurs who use illegal immigrants to develop the land in Orange County in San Diego?
4. Why is Schlosser critical of the theory "bowing down to the market"? Why is he critical of a free market economy? Explain why you agree or disagree with Schlosser's point of view?

Ideas for Writing

1. Research the social status and level of poverty of illegal immigrant workers on the Internet or from interviews with workers and farmers in your own community. Write an argument supporting Schlosser's position that conditions could be improved for immigrant workers in the United States. In what specific ways can these conditions be improved?

2. Do some research to find out where and how solutions to the problems of immigrant workers have been implemented in this country. Write an essay that presents a plan for helping more immigrant workers.

Media Magic: Making Class Invisible
GREGORY MANTSIOS

Gregory Mantsios, Ph.D., is the Director Worker Education and the Labor Resource Center at Queens College, CUNY. He is the author of Class in America: Myths and Realities *(1992) and the editor of* A New Labor Movement for a New Century *(1998). Mantsios is also the editor of an academic journal* New Labor Forum, *which "provide[s] a place for labor and its allies to test new ideas and debate old ones." His writings on unions and other labor movements are read at many schools and by numerous organizations throughout the country. The selection that follows from Mantsios's essay "Media Magic: Making Class Invisible" (2001) explores how the media use various techniques to hide the realities of vast numbers of poor people living in America.*

———————— ✦ ————————

Of the various social and cultural forces in our society, the mass media is arguably the most influential in molding public consciousness. Americans spend an average twenty-eight hours per week watching television. They also spend an undetermined number of hours reading periodicals, listening to the radio, and going to the movies. Unlike other cultural and socializing institutions, ownership and control of the mass media is highly concentrated. Twenty-three corporations own more than one-half of all the daily newspapers, magazines, movie studios, and radio and television outlets in the United States.[1] The number of media companies is shrinking and their control of the industry is expanding. And a relatively small number of media outlets is producing and packaging the majority of news and entertainment programs. For the most part, our media is national in nature and single-minded (profit-oriented) in purpose. This media plays a key role in defining our cultural tastes, helping us locate ourselves in history, establishing our national identity, and ascertaining the range of national and social possibilities. In this essay, we will examine the way the mass media shapes how people think about each other and about the nature of our society.

The United States is the most highly stratified society in the industrialized world. Class distinctions operate in virtually every aspect of our lives, determining the nature of our work, the quality of our schooling, and the health and safety of our loved ones. Yet remarkably, we, as a nation, retain illusions about living in an egalitarian society. We maintain these illusions, in large part, because the media hides gross inequities from public view. In those instances when inequities are revealed, we are provided with messages that obscure the nature of class realities and blame the victims of class-dominated society for their own plight. Let's briefly examine what the news media, in particular, tells us about class.

ABOUT THE POOR

The news media provides meager coverage of poor people and poverty. The coverage it does provide is often distorted and misleading.

The Poor Do Not Exist

For the most part, the news media ignores the poor. Unnoticed are forty million poor people in the nation—a number that equals the entire population of Maine, Vermont, New Hampshire, Connecticut, Rhode Island, New Jersey, and New York combined. Perhaps even more alarming is that the rate of poverty is increasing twice as fast as the population growth in the United States. Ordinarily, even a calamity of much smaller proportion (e.g., flooding in the Midwest) would garner a great deal of coverage and hype from a media usually eager to declare a crisis, yet less than one in five hundred articles in the *New York Times* and one in one thousand articles listed in *Readers Guide to Periodic Literature* are on poverty. With remarkably little attention to them, the poor and their problems are hidden from most Americans.

5   When the media does turn its attention to the poor, it offers a series of contradictory messages and portrayals.

The Poor Are Faceless

Each year the Census Bureau releases a new report on poverty in our society and its results are duly reported in the media. At best, however, this coverage emphasizes annual fluctuations (showing how the numbers differ from previous years) and ongoing debates over the validity of the numbers (some argue the number should be lower, most that the number should be higher). Coverage like this desensitizes us to the poor by reducing poverty to a number. It ignores the human tragedy of poverty—the suffering, indignities, and misery endured by millions of children and adults. Instead, the poor become statistics rather than people.

The Poor Are Undeserving

When the media does put a face on the poor, it is not likely to be a pretty one. The media will provide us with sensational stories about welfare cheats, drug addicts, and greedy panhandlers (almost always urban and Black). Compare these images and the emotions evoked by them with the media's treatment of middle-class (usually white) "tax evaders," celebrities who have a "chemical dependency," or wealthy businesspeople who use unscrupulous means to "make a profit." While the behavior of the more affluent offenders is considered an "impropriety" and a deviation from the norm, the behavior of the poor is considered repugnant, indicative of the poor in general, and worthy of our indignation and resentment.

The Poor Are an Eyesore

When the media does cover the poor, they are often presented through the eyes of the middle class. For example, sometimes the media includes a story about community resistance to a homeless shelter or storekeeper annoyance with panhandlers. Rather than focusing on the plight of the poor, these stories are about middle-class opposition to the poor. Such stories tell us that the poor are an inconvenience and an irritation.

The Poor Have Only Themselves to Blame

In another example of media coverage, we are told that the poor live in a personal and cultural cycle of poverty that hopelessly imprisons them. They routinely center on the Black urban population and focus on perceived personality or cultural traits that doom the poor. While the women in these stories typically exhibit an "attitude" that leads to trouble or a promiscuity that leads to single motherhood, the men possess a need for immediate gratification that leads to drug abuse or an unquenchable greed that leads to the pursuit of fast money. The images that are

seared into our mind are sexist, racist, and classist. Census figures reveal that most of the poor are white, not Black or
Hispanic, that they live in rural or suburban areas, not urban
centers, and hold jobs at least part of the year.[2] Yet, in a fashion
that is often framed in an understanding and sympathetic tone,
we are told that the poor have inflicted poverty on themselves.

The Poor Are Down on Their Luck

10   During the Christmas season, the news media sometimes provides us with account of poor individuals or families (usually
white) who are down on their luck. These stories are often linked
to stories about soup kitchens or other charitable activities and
sometimes call for charitable contributions. These "Yule time"
stories are as much about the affluent as they are about the poor:
they tell us that the affluent in our society are a kind, understanding, giving people—which we are not.[3] The series of unfortunate
circumstances that have led to impoverishment are presumed to
be a temporary condition that will improve with time and a
change in luck.

Despite appearances, the messages provided by the media are
not entirely disparate. With each variation, the media informs us
what poverty is not (i.e., systemic and indicative of American society) by informing us what it is. The media tells us that poverty is
either an aberration of the American way of life (it doesn't exist, it's
just another number, it's unfortunate but temporary) or an end
product of the poor themselves (they are a nuisance, do not deserve
better, and have brought their predicament upon themselves).

By suggesting that the poor have brought poverty upon themselves, the media is engaging in what William Ryan has called
"blaming the victim."[4] The media identifies in what ways the poor
are different as a consequence of deprivation, then defines those
differences as the cause of poverty itself. Whether blatantly hos-
tile or cloaked in sympathy, the message is that there is something fundamentally wrong with the victims—their hormones,
psychological makeup, family environment, community, race, or
some combination of these—that accounts for their plight and
their failure to lift themselves out of poverty.

But poverty in the United States is systemic. It is a direct result of economic and political policies that deprive people of jobs,
adequate wages, or legitimate support. It is neither natural nor
inevitable: there is enough wealth in our nation to eliminate

poverty if we chose to redistribute existing wealth or income. The plight of the poor is reason enough to make the elimination of poverty the nation's first priority. But poverty also impacts dramatically on the nonpoor. It has a dampening effect on wages in general (by maintaining a reserve army of unemployed and underemployed anxious for any job at any wage) and breeds crime and violence (by maintaining conditions that invite private gain by illegal means and rebellion-like behavior, not entirely unlike the urban riots of the 1960s). Given the extent of poverty in the nation and the impact it has on us all, the media must spin considerable magic to keep the poor and the issue of poverty and its root causes out of the public consciousness.

ABOUT EVERYONE ELSE

Both the broadcast and the print news media strive to develop a strong sense of "we-ness" in their audience. They seek to speak to and for an audience that is both affluent and like-minded. The media's solidarity with affluence, that is, with the middle and upper class, varies little from one medium to another. Benjamin DeMott points out, for example, that the *New York Times* understands affluence to be intelligence, taste, public spirit, responsibility, and a readiness to rule and "conceives itself as spokesperson for a readership awash in these qualities."[5] Of course, the flip side to creating a sense of "we," or "us," is establishing a perception of the "other." The other relates back to the faceless, amoral, undeserving, and inferior "underclass." Thus, the world according to the news media is divided between the "underclass" and everyone else. Again the messages are often contradictory.

The Wealthy Are Us

Much of the information provided to us by the news media focuses attention on the concerns of a very wealthy and privileged class of people. Although the concerns of a small fraction of the populace, they are presented as though they were the concerns of everyone. For example, while relatively few people actually own stock, the news media devotes an inordinate amount of broadcast time and print space to business news and stock market quotations. Not only do business reports cater to a particular narrow clientele, so do the fashion pages (with $2,000 dresses), wedding announcements, and the obituaries. Even weather and sports   15 news often have a class bias. An all news radio station in New York City, for example, provides regular national ski reports. International news, trade agreements, and domestic policies issues are also reported in terms of their impact on business climate and the business community. Besides being of practical value to the wealthy, such coverage has considerable ideological value. Its message: the concerns of the wealthy are the concerns of us all.

The Wealthy (as a Class) Do Not Exist

While preoccupied with the concerns of the wealthy, the media fails to notice the way in which the rich as a class of people create and shape domestic and foreign policy. Presented as an aggregate of individuals, the wealthy appear without special interests, interconnections, or unity in purpose. Out of public view are the class interests of the wealthy, the interlocking business links, the concerted actions to preserve their class privileges and business interests (by running for public office, supporting political candidates, lobbying, etc.). Corporate lobbying is ignored, taken for granted, or assumed to be in the public interest. (Compare this with the media's portrayal of the "strong arm of labor" in attempting to defeat trade legislation that is harmful to the interests of working people.) It is estimated that two-thirds of the U.S. Senate is composed of millionaires.[6] Having such a preponderance of millionaires in the Senate, however, is perceived to be neither unusual nor antidemocratic; these millionaire senators are assumed to be serving "our" collective interests in governing.

The Wealthy Are Fascinating and Benevolent

The broadcast and print media regularly provide hype for individuals who have achieved "super" success. These stories are usually about celebrities and superstars from the sports and entertainment world. Society pages and gossip columns serve to keep the social elite informed of each others' doings, allow the rest of us to gawk at their excesses, and help to keep the American dream alive. The print media is also fond of feature stories on corporate empire builders. These stories provide an occasional "insider's" view of the private and corporate life of industrialists by suggesting a rags to riches account of corporate success. These stories tell us that corporate success is a series of smart moves, shrewd acquisitions, timely mergers, and well thought out executive suite shuffles. By painting the upper class in a positive light, innocent of any wrongdoing (labor leaders and union organizations usually get the opposite treatment), the media assures us that wealth and power are benevolent. One person's capital accumulation is presumed to be good for all. The elite, then, are portrayed as investment wizards, people of special talent and skill, whom even their victims (workers and consumers) can admire.

The Wealthy Include a Few Bad Apples

On rare occasions, the media will mock selected individuals for their personality flaws. Real estate investor Donald Trump and New York Yankees owner George Steinbrenner, for example, are admonished by the media for deliberately seeking publicity (a very un-upper class thing to do); hotel owner Leona Helmsley was caricatured for her personal cruelties; and junk bond broker Michael Milkin was condemned because he had the audacity to rob the rich. Michael Parenti points out that by treating business wrongdoings as isolated deviations from the socially beneficial system of "responsible capitalism," the media overlooks the features of the system that produce such abuses and the regularity with which they occur. Rather than portraying them as predictable and frequent outcomes of corporate power and the business system, the media treats abuses as if they were isolated and atypical. Presented as an occasional aberration, these incidents serve not to challenge, but to legitimate, the system.[7]

The Middle Class Is Us

By ignoring the poor and blurring the lines between the working people and the upper class, the news media creates a universal middle class. From this perspective, the size of one's income becomes largely irrelevant: what matters is that most of "us" share an intellectual and moral superiority over the disadvantaged. As *Time* magazine once concluded, "Middle America is a state of mind."[8] "We are all middle class," we are told, "and we all share the same concerns": job security, inflation, tax burdens, world peace, the cost of food and housing, health care, clean air and water, and the safety of our streets. While the concerns of the wealthy are quite distinct from those of the middle class (e.g., the wealthy worry about investments, not jobs), the media convinces us that "we [the affluent] are all in this together."

The Middle Class Is a Victim

20   For the media, "we" the affluent not only stand apart from the "other"—the poor, the working class, the minorities, and their problems—"we" are also victimized by the poor (who drive up the costs of maintaining the welfare roles), minorities (who commit crimes against us), and workers (who are greedy and drive companies out and prices up). Ignored are the subsidies to the rich, the crimes of corporate America, and the politics that wreak havoc on the economic well-being of middle America. Media magic convinces us to fear, more than anything else, being victimized by those less affluent than ourselves.

The Middle Class Is Not a Working Class

The news media clearly distinguishes the middle class (employees) from the working class (i.e., blue collar workers) who are portrayed, at best, as irrelevant, outmoded, and a dying breed. Furthermore, the media will tell us that the hardships faced by blue collar workers are inevitable (due to progress), a result of bad luck (chance circumstances in a particular industry), or a product of their own doing (they priced themselves out of a job). Given the media's presentation of reality, it is hard to believe that manual, supervised, unskilled, and semiskilled workers actually represent more than 50 percent of the adult working population.[9] The working class, instead, is relegated by the media to "the other."

In short, the news media either lionizes the wealthy or treats their interests and those of the middle class as one in the same. But the upper class and the middle class do not share the same interests or worries. Members of the upper class worry about stock dividends (not employment), they profit from inflation and global militarism, their children attend exclusive private schools, they eat and live in a royal fashion, they call on (or are called upon by) personal physicians, they have few consumer problems, they can escape whenever they want from environmental pollution, and they live on streets and travel to other areas under the protection of private police forces.[10,11]

The wealthy are not only a class with distinct life-styles and interests, they are a ruling class. They receive a disproportionate share of the country's yearly income, own a disproportionate amount of the country's wealth, and contribute a disproportionate number of their members to governmental bodies and decision-making groups—all traits that William Domhoff, in his classic work *Who Rules America*, defined as characteristic of a governing class.[12]

This governing class maintains and manages our political and economic structures in such a way that these structures continue to yield an amazing proportion of our wealth to a minuscule upper class. While the media is not above referring to ruling classes in other countries (we hear, for example, references to Japan's ruling elite),[13] its treatment of the news proceeds as though there were no such ruling class in the United States.

Furthermore, the news media inverts reality so that those who are working class and middle class learn to fear, resent, and blame those below, rather than those above, them in the class structure. We learn to resent welfare, which accounts for only two cents out of every dollar in the federal budget (approximately $10 billion) and provides financial relief for the needy,[14] but learn little about the $11 billion the federal government spends on individuals with incomes in excess of $100,000 (not needy),[15] or the $17 billion in farm subsidies, or the $214 billion (twenty times the cost of welfare) in interest payments to financial institutions.

Middle-class whites learn to fear African Americans and Latinos, but most violent crime occurs within poor and minority communities and is neither interracial[16] nor interclass. As horrid as such crime is, it should not mask the destruction and violence perpetrated by corporate America. In spite of the fact that 14,000 innocent people are killed on the job each year, 100,000 die prematurely, 400,000 become seriously ill, and 6 million are injured from work-related accidents and diseases, most Americans fear government regulation more than they do unsafe working conditions.

Through the media, middle-class—and even working-class—Americans learn to blame blue collar workers and their unions for declining purchasing power and economic security. But while workers who managed to keep their jobs and their unions struggled to keep up with inflation, the top 1 percent of American families saw their average incomes soar 80 percent in the last decade.[17] Much of the wealth at the top was accumulated as stockholders and corporate executives moved their companies abroad to employ cheaper labor (56 cents per hour in El Salvador) and avoid paying taxes in the United States. Corporate America is a world made up of ruthless bosses, massive layoffs, favoritism and nepotism, health and safety violations, pension plan losses, union busting, tax evasions, unfair competition, and price gouging, as well as fast buck deals, financial speculation, and corporate wheeling and dealing that serve the interests of the corporate elite, but are generally wasteful and destructive to workers and the economy in general.

25

It is no wonder Americans cannot think straight about class. The mass media are neither objective, balanced, independent, nor neutral. Those who own and direct the mass media are themselves part of the upper class, and neither they nor the ruling class in general have to conspire to manipulate public opinion. Their interest is in preserving the status quo, and their view of society as fair and equitable comes naturally to them. But their ideology dominates our society and justifies what is in reality a perverse social order—one that perpetuates unprecedented elite privilege and power on the one hand and widespread deprivation on the other. A mass media that did not have its own class interests in preserving the status quo would acknowledge that inordinate wealth and power undermines democracy and that a "free market" economy can ravage a people and their communities.

Endnotes

1. Martin Lee and Norman Solomon, *Unreliable Sources*, Lyle Stuart (New York, 1990), p. 71. See also Ben Bagdikian, *The Media Monopoly*, Beacon Press (Boston, 1990).
2. Department of Commerce, Bureau of the Census, "Poverty in the United States: 1992," *Current Population Reports, Consumer Income*, Series P60–185, pp. xi, xv, 1.
3. American households with incomes of less than $10,000 give an average of 5.5 percent of their earning to charity or to a religious organization, while those making more than $100,000 a year give only 2.9 percent. After changes in the 1986 tax code reduced the benefits of charitable giving, taxpayers earning $500,000 or more slashed their average donation by nearly one-third. Furthermore, many of these acts of benevolence do not help the needy. Rather than provide funding to social service agencies that aid the poor, the voluntary contributions of the wealthy go to places and institutions that entertain, inspire, cure, or educate wealthy Americans—art museums, opera houses, theaters, orchestras, ballet companies, private hospitals, and the elite universities. (Robert Reich, "Secession of the Successful," *New York Times Magazine*, February 17, 1991, p. 43.)
4. William Ryan, *Blaming the Victim*, Vintage (New York, 1971).
5. Benjamin Demott, *The Imperial Middle*, William Morrow (New York, 1990), p. 123.
6. Fred Barnes, "The Zillionaires Club," *The New Republic*, January 29, 1990, p. 24.
7. Michael Parenti, *Inventing Reality*, St. Martin's Press (New York, 1986), p. 109.

8. *Time*, January 5, 1979, p. 10.
9. Vincent Navarro, "The Middle Class—A Useful Myth," *The Nation*, March 23, 1992, p. 1.
10. The number of private security guards in the United States now exceeds the number of public police officers. (Robert Reich, "Secession of the Successful," *New York Times Magazine*, February 17, 1991, p. 42.)
11. Charles Anderson, *The Political Economy of Social Class*, Prentice Hall (Englewood Cliffs, N.J., 1974), p. 137.
12. William Domhoff, *Who Rules America*, Prentice Hall (Englewood Cliffs, N.J., 1967), p. 5.
13. Lee and Solomon, *Unreliable Sources*, p. 179.
14. A total of $20 billion is spent on welfare when you include all state funding. But the average state funding also comes to only two cents per state per dollar.
15. *Newsweek*, August 10, 1992, p. 57.
16. In 92 percent of the murders nationwide the assailant and the victim are of the same race (46 percent are white/white, 46 percent are black/black), 5.6 percent are black on white, and 2.4 percent are white on black. (FBI and Bureau of Justice Statistics, 1985–1986, quoted in Raymond S. Franklin, *Shadows of Race and Class*, University of Minnesota Press, Minneapolis, 1991, p. 108.)
17. *Business Week*, June 8, 1992, p. 86.

Questions for Discussion

1. In what ways do the media desensitize the public to the reality of the poor in America? What is that reality, according to the author, and how does he argue for its existence?
2. How do the media make the poor "faceless?" If the media use a face or faces for the poor in a report, what images do they portray? How do the media show the public that poor people are to blame for their own situation?
3. How do the media create "a sense of we or us"? Who is the "we" and who is the "other?" What is the perceived advantage of creating this sense of separation?
4. According to this reading, why do the media seek to "make class invisible"? Who does the author imply owns the media and why?

Ideas for Writing

1. Examine several examples of newsprint and television, paying close attention to the treatment of the poor, blue-collar workers, and the wealthy. Write an essay that relates your findings to the information presented in

this article. Do your findings support the author's point of view or not? What is your point of view on the media's presentation of the poor, blue-collar workers, and the wealthy?

2. Pick one newsworthy event in which the poor are portrayed. Examine several sources, including television and the print medium, and write about which "face" (if any) the poor are given. Do all your sources report in the same fashion or not? Do your findings coincide with the author's ideas in this reading?

Extending the Theme

1. Discuss an experience you have had as a low-wage worker. How did you break away from the trap of only working to survive? If you have not had this experience, discuss what you know about someone close to you who was trapped in a "dead end" job. Write an essay in which you argue that it is or is not possible for the working poor to break out of their cycle of poverty. Refer to writers in this chapter and to your own experiences to support your position.

2. Write an essay that explains how your understanding of the blue-collar American worker was changed by reading these selections. How do you feel about what you have learned? What do you think should be done to improve the lives of the working poor? Do all Americans have a responsibility to help in equalizing the standard of living in our country? What can you do as an individual to change this situation that you encounter in some way every day in your community?

3. Write a research paper that examines the problems of immigrant workers on a national level. Find out more about why the United States and Mexico have made so little progress in solving the problems of immigrant labor in the United States.

4. After considering the points of view presented in the various essays in this chapter, write an essay that discusses several ways an individual citizen can work to help solve the problem of the working poor that affects the nation as a whole.

CHAPTER 5

Working
for Change

Technology has changed the world of work so that businesses around the world can communicate with one another instantaneously. Products that were once made in the United States can now be created more cheaply overseas and then shipped here enabling corporations to make larger profits. However, many American people have also lost their jobs because of this shift in the labor source to Third World countries, while those who hang onto their jobs feel increasingly alienated from their labors in computer-controlled workplaces where the overall health and happiness of workers are neglected at stressful jobs done in isolation from coworkers.

The purpose of this chapter is to present you with readings that will help you to think about alternatives to counteract the problems caused by today's rapidly changing workplaces. Our first reading, "The Obliteration of Alienation" by anthropologist Elliott Leyton, shows the lengths that some individuals, many considered privileged and economically secure in their employment settings, will go to escape the numbing sense of alienation that pervades most jobs and careers today. Leyton writes about a global organization of physicians, *Medecins sans Frontiers* (Doctors without Borders) that takes on the most dangerous projects in countries ravaged by war, disease, natural disasters, and poverty, in order to make a difference in people's lives. Doctors without Borders is one of many organizations today whose minimally compensated workers are devoted to helping people who are poor and lack proper education, job training, or medical attention.

Next we present two projects that originated in the business world which demonstrate the courage of some to change the way work and workers in particular fields have been stereotyped and treated. In "Made in the U.S.A.," Jenny Strasburg of the *San Francisco Chronicle* profiles a businessman in Los Angeles, Dov Charney, who has opened a garment business that has been financially successful while managing to accommodate employee needs: fair salaries, health-care benefits, and a pleasant working environment. Charney hopes to become a new model for the equal treatment of immigrant or lower-class workers, bringing back to the United States an industry that has been decimated by job outsourcing in overseas sweatshops. He has a banner outside of his workplace that proclaims, "an industrial revolution." Charney has worked for change and wants his workplace to become a model for other businesses in the nation.

In "Secondary Five" by Rodney J. Carroll, we learn how the author's struggles as a welfare recipient motivated him to help other welfare recipients to reclaim their independence by proving themselves to be reliable workers at a UPS facility in Philadelphia. UPS was the employer that gave Carroll a chance to prove himself when he was first getting off of welfare. The benefits of "welfare to work" hiring and retraining programs are enormous. They help to create more jobs and bolster the economy. Most of all, by holding down jobs, those who have been unemployed for many years can regain a sense of self-confidence and self-worth.

Our next selection, "A Pioneer of Community Wealth," is written by Bill Shore, the activist and founder of Share Our Strength, a philanthropic group that helps fund and coordinate many non-profit organizations which employ the poor, the homeless, ex-convicts, and people with AIDS. In this selection from his book *The Cathedral Within: Transforming Your Life by Giving Something Back*, Shore profiles Gary Mulhair, an entrepreneur from a small town in Washington state. Mulhair developed a successful, "self-sustaining" non-profit business, Pioneer Human Services, that has helped to shatter stereotypes about both non-profit businesses and ex-convicts, by training and employing former prisoners as the primary workers in his company.

Another possible solution to the alienation and other problems created by an economic system that places profits before people is employee ownership of businesses. Workers who own the means of production are happier, more involved in the workplace, and the profits from such a business, if managed correctly, can also be high, resulting in fewer lay-offs. This new type of workplace model presents yet another creative answer to the challenges that now face the world of work. We learn how workers can become the owners of businesses by reading the selection "Work Rules" from William Greider's recent book, *The Soul of Capitalism*.

What a sharp contrast we experience in reading about the groups and individuals in this chapter who have helped others to build better lives rather than remaining complacent in the face of the overwhelming force of the free market economy that is dehumanizing us and the communities around us. We hope that after thinking about the readings included in this chapter, you will try to find a vision for your own work that is meaningful and conscious of the plight of other workers, both here and abroad.

The Obliteration of Alienation
ELLIOTT LEYTON

Elliott Leyton is a Canadian anthropologist who received his Ph.D. from the University of Toronto in 1972. He has written several studies of serial killings and genocide, including Hunting Humans *(1986) and* Men of Blood: Murder in Everyday Life *(1995). After studying the genocide that occurred in Rwanda in 1996, Leyton learned of the organization* Medecins sans Frontiers *or MSF (Doctors Without Borders), an international group of physicians dedicated to helping victims of genocide, war, disasters, and epidemics, often in impoverished Third World countries. After observing the work of members of this group, who do their jobs under conditions of extreme danger, Leyton wrote a book about them:* Touched by Fire: Doctors Without Borders in a Third World Crisis *(1998), a study of their accomplishments and motivations. In the selection from that book that follows, Leyton describes how social and workplace alienation drives these heroic individuals to risk their lives in unsettled areas of the world.*

———————————— ✦ ————————————

A primary quality of life in the modern urban, industrial world is alienation. People are brought to work in the cities, packed together in anonymous apartments, often disconnected from family, from neighbourhood, and, more importantly, from themselves. This process of progressive alienation has its roots in modernity, in the industrialization of the economy, the urbanization of the landscape, and the stratification of society that began in the late eighteenth century and reached its fullest flowering in our time.

The Industrial Revolution was one of the great human achievements. On the one hand, it liberated people, freeing them from otherwise unbreakable social commitments to kin and neighbours, as well as from the unthinkable slaveries of caste, race, gender, and class. Anthropologist Eric Wolf wrote that in liberating people, it made them independent actors, directors of their own lives. Yet it also created its own reservoir of anguish. In the industrializing nineteenth century, both conservative and radical social critics were appalled at the new alienation they saw. In the transformed industrial order, people were alienated from "the product of their work which disappeared into the market"; alienated from "their fellow men who had become actual or potential competitors in the market"; and from "themselves to the extent to which they now had to look upon their own capabilities as marketable commodities," no longer the qualities of a full human being.

This alienation of modern industrial man can cut the spirit like a machete. John Berger, writing of an extreme form of this dilemma in *A Seventh Man*—migrant labouring in wealthy Europe—speaks of it as a form of "imprisonment," wherein a man imported for his labour from the Third World is hermetically sealed off from all natural social and sexual intercourse—with his lover, his family, and his home—and is thus transformed into a kind of non-person. Many MSFers also felt like non-persons when trapped in their dull previous lives.

Becoming an MSFer is the opposite of this experience: it is a kind of *dis*alienation. Membership liberates them as human beings, allows them to explore fully their potential as they seize the opportunity to act. With that liberation comes a profound conviction of the purity of what they do, of the moral superiority of their agency and themselves—a belief so powerful, a satisfaction so intense, that it sustains them through whatever they must do. To witness atrocity and fear, to treat vile diseases, to heal terrible wounds, to dig the latrine or deliver clean water are all part of a process in which they confront reality and construct their identities. In acting thus with such purpose and moral clarity, all other dilemmas dissolve. To act without ambivalence or regret, to cut through the mindlessness of conventional life, to revel in what one is and what one does is for them the only way to become whole.

5   MSFers do not of course usually discuss their lives in terms of social philosophy. Yet they consistently allude to the trivialization, even negation, of self that comes with being a replaceable "cog in a machine" in Europe or America. Clive speaks for them all when he reminds us of his gift from MSF—to be permitted to do something of value, to act with confidence, to create his identity, to seize control of his life. Through MSF, he can achieve a kind of internal peace through meaningful labour. He heals

himself as he gives the suffering the means to heal, as he sees firsthand the results of setting up a water station, supervising the digging of a latrine. When he works in his characteristic state of total concentration, he is always smiling.

Now they are with MSF, the elite shock troops of the unarmed armies of international aid, the firefighters who are parachuted into a crisis at the first sign of trouble, women and men who routinely go where modern armies and their political masters fear to tread. Now there is no endless waiting as a bureaucracy creeps towards an always meaningless and already outdated decision: MSF makes decisions according to circumstance, and MSF makes them *now*. If they are at home on leave, a packed suitcase sits ready by the door, because the recall could come at any time.

Their work will drain every ounce of their energy. They will eat and sleep when and where they can, but their being is engorged with a sense of purpose that transcends their experience, electrifying their muddy and repellent insect- and reptile-infested environment. We see it all at once on our very first full day in Africa, as we sit in an outbuilding behind MSF's East African Logistics Centre in Nairobi. It is now what the Irish call the edge of dark, and a lone fluorescent bulb on a wall partly illuminates the shadowy room. All we can hear in the background is the song of unfamiliar birds and the sudden onset of this minor rainy season's windswept showers. Leaning over Harry's shoulder we surmise that Zaire, the rotten Empire of the Equator, is indeed imploding and a million refugees are about to pour across the border. What rivets our attention is the clicking of Harry's computer keys, and his rapid switches from Dutch to English on the radio-telephone as MSF struggles to estimate the scale of the disaster. In the main building in front of us, Robert is making a flurry of telephone calls around the world to orchestrate emergency flights into Rwanda. Two rooms away, other MSF workers are on radio-telephones, straining for up-to-the-moment information from their workers in the jungle—"Allo? Allo? Allo?" Lizards wait patiently on the wall and gorge on the insects that swarm the light. Thousands of white-winged moths swirl and dance in front of the outdoor lamps. "Stand by . . . over," sputters through the radio. Nothing else for them will ever be so complete, so focused, so absorbing.

When they arrive at their new posting—into the throat of a flood in Somalia, an epidemic in Cambodia, a plague in the Sudan, or a bloody civil war in what once was Yugoslavia—they become part of a self-confident elite. They lose all sense of alienation, they fuse with both their inner beings and their fellows, and become what they wish to be. We're the best; we don't panic; we know what's going on, and we know what we're doing; we're politically and financially independent; and we tell the others just what we think of them. But most of all we work.

We are back in Rwanda with a million refugees pounding down the road from Zaire. As we leave to check the MSF installations, the inexperienced young woman from a UN relief camp radios in a panic: "The refugees are all here, we don't know if we can handle it!" "Ridiculous!" exclaims MSF nurse Monique. "Don't panic! Everything is fine, at least until tomorrow morning. We're not panicking." Later, as the moving wave of refugees appears below our way station, she phlegmatically announces over the radio-telephone, "Okay, they are coming. We are ready for them."

10   Contact! Not the mindless handing out of food and medicines, but witnessing against evil. Not the soul-less merchandising of public health, but eye and hand contact with the victims of unthinkable deprivation. Their job is clear: Feel the suffering with your hands. Witness, food, water, latrines, medicine!

Contact with the humanity of others and the self's full potential, contact with those who need and feel your human help—the crippled, raped, torn, and traumatized, the victims of ruthless political manipulators. The space around you has become the centre of the world, regardless of whether the eyes of the world are turned in horror on the suffering people before you, as in Rwanda and Zaire in November 1996, or when no one else is watching, as in the unknown wars and genocides in Asia, South America, and Africa. These are the disremembered and unacknowledged tortures, plagues, and famines that only you and your most intimate friends can reach out and touch, and heal. This is the meaning of humanity.

They all share in the intoxication of focused collective action. Make decisions, act to soothe suffering, save lives, to hell with everybody else. A thirsty crowd gathers to watch Clive finish connecting the giant water bladder to its pipes: an audible moan escapes their lips when a tap is turned and a faucet gushes. A few weeks ago, I had thought MSFers were exercising some kind of false modesty when they balked at being called heroes, but now I understand that they are merely experiencing what it is to be fully alive. This is disalienation, the antithesis of the programmed numbness that life in a modern industrial city can be, commuting alone to anonymous work with strangers.

Weeks later, Interhamwe death squads will come with murderous intent to the gate of our emergency team's house in Ruhengeri, but will find the doors too awkward to break, the unarmed MSF guards too stubborn. They will go instead a few metres down the road, drag three Spanish medical workers and an American to the lawn, check their passports to ensure they are the inconvenient foreign witnesses to their genocidal evil, and shoot them on the spot. Only the American will escape death, but his leg will be amputated to save his life. As the death squad flees, it will kill three Rwandan soldiers and many civilians.

This night, around a hurried meal in the MSF compound, an intolerable screeching bursts from the hallway, where rats are fighting for food. Monique runs through the kitchen, past the enormous insects in the air and on the table, and confronts the rats as she would the killers. "Fuck off!" she shouts. Other aid agencies will withdraw from the country immediately after the murders, but MSF workers vote to stay in place for the time being, unarmed, only reminding themselves they are free to leave at any time if they feel insecure.

Questions for Discussion

1. How, according to Leyton, did the Industrial Revolution and the more recent technological revolution intensify the sense of alienation among many workers from different classes in society?
2. How, in Leyton's view, does alienation motivate the doctors in MSF? How is their work in MSF "disalienating"? How does it help them to "construct their identities"?
3. How do the testimony of Clive and Leyton's own observation of MSF workers on site in Nairobi help Leyton to make his point about the disalienation of MSF work? Do you find his evidence persuasive?
4. Why do MSF workers balk at being called heroes? What is the relationship between this "balking" and the disalienation they are experiencing, in Leyton's view?

Ideas for Writing

1. Write an essay in which you evaluate Leyton's essay. Does his portrait of the Doctors Without Borders physicians seem objective to you? Does it demonstrate his thesis that the doctors perform their dangerous duties, not to be "heroic" but to further the "obliteration of alienation"? What other motives might they have for their work?
2. Update Leyton's essay by doing further research into the Doctors Without Borders group today: Is it still a thriving organization? Are there conditions under which the doctors will not work, and have there been recent situations in which they have "pulled out" of a country altogether? Write an essay about your findings.

Made in the USA

JENNY STRASBURG

Jenny Strasburg is a business reporter with the San Francisco Chronicle, *where for the past two years she has focused on retail companies, industry trends, and legal issues. Prior to coming to San Francisco in 1999, she worked as a news and features writer in Texas. She attended New Mexico State University in Las Cruces and grew up in Albuquerque. In the following article, first published in the* San Francisco Chronicle, *Strasburg profiles a successful small business owner who provides for his employees' welfare through good salaries, health-care benefits, and a comfortable work environment.*

— ✦ —

In a business better known for dull uniformity than bold personality, Dove Charney is a dynamo who has found success selling an unlikely mix of T-shirts, sex and social responsibility.

On the factory floor at American Apparel—the company he runs just outside of the Garment District here—he's the loud, lanky boss with mutton chops, a rock-star demeanor and an often-discussed love life that seems outsized even by Los Angeles standards. But in an industry that has all but fled American soil for cheaper labor elsewhere, he's also the businessman who has pledged his loyalty to homegrown apparel, above-average wages and worker-friendly factory conditions.

On billboards and in magazines, Charney sells youth and sex appeal packaged in extra-soft, snug T-shirts. Through shrewd marketing, he has commandeered a significant slice of the market, infusing a high level of fashion into an everyday wardrobe item. The formula has brought American Apparel rising sales and national attention.

But the question remains: Can he continue to do well and do good? His marketing acumen could falter, his rivals could offer similar high-fashion T-shirts at lower prices, and fleeting styles and tastes could shift. Pressure could build to compromise the workplace ideals on which he has built the business.

5   "His goals are very, very laudable, but I think a lot of people in the industry are watching to see if he's going to be able to survive," says Jack Kyser, chief economist with the Los Angeles County Economic Development Corp., a private nonprofit that promotes jobs and industry.

With his edgy, out-front image, Charney doesn't seem like a man who is worried. He is a portrait in confidence, an unsubtle and sometimes off-color company spokesman prone to manic populist discourses. He's unapologetic about American Apparel's in-your-face marketing, his confrontations with unions, and his love affairs with employees and women who model his T-shirts.

Stories about Charney's personal life, which circulate in industry circles and have been featured in media coverage of American Apparel, sometimes overshadow more-serious portrayals of the business he's building, he says.

"There's a lot of love, and a lot of commitment, and a lot of passion and blood and tears that have gone into this company," Charney says. "And there are many hardworking people there that are extremely passionate that I've never had any romantic relationship with."

Four years ago, he pulled his then-little-known rag business into profitability after years of red ink. He didn't do it selling boxy, mass-market T-shirts. Instead, he weaves thin-fiber cotton yarn into styles favored by urban trend-seekers in cities such as San Francisco and New York. A basic women's T-shirt from American Apparel is priced at about $16 retail. Much of the company's business comes from small, independent designers who buy the shirts wholesale, embellish them with original touches and resell them in boutiques for $30 or more.

It's a niche market that distantly trails the multibillion-dollar 10 reach of brands such as Hanes and Fruit of the Loom. But American Apparel reported $80 million in sales last year, and Charney says he expects to reach $140 million this year.

The company opened its first retail stores last year, in New York and Los Angeles, and Charney plans to have 25 locations by the end of the year, possibly including San Francisco.

BUCKING THE OFFSHORE TREND

American Apparel weaves its fabric and cuts and stitches its T-shirts, fleece pants, pullovers and panties in an immense, adobe-pink former railroad warehouse in downtown Los Angeles. A huge banner that hangs outside proclaims the company "an industrial revolution."

Its sewing-machine operators commonly make more than $500 a week working fewer days and shorter hours, with more-generous benefits and generally better working conditions, than most other garment workers in the city, according to industry observers and independent worker advocates.

In recent years, much of the Los Angeles garment industry has moved away from manufacturing in favor of importing. At the same time, American Apparel has grown from 1,200 workers a year ago to nearly 2,000, most of them Latinos who live in low-income neighborhoods.

15   "I'm only 35. You name another 35-year-old who's changing this many lives." Charney says during a factory walk-through, in the midst of a running commentary that ranges from free-market trade to cotton shrinkage and prisons in Iraq.

Yet questions remain whether Charney's business model can be broadly adopted to bring large-scale apparel manufacturing back to the United States. Charney argues that higher labor costs can be off-set by happier and more-efficient workers, generating higher profit.

Two decades of industry trends refute the notion. Major apparel brands such as Gap and Ralph Lauren subcontract with factories in dozens of countries outside the United States in their search for the right balance of design, quality and labor costs.

"American Apparel is an anomaly. It's not the status of the industry, nor is it the future of where the industry is going, but it is functioning extremely well based on the model it has designed for itself," says Ilse Metchek, executive director of the industry-backed California Fashion Association, and LA By Design, a marketing program under the private Los Angeles County Economic Development Corp.

"SWEATSHOP FREE" MARKETING

American Apparel keeps things simple, sticking with cotton tops and bottoms that require a narrow range of machinery and skills to produce.

20   The company stresses the made-at-home mantra. American Apparel clothing tags, catalogs and billboards declare the goods "Sweatshop Free." Yet, it's unclear how much that message registers with its wholesale customers and individual shoppers.

"Customers are more attuned to quality" than to anti-sweatshop marketing, says Roxy Buu, who owns the San Francisco boutique Buu, in San Francisco's Hayes Valley, which carries designers who use Charney's T-shirts. "When I see that a shirt is American Apparel, I know it's good."

Los Angeles County's roughly 67,000 apparel workers don't make many commodity clothing products, says Kyser, the economic-development economist. The region's garment shops more routinely churn out quick-turnaround, inexpensive fashions for specialty retailers such as Forever 21 and Wet Seal, or higher-end goods for upscale retailers such as St. John Knits. Basic apparel competes heavily on price, which generally means overseas production, Kyser says.

On the factory tour, Charney—dressed in pink cotton-jersey leisure shirt made by his company—seems confident that he can thrive. The company is built on more than some do-gooder social mission, he insists.

"No one can stop this," Charney says over the hum of sewing machines, punching the air with his fist and whooping at his workers, inviting them to shout back in a kind of impromptu pep rally. "I'm paving a new method of distribution.... I have to rebuild part of America!"

Some workers grin. They say that theatrics are typical for the boss.   25

A LIFETIME IN T-SHIRTS

Charney's mother is a painter and his father a Harvard-educated architect. He first sold T-shirts as a Montreal high-school student, buying them at U.S. Kmarts and trucking them back to Canada.

T-shirt brokering led to manufacturing, which led Charney to South Carolina in the early 1990s. The industry was highly competitive and increasingly moving offshore. Charney moved to Los Angeles in the summer of 1997 and partnered with Sam Lim and other garment-industry veterans to get American Apparel off the ground. The company turned a profit in 2000 after shifting its focus to fashion-conscious youth, Charney says.

A tireless promoter, he has worked the floors at major trade shows such as the Magic Marketplace in Las Vegas, often flanked by models handing out American Apparel ClassicGirl Ts and women's briefs.

According to Charney, the "Sweatshop Free" tag has built up the company's image but also caused headaches. The designation, combined with the company's success, makes him a prime target of what he calls "the liberal, PC-oppressed left."

"Is it a cooperative? Is it unionized? Are you objectifying women?" he says, listing the questions he says he gets from anti-sweatshop activists and union organizers. "Of course we're objectifying women. You want a smock? Go to the Middle East."   30

LIFE ON THE FACTORY FLOOR

The factory is not unionized. Last year, Charney and the Union of Needletrades, Industrial and Textile Employees, AFL-CIO, or UNITE, tangled over an organizing drive. The effort failed, and at one point hundreds of American Apparel workers staged a protest against the drive. The union says that the company management intimidated workers.

"By the third day of our campaign, people were not receptive. They were very afraid," says Cristina Vazquez, UNITE's regional manager in California and international vice president. She contends that American Apparel should set an example for other, smaller factories in the city by embracing the union.

UNITE, in a complaint to the National Labor Relations Board, contended that Charney had meddled in union talks with employees. In a non-monetary settlement. Charney, who denied wrongdoing, agreed to post flyers spelling out workers' collective-bargaining rights, have the list of rights read aloud to employees and stay out of future talks.

Kimi Lee, director of the independent, nonprofit Garment Worker Center in Los Angeles, says that the center typically supports UNITE's organizing efforts. But, in the case of American Apparel, the center did not believe that workers would benefit.

35   The Garment Worker Center hears few complaints from American Apparel workers, and those that come up are typically minor and resolved relatively easily, Lee says. They tend to stem from a lack of management experience among floor supervisors who have been promoted with little training, as a result of the company's fast growth, she says.

"Dov believes in a happy workforce," and that's reflected in the factory conditions and salaries, Lee says.

American Apparel workers can take free English-language classes and yoga classes on-site. They have free Internet access and massage therapy and subsidized lunches and bus passes. Employee health care has been privatized and subsidized by the company for about a year and a half, Charney says.

"This is the only factory where I've been content, where I have been happy," says Benigno Navarro, 36, of Los Angeles, who has worked there a year. He sews T-shirt hems.

During his decade in the city's garment factories, the husband and father of three rarely earned more than $30 or $40 a day at other factories, often working from 6 a.m. to 6 p.m., and had no health benefits, he says in Spanish.

At American Apparel, he says that he works 7:45 a.m. to 4 p.m.   40
most days, with a lunch break, and makes anywhere from $80 to
$120 per day. In Los Angeles, Navarro says, "This is the company
people say is the best."

The average hourly pay is about $13, with some workers
making more than $18, Charney says. He vows that if he ever
expands production overseas, he'll pay those workers above-
standard wages as well. Workers who can't afford hot water and
an Internet connection aren't making a living wage, he says.

American Apparel isn't the only Los Angeles clothing-maker
that has stressed social values. A company called TeamX marketed its "union-made, sweatshop-free clothes (produced) in the
most socially responsible manner" under a label called SweatX.
It was founded by UNITE in 2002 with a reported $1 million
seed investment from the Hot Fudge Social Venture Capital
Fund established by Ben & Jerry's co-founder Ben Cohen. The
workers made at least $10 an hour and had medical coverage.

But the company wasn't profitable, and it folded in May, says
Rick Roth, who was hired in October as chief executive. By then,
TeamX was debt-ridden and beyond saving, he says.

"It was all about the social premise, and the only thing that
works in this business is the product," says Metchek, of the
California Fashion Association.

After SweatX folded, Charney bought some of its sewing ma-   45
chines. He says he'll use them to expand his operation.

American Apparel, Los Angeles made 80 million dollars in 2003.

Questions for Discussion

1. The writer tells us a lot about Charney's personality and dreams. Does this
    information help to support your belief in his ability to succeed? Why or
    why not? Why does he think that the cost of paying his workers a fair salary
    and giving them better working conditions as well as benefits will pay off in
    the end? Do you agree with his point of view? Explain your response.

2. Strasburg quotes from Charney when he speaks of values. Does this strategy
    help to engage the readers' interest in Charney's company and convince
    them that he wants to change the current way the garment industry has
    been successful, through its exploitation of workers? Although he is but one
    individual, Charney hangs a banner outside his business that says "an indus-
    trial revolution." What is the effect of this banner? What do his opponents be-
    lieve? Do you believe that one man can be the catalyst for crucial social
    change?

3. Why isn't Charney's business unionized? Why does the writer contrast American Apparel with the failure of TeamX, a unionized and "socially responsible" business? Speculate on why Charney's business has been able to continue to grow while TeamX failed.

4. Charney says, "I'm paving a new method of distribution. . . . I have to rebuild part of America!" Explain why you agree or disagree with Charney. Then present reasoning and evidence to support your point of view.

Ideas for Writing

1. Do some research on the lives of the workers who produce garments for a particular company such as the Gap, which employs workers outside of the United States. Then write a paper in the form of an argument that supports the Gap's practices (or any company that you choose which employs workers from Third World countries) or one that points out why their policy and business strategy will ultimately fail.

2. Interview a person who has been exploited by his or her employer. Try to find out why the person stayed at the job and what impact the job had on his or her self-esteem and ability to be productive. Before writing your essay, brainstorm with your classmates to come up with ways employee exploitation could be mitigated.

Secondary Five
RODNEY J. CARROLL

Raised in an impoverished neighborhood in North Philadelphia, Rodney J. Carroll is himself a welfare-to-work success story. He started his career at (UPS) United Parcel Services in 1987, working part-time unloading packages, and eventually he rose to the position of UPS Operations Division Manager at the Philadelphia Air Hub. His motivational and inspirational presence has made him a highly requested public speaker. In August 1999, his reputation was established on a truly national scale when he co-moderated a Town Hall meeting on welfare reform with former President Bill Clinton at the Partnership's One America Conference in Chicago. After a 22-year career at UPS, he was named the president and CEO of the Welfare to Work Partnership in December 2000. Carroll's book No Free Lunch *(2002), from which the selection that follows is excerpted, describes his own struggles and the challenges faced by welfare recipients who want to reclaim their independence through work.*

✦

I knew what it was like to be a welfare recipient looking for a chance and I knew what it was like to be part of a business looking for good workers.

When I got back to my office, I opened the top left-hand drawer of my desk and pulled out the e-mails.

I'll show them, I thought to myself. And I got to work.

I felt like I didn't stop working for two months.

"Okay," I said to myself. "Transportation." 5

We had people in Camden who needed jobs and a facility in Philadelphia that needed good workers. I was not going to let a little thing like a lack of transportation stand in our way.

I went back to the office and called the New Jersey Transit Authority.

"No way," they said. "We can't go across state lines."

I called the Southeastern Pennsylvania Transit Authority. They cited union problems. Neither place would budge. Finally I decided to try UPS. I called Bill Riggans, District Manager. I told him that I had an idea to solve our staffing problems. I explained the situation, including the transportation hassle, and suggested a solution.

"Why don't we charter a bus to pick them up," I said. 10

"Who's going to pay for that?" asked Riggans.

"Well, the welfare recipients don't have the money to pay for it," I said. "I was thinking that UPS could pay."

"You're very generous with UPS's money," He said. "But what's in it for UPS?"

A great question. Even today as I travel across the county speaking to companies about the value of welfare-to-work hiring programs, I bring this up because corporate America always wants to know, "What's in it for us?" And they are right. They have a responsibility to the shareholders. As nice as it would be to help people in need, businesses can't start programs that don't make good sense. They have to be able to say, "This is a sound investment."

"I think it could be extremely profitable for UPS," I said. 15

"I'm listening."

"People on welfare are hungry. They want to work and I believe that if we train them properly, they will have higher retention rates than our other workers. They'll stay around longer and that will turn into positive UPS dollars."

Riggans wasn't a champion of welfare-to-work as much as he liked the idea of doing things that were noteworthy. And transporting people on welfare across state lines to available jobs was most definitely noteworthy. "Alright," Riggans said. "I'll tell you what. We'll try it for three months, and after three months if it's not working, it's gone. So tell them up front, we're only doing this for three months."

"Done," I said.

20   The next day, Al, Rich, and I headed back to the facility in Camden.

"Did you solve the transportation problem?" Peter asked.

"We took care of it," I said, and explained the arrangement.

"Great," said Peter. "Our next responsibility is to get them jobs."

A week later we came back with human resource representatives to interview the candidates. During the interviews, I noticed a tall, straggly-looking man standing off to one side. His battered construction boots had no laces. He wore ripped and tattered overalls, and even though it was a warm day, he wore a flannel shirt. I saw old punctures on his arms that were unmistakably from drugs. He had an unkempt mustache and his long, stringy hair covered most of his face. He was watching us.

25   "Hi," I said, sticking out my hand. "My name's Rodney."

"Billy," he answered.

"We're from UPS."

"I didn't see any UPS trucks outside," he said. I chuckled although I wasn't sure he was joking.

"We hear you guys are looking for jobs."

30   "Is that right?" he said, his voice rising.

"Do you think you would be a good candidate to work at UPS?" I always asked that question in interviews and usually got the same answer: "There's nobody better than me."

But Billy was different.

"To be honest," he said. "I have no idea why you would hire me."

With his hands in his pockets, he told me he was sure that there were people with a better education. He told me that he had to drop out of high school when he was sixteen to support his family—although he made sure to mention that he received his GED. He told me that he was embarrassed to be on welfare.

35   "But at thirty years old, I need to be a man again," he said. Then he picked up his head and looked me in the eye.

"I'm not the smartest guy you're going to hire, Mr. Carroll. But because I'm not as smart, I'm going to work twice as hard. I'm just hoping that somehow I'll get a chance to prove I'm worth something, not only to myself but to my family and my children. If I had an opportunity, I know I would make the best of it."

Billy reaffirmed my belief in the human spirit. He sincerely wanted to work and that meant more to me than a college degree or work history. That is why I strongly object when some welfare recipients are called the "hardest to place." We sometimes fall into the trap of profiling people. The social scientists do it when they refer to people with specific skill levels or educational backgrounds. They give names for these categories, including the "hardest to place," meaning the background prohibits a person from becoming a successful employee. This usually includes people who use drugs and alcohol, women who are victims of spousal abuse, and ex-felons.

Chris Wilcox and Gale Hagan are two classic examples of what social scientists call the "hardest to place." For years Chris had a drug problem. His three children suffered from the instability of their parents and the limitations of welfare.

Finally, Chris got "sick and tired of being sick and tired." Fortunately for Chris, Cessna Aircraft Company in Wichita, Kansas is another company that believes everyone has the potential to be a good employee—regardless of past mistakes. One of the workers at the KanWorks program, the welfare program in Kansas, introduced Chris to Cessna's 21st Street Facility, a program designed to train welfare recipients for jobs at Cessna Aircraft Company.

The 21st Street program was started in 1990 in a single build-   40
ing, which was eleven thousand square feet. Seven years later, Cessna had added fifty-eight thousand square-foot learning center, including five thousand feet for day care. They built safe housing, where trainees could temporarily live to avoid dangerous circumstances at home.

The 21st Street program has provided more than two hundred loyal and dedicated employees who have a higher retention rate than more traditionally hired employees.

"We have found that there are an awful lot of people who have led their life in a particular way for a number of years, but who are willing and want very badly to lead the rest of their life differently," said John Moore, senior vice president of human resources.

Chris Wilcox is one of those people. Today, Chris is the final assembly mechanic on the Citation 750 line at Cessna Aircraft. He has already been promoted and is now trusted with building Cessna's most advanced aircraft. But most important, Chris has custody of his three children. They have a safe, stable home with a father who loves and supports them.

"To me, every day that I wake up and am able to breathe is a good day, from where I came from," said Chris. "It's pretty neat to be able to say to my kids, 'There's one of the planes that I built.' Now when somebody asks, 'Where's your dad work?,' they've got an answer. 'At Cessna.' "

45   Gail Hagan was a victim of domestic violence and she now works for Salomon Smith Barney, a subsidiary of CitiGroup. For two years, Gail had struggled with an alcohol problem. After almost losing her daughter to social services, Gail decided to turn her life around.

She entered a program at Wildcat Services, a nonprofit service provider that trains welfare recipients for jobs. Wildcat is one of the best service providers in the country.

"We're in the business of training people who others thought were untrainable, and making them into good citizens who will do well at their jobs," said Amalia Betanzos, president of the Wildcat Service Corporation.

The best part of the partnership is that Wildcat knows exactly what skills the trainees need to succeed at Salomon Smith Barney and they tailor their training program accordingly. After a sixteen-week training program, trainees are guaranteed an opportunity for work. It took Gail only eight weeks before she graduated to an internship in the financial services industry at Salomon Smith Barney. After two more months, she had a full-time job.

Now Gail, someone who most companies wouldn't have even considered because of her background, works for a company that pays her more than thirty-thousand dollars a year. She's earning stock options and has a 401(k). One day, Gail is waiting by her mailbox for a welfare check, four months later she's waiting for her retirement statements.

50   "This is not charity," said Michael Schlein, the director of corporate affairs at CitiGroup. "Gail is working for a living. She's getting paid, and she deserves to be well paid. We give a lot of people an opportunity, but people like Gail are the ones who are making the most of that opportunity."

As more and more people like Chris and Gail succeed, more and more business leaders are willing to look beyond the stereotypes of people with substance-abuse problems and criminal records, to see people who have made mistakes and now want to change their lives. Most drug addicts or criminals were like Courtney at one point. Not all of them, but most of them were nice kids who tried to do the right thing before getting overwhelmed by societal pressures.

It's not up to corporate America to help welfare recipients. As I learned through Courtney, that's a job that only they could do for themselves. But if a person can break an addiction or climb out of welfare, then they can do anything.

"These are exactly the type of people we're looking for," I told Al and Rich on the drive home. "People who have something to prove."

Like everyone else at UPS, Al had his own theories on why retention was low. He believed that the five-day training program was insufficient for employees to learn the many intricacies of the job.

"This will be a good opportunity to revamp the program," he told me.   55

"I was thinking the same thing," I responded.

Over lunch, we discussed how to change the program. Then, unilaterally, we agreed to extend it from five days to six weeks. Al and I believed that six weeks gave us enough time to thoroughly teach the trainees the job. We also knew that by working six weeks, employees were eligible to join the union—an important benefit to working at UPS. I knew many good people who would still be working at UPS today, if they could have just made it into the union.

"Six weeks it is," said Al, as he wiped his mouth and prepared to leave.

"Just one more thing," I said. "We need to create some demand for the jobs at UPS. Instead of hiring fifty employees a week, we are only going to hire forty to fifty employees every six weeks."

Al knew how hard I was working on the program. And he knew that, at this point, I wasn't going to compromise. I would have a tough enough time convincing the other managers to reduce hiring so drastically, so Al didn't respond.   60

"Thanks for the lunch, Rodney," he said and, as usual, left the check to me.

At the next employment meeting, Al and I made our case for a six-week training course. It was well received. When we were done, I kept the floor.

"For the last several years, people thought they could get a job at UPS anytime they wanted," I said. "Therefore the value of a job at UPS diminished. We have to create a perception—and ultimately the reality—that it's prestigious to work at UPS. And we don't do that by hiring anybody that applies every week."

"Then how do we do it?" a manager asked.

"By hiring once every six weeks."   65

"You're out of your mind," said an area hub manager. "There's no way we can make it once every six weeks. I won't have any people left."

"You'll have to value your people more," I responded.

"How are we going to keep people waiting for six weeks?" asked a human resource director.

"The people that are really interested in UPS will wait," I said. "You have to trust me on this."

70 The debate over the dramatic change in hiring practice continued for thirty minutes. Al didn't say a word and the idea passed. After the meeting. Al approached me privately.

"Keep trusting your instincts," he said. "We're almost there."

Managers at UPS are evaluated solely on performance. If production is down, they don't get bonuses. If service doesn't keep increasing, they can forget about a raise. If there were too many missorts, they could lose their job. The basic fact was that if employees didn't do well, then managers didn't either.

When I informed the managers that forty-one of their new employees were coming from welfare, they were livid.

"Why don't we bring in blind and crippled people, too," cried Scott Conaway, an outbound manager.

75 Dan Havaford, who ran the small sort, was especially upset because his area was close to reaching his goals. "You're trying to sabotage my area," Dan yelled.

"The decision has already been made," I said. "You guys are going to have to trust me. This will work."

Normally, each trainee is assigned to a different area of the operation for "on-the-job training." I asked the managers who needed workers.

Silence.

I turned to Mondel, the primary direct manager. "You don't want anybody, Mondel? You have the highest turnover in the group."

80 "Nope," answered Mondel. "We're alright, we're good."

"Wes," I continued. "You're turning over people like flapjacks. You don't need anybody?"

"I'm cool," answered Wes.

I asked every manager and everyone said, "Nope." I shook my head. I was frustrated. Ninety-nine times out of one hundred, I wouldn't have said anything, but this time was different. This was too important.

I slammed my notebook on the table.

85 "Let me make sure I understand this," I said. "Nobody needs any workers? And you realize we're not getting anyone in for six weeks?"

"Nope," they said. "We don't want anybody."

"If I didn't know any better," I said, "I would think that this has something to do with the group of people that we are hiring. People coming from welfare."

Again, silence.

"But I know better than that," I continued. "Because for three months now, we've been talking about how to value our employees and what it means to give someone a chance. I know you were listening to me, so it can't be that you don't want to hire welfare recipients. Can it, Dan?"

Dan was rattled and I didn't let him wriggle out.   90

"Dan, that can't be what you guys are thinking. Could it?"

"Well, no," Dan replied. "I just happen to be in good shape. I'll take one if you want me to have one."

"One what?" I said glaring down at him.

"One person," he said.

"No," I snapped back. "If you say you don't want anyone, then   95 you're not getting anyone. I just want to tell you guys, I'm very disappointed. I have a mind to tell each of you to take five people from this new class, but I'm not going to do that. It's not fair to the people who are really trying to make it. They're not here as guinea pigs. They're here to turn their lives around."

I stormed out of the room. I paced up and down the hallway.

A few of the managers thought the meeting was over and tried to leave the room.

"This meeting is not over," I said. "Just stay in there and wait until I get back."

I went down to my office to calm down. I leaned back on my chair and stared out of the window toward the operation. It was a down time. The two belts right in front of my office in Secondary Five were vacant. I racked my brain trying to think of a solution. I had forty-one welfare recipients starting in two weeks and I had managers that didn't want them. If I forced the managers to participate, the program wouldn't work.

I swung back and forth on my swivel chair, just thinking and   100 staring. Then it came to me. I went back upstairs and walked calmly into the conference room. When the managers saw me, they stopped talking and took their seats.

"We're making Secondary Five a training area," I proclaimed. It was perfect. Not only was Secondary Five right outside my office, it was also a highly visible area. The first thing anyone coming down from the parking lot or in from the buses saw was Secondary Five. It was the ideal location for a program that I wanted everyone to recognize.

"Scott, we're going to take you off the Secondary Five red and blue belts. They're no longer going to be part of your area," I instructed. "I'm going to have them report to Nan Miland."

"What?" he said. "Are you promoting Nan?"

"No, she is just going to run this area. This is now going to be a training area."

105   As it turned out, this was much better than spreading the trainees throughout the operation. Nan was the ideal supervisor. She was caring and compassionate, but tough enough to get the job done.

I called Nan at home. Before I finished describing the program, she said, "I'll be honored."

I lay in bed that night feeling good. We had workers. They had a way to get to work and they had a supportive place to work.

Now for the training, I thought.

The training program was the easy part. Through all the different stops on my road to division manager, I had developed strong opinions and strategies for the best way to train workers. It had started on my second day of work, eighteen years earlier, when I learned the most important thing for any new employee: Dominic Palvino.

110   Every new worker deserved their own Dominic. As abrasive as he was, I remembered how comfortable I felt at work with him by my side. He wasn't my supervisor. He was just someone who gave me the inside scoop about working at UPS.

I knew that our training program needed to include this mentoring aspect. We had forty-one welfare recipients. We needed forty-one mentors.

The selection process for the mentors was rigorous. To encourage the workers to apply, I suggested that the mentor position was a stepping-stone to supervisor. "So if you want to be a supervisory candidate, I suggest you apply to be a mentor," the flyer read.

There was a great demand to be a mentor and we had more than one hundred excellent candidates apply. I outlined my vision for the mentors: "They are there to be a friend. To help the new hire get over any bumps in the road; to give practical workplace advice; or just be a sounding board or a cheerleader."

I then personally interviewed all the candidates. I wasn't looking for the hardest workers. I looked for workers with good communication skills, patience, and compassion. After a solid week of interviews and second interviews, I handpicked forty-one workers to be our first class of mentors.

115   "It takes courage to try to change your life," I told the training coordinators—they preferred to be called training coordinators over mentors. "Many times, it's safer to stay on welfare."

I placed incredible pressure on the training coordinators. They spent five weeks helping me create the training program. They spent two weeks mastering the flow of the blue and red belts in Secondary Five. I held them professionally responsible for the progress of the trainees.

"Don't you give them an excuse to quit," I warned. "They're waiting for you to say that they can't do it, or give them some negative vibe. That's what they've gotten their entire lives. We're going to beat them to the punch and tell them why they *can't* quit."

We made sure to keep the same basic standard for the welfare recipients as we had for other employees—no tardiness, no absenteeism.

The class would be divided into two teams—a red team and a blue team—coinciding with their belts. For each week the entire group remained on the job, they would earn a pizza party—including toppings—if no one was tardy. The extra topping incentive may seem odd, but when you're poor, mushrooms and pepperoni on your pizza is not an option. You get cheese.

If the group went a week with perfect service—no missorts—   120
they would earn a T-shirt. Two weeks in a row earned a hat. Three weeks a UPS jacket.

Aside from learning the intricacies of the job, the training program was designed to build self-esteem. Many companies say they don't want to be social workers, and I don't think they should be. But the fact is that if you take the time to address the concerns of your employees—whether they are on welfare or not—they will feel valued, they will work harder, and they will stay on the job.

The training coordinators did role-plays concerning challenges for the jobs: the packages are too heavy. The flow is moving too quickly. And role-plays concerning non-job-related issues: I have personal problems at home. I didn't get any sleep last night because my child kept me up.

We incorporated a lesson I learned from Willow Grove. "We want the trainees to know more about UPS than most of the people in this hub," I said. "The more they know, the better they'll be able to do their jobs."

So we scheduled representatives from all facets of the organization to speak to the trainees each week. First, accounting would talk about stock programs, the 401(k) and retirement plans. Two weeks later, human resources would discuss benefits, including the difference between welfare benefits and UPS benefits.

When I was growing up, we didn't visit a doctor's office   125
with comfortable chairs, music, and *Sports Illustrated* to browse

through. Our only option was the emergency room, where we waited and waited and waited. At UPS, employees could make an appointment with a doctor of their choice. There was 100 percent prescription drug coverage.

The next week, representatives from our airline would speak about opportunities in the planes. Many people probably don't realize that UPS is the largest cargo airline in the world.

We scheduled people to talk about computers and marketing and tractor trailers. The program was choreographed so that while one group was doing on-the-job training, the other was in the classroom.

In the end, the program was created exactly as I had visualized it. It was challenging enough so the trainees would be valuable when they graduated, but forgiving enough so they wouldn't get discouraged during the process.

On July 17, 1996, a class of forty-one welfare recipients began the first six-week training program at UPS.

Questions for Discussion

1. How does Carroll succeed in getting work to welfare people from Camden to Philadelphia? How many obstacles does he have to overcome before he convinces UPS to help his clients? What impression do the opening pages of the selection give you of Carroll's personality and values? What rhetorical strategies does the author use to achieve this effect?
2. Billy's success exposes the dangers of profiling welfare recipients. How does Carroll's use of this information help to persuade you of his argument?
3. How does Carroll succeed in convincing UPS bosses to accept his plans that they do not think will work? What are its guiding principles? What does Secondary Five refer to? Why do you think Carroll titled this selection "Secondary Five"?
4. In what ways do welfare-to-work programs challenge the traditional definitions of a good worker? Did Carroll convince you that people can go from welfare to work successfully? What was persuasive about his presentation of his victory?

Ideas for Writing

1. Write a research paper that explains the development and concept of welfare-to-work. Profile the evolution and success of one or two welfare-to-work programs as Carroll has in this article.

2. Write a research argument in favor of welfare-to-work programs or one that opposes this type of reform. In either case, use examples to support your main ideas.

A Pioneer of Community Wealth

BILL SHORE

A former political campaign director turned community activist, Bill Shore (b. 1957) is the founder of Share Our Strength, one of the most successful fundraising organizations serving people who suffer from poverty and disease. Since 1984 when the foundation began helping people, it has raised more than $82 million, which has been distributed to 1,000 hunger and poverty associations. Shore recently founded Community Wealth Ventures, Inc., an advisory board that works with corporations and non-profits to develop jobs for the unemployed. He has been honored with many awards, and in 1999 he published two books: Revolution of the Heart: A New Strategy for Creating Wealth and Meaningful Change *and* The Cathedral Within: Transforming Your Life by Giving Something Back, *from which the following selection is taken. The portrait of an entrepreneur who founded a successful non-profit business designed both to provide useful services to the community and to help ex-convicts by providing them with good jobs is inspiring and thought-provoking.*

———————— ✦ ————————

Walla Walla, Washington, is a small city of less than thirty thousand at the foot of the Blue Mountains in the southeast corner of the state. Its entire population could be comfortably seated on one side of an NFL football stadium. It lies so close to the Oregon border that on a map, the second "Walla" almost spills across the state line. You can tell from the names of the surrounding geography that there was a time when life in this territory was not for the timid: Rattlesnake Flat, Ice Harbor Dam, Diamond Peak, Huntsville, Echo. Known today for little more than the Walla Walla Sweet Onion Harvest, it was once the largest city in what was called the Washington Territory.

Built by fur traders on the famous Native American Nez Percé trail, Walla Walla was officially founded in 1856, but it had seen Lewis and Clark's footsteps half a century earlier. The gold rush made it a commercial, banking, and manufacturing center, none of which outlasted the farms that still dominate its economy today. As one of the first areas settled between the Rockies and the Cascades, Walla Walla played a historic role in the development of the Pacific Northwest.

Walla Walla not only attracted the West's earliest pioneers, it bred a few as well. Gary Mulhair was born there in 1941. He spent his boyhood exploring the river valleys and working on farms. He can remember summers irrigating cornfields, pulling the pipes through thick rows of wet and heavy cornstalks and coming out drenched into the cold September air. In the fall, his mother sent him out to find and shell black walnuts that she wanted for cakes and pies. "They're very hard, and after cracking them, scraping the meat out of those was murder," he recalls. "Your fingers would be stained for maybe a week." She expected to receive the amount she'd asked for, often an entire bushel, no matter how hard it was or how long it took. From an early age, he understood that outcomes were what counted, that deliverables are how you measure value.

He stayed through college and eventually journeyed as far as Seattle, some 270 miles west, but no further. He never had to. The region's culture of rugged individualism has been defined by a spirited entrepreneurship and innovation that has changed the course of human history. Gary Mulhair helped do the defining. Many entrepreneurs have been at home there, from Bill Gates at Microsoft to Howard Schultz at Starbucks, as well as hundreds of others who are part of the region's flourishing high-tech economy. But when it came to social entrepreneurship, Gary Mulhair beat them all to the punch.

5   Since 1975, Mulhair has been creating jobs and saving lives through a unique model that is the envy of organizations across the nation. Under his leadership, Seattle's aptly named Pioneer Human Services has become the largest and most self-sustaining human service agency of its kind. He has revolutionized the way human service organizations operate through self-supporting enterprises and programs that integrate jobs, housing, training, and other support services for at-risk individuals. With revenues in excess of $50 million a year, Mulhair has created wealth of a magnitude previously unheard of in the nonprofit world.

He did it the toughest way possible, not by begging for foundation grants or government support, but by manufacturing and selling high-quality products and services with a workforce made up entirely of ex-offenders and former substance abusers. As he explained to the *Seattle Post-Intelligencer:* "These are people who have broken the law, folks most people are frightened of. They've been in prison or they're recovering from alcohol or drugs. They haven't held a job. When they apply for a job they get screened out pretty quickly. . . . We're going to hire people you wouldn't," Mulhair asserts, "but in a year or so, you will—because they'll be citizens."

What Pioneer's success means is that for the first time, a non-profit organization is not dependent solely upon the charity of others. Its leaders do not have all of their energies diverted and usurped by the relentless demands of fund-raising—the meetings, phone calls, dinners, and events designed to meet and win the hearts of wealthy individual donors. Instead, they can focus on what attracted them to the job in the first place: developing effective programs to help the people they serve. Pioneer has proved that nonprofits can do more than just redistribute wealth, which they are typically quite good at. They can also create wealth, though it is a different kind of wealth—community wealth—that is used to directly benefit the community.

Shattering stereotypes is a fundamentally subversive activity. Initially, Mulhair's role in inventing a new model for nonprofits to grow to scale was so quiet as to be almost unnoticed outside of the Seattle area. Running a factory, building a profitable business, and delivering comprehensive social services to a severely challenged population—all at the same time—is complicated, taxing work. Mulhair couldn't find the time to both do the work and talk about it, so he kept his focus on the former. Gradually, through word of mouth, visitors, and the circulation of a few local press clips, the story of what he'd accomplished began to spread.

I called Gary Mulhair in 1996. I asked him to come to Washington to join in a discussion about redefining civic responsibility with people like Jeff Swartz of Timberland, former New Jersey senator Bill Bradley, and Michael Kennedy from Citizen's Energy. Leaders in various fields who were helping to create this new kind of community wealth did not yet know one another, and were not sharing, collaborating, or even talking. Share Our Strength saw value in playing the simple role of convener.

"Why do you want me?" he asked with characteristic reti- 10
cence. The tone of his voice was stern. I couldn't tell whether he was genuinely curious or whether the question was some kind of test, but I was conscious of choosing my words carefully.

"Because you've been doing what everyone else only talks about."

"Okay," he said, ending the conversation. It meant he would come.

I learned then that Gary doesn't usually say more than he needs to. But when he came to Washington a few months later, he said enough.

Fifty-six years old and neatly if conservatively dressed, he maintains a steady gaze through large round lenses as if searching for the real you and pretty much expecting to find it. He is cautious with his broad smile, but friendly in the way of a small-town pharmacist. You can trust that whatever he's telling you is for you own good. He's given to short declarative statements that you can take or leave.

15   In his plainspoken way, and without the pretense that usually accompanies a Washington presentation, Mulhair described for the group the history of Pioneer, which began in Seattle in 1962 when an attorney named Jack Dalton was released from prison after serving a sentence for embezzling from his clients. "Jack came out of prison," Mulhair explained, "and he realized he was disbarred, disowned, and disenfranchised. He had nothing going for himself except the fact that he had nothing going for himself. Along with half a dozen other former prisoners who were struggling to build new lives, he started a halfway house with a budget of less than a thousand dollars that he raised by going to the very friends from whom he had embezzled. Jack had a lot of chutzpah."

Pioneer now serves more than five thousand clients each year, employing nearly seven hundred people in its programs. Its largest business is a precision light-metal fabricator that has become the sole supplier to Boeing sheet-metal liners for the cargo bays of Boeing aircraft. On a visit there, I walked with Mulhair across a factory floor the size of a football field, listening to him chat with workers whose skills once included forging checks, trafficking cocaine, and burglary. He is able to explain each stage of the production process and how each custom-made machine operates. He describes the flow of water jets, laser cutters, and electrostatic paint machines as the workers move large, flat sheets of plastic and metal among them, cutting them into as many as three hundred precision pieces, depending on the configuration of the plane. "It's like a big jigsaw puzzle."

Thanks to Pioneer, this workforce of ex-offenders has acquired new skills in a first-rate production setting that offers the patience and support few conventional businesses can afford. Operating computer-controlled machine tools to fabricate parts according to designs transmitted electronically by their customers, the employees are held to the most exacting standards. I asked Mulhair what kind of problems they have on the factory floor with a workforce that has such a history as this one, assuming the problems would be fighting and stealing. I assume wrong. "For about half of 'em, there comes a day where they just stop showing up. Problems with authority or what have you. That's about the only difficulty we have. But we can plan for it now and build it into the cost of doing business."

Mulhair is emphatic that quality is not sacrificed. He's got convincing evidence. In 1996, Pioneer's plant became the first nonprofit in the United States to win ISO-9002 certification, a benchmark for quality in the private sector. Even more convincing, Boeing keeps expanding its contract year after year.

In fact, Gary would argue that market forces ensure higher quality. As he told *The Chronicle of Philanthropy:*

> Most of our activities are customer-driven, and it gives us a different relationship with the people we're providing services for than if we were getting government money or foundation money. What you care about when you are talking to a foundation officer is getting his or her money into your organization, and that's input-driven. Our activities are output-driven. . . . I don't think nonprofits in this country have done a very good job of understanding the management side of things, understanding that their businesses should succeed or fail not on how much money they raise, but on how good a job they do. And that means understanding who your customers are and always focusing on satisfying your customers.

Pioneer also operates a wholesale food distribution enter- 20
prise that reaches four hundred food banks in twenty states. Other businesses include a real estate division that develops and manages more than 500,000 square feet of residential and commercial properties, and the Mezza Café—a 150-seat cafeteria for the corporate headquarters of Starbucks. In 1986, Pioneer bought the St. Regis Hotel in the heart of Seattle's popular Pike Place Market district. Today, it has been transformed into an unusual hybrid, serving tourists on a budget and recovering substance abusers participating in Pioneer's rehabilitation programs.

Ten years ago, 75 percent of Pioneer's revenues came from government, mostly in the form of grants. Today, that has been reduced to 25 percent, and most of that is from government contracts for services. Fifty million dollars in revenue is a lot of money for a nonprofit, and it attracts more. The Ford Foundation just wrote a check for $2.4 million so that Pioneer can continue to acquire other businesses and convert them into sheltered non-profit workshops. As a result, Pioneer bought Greater Seattle Printing & Mailing in Redmond, Washington, a six-million dollar business with lots of entry-level jobs, particularly on the mailing and fulfillment side.

There is one fundamental reason that nonprofits have only rarely started or owned business for the purpose of generating revenues for growth and sustainability: They only rarely thought they could. It has been a colossal failure of imagination pervasive to the nonprofit sector. That's not to say there are not financial, managerial, and regulatory hurdles to overcome; there are in any business venture. But the limitations on nonprofits starting businesses have by and large been self-imposed.

Gary Mulhair managed to get around that. "Growing up in such a small town like Walla Walla made me feel that there were no limitations," he told me over dinner during a visit to New York. "I've never accepted that things had to be just one way or another."

Questions for Discussion

1. What were Gary Mulhair's earliest work experiences, and what impression did they leave him with? How did these experiences and the unique region he grew up in influence his desire to become an entrepreneur?
2. How did Mulhair's association with ex-convict Jack Dalton influence his ideas about developing the Pioneer program? How do Mulhair's experiences working with ex-convicts help to dispel popular stereotypes of such individuals?
3. Why is Mulhair's non-profit less reliant on the charity of others than the typical non-profit organization? What does it take for a non-profit to be "self-sustaining"?
4. Based on this essay, how would you define Shore's vision of social entrepreneurship and non-profit philanthropy?

Ideas for Writing

1. Do some research on other organizations similar to Gary Mulhair's that would meet the approval of Shore. What do such organizations have in common? What makes some of them successful, and others less so?
2. Expanding beyond the philanthropic organizations discussed in this essay, do you believe that such groups have the potential for revolutionizing the nature of capitalism and work in this country? Why or why not? Explain your position.

Work Rules

WILLIAM GREIDER

William Greider has done reporting and articles for newspapers, magazines, television, and has written several books. He has been an assistant managing editor for The Washington Post *and is currently a national affairs correspondent for* The Nation. *His books include* Who Will Tell the People: The Betrayal of American Democracy *(1992),* One World, Ready or Not: The Manic Logic of Global Capitalism *(1997), and* Fortress America: The American Military and the Consequences of Peace *(1998). In the following selection from his newest book,* The Soul of Capitalism: Opening Paths to a Moral Economy *(2003), Greider presents a way that Americans can help change our current economic system's values and power structures by involvement in employee-owned businesses.*

-------------------- ◆ --------------------

Thorstein Veblen, whose corrosive critiques of American capitalism in the early twentieth century remain relevant and wickedly entertaining today, had one tender spot in his thinking. Veblen believed in engineers. The engineer, he wrote, is not captive to the money compulsion and other malignant illusions associated with capitalism. Engineers gain their satisfaction and status mainly from figuring out how to make things work better. Veblen's romantic notion was that someday engineers and the other dedicated technicians in business would rise up and take control from the absentee owners. Then they would redesign the production system so that it works better for humanity. I share Veblen's soft spot for engineers and similar types. My father, Harold W. Greider, was a research chemist and chemical engineer in a midsize manufacturing company, a prolific inventor and practical-minded optimist of twentieth-century industry who believed problems could be solved if people applied their minds rigorously (at the end of his long life, his mind was working on the ecological crisis).

I was reminded of Veblen's vision when I talked with Joseph Cabral, the CEO of Chatsworth Products Inc., a small and very successful California manufacturer owned 100 percent by its employees. Joe Cabral was schooled in accounting—"I'm one of the bean counter guys," he says—but became an executive whose business sensibilities harmonize with Veblen's. Cabral's manner is can-do practicality and rigor with the facts, yet he also nurtures a big-think understanding of how the system should be reformed. Experience tells him that making capitalist enterprise more equitable and human scale—more like "family"—actually makes it more productive and enduring.

"We have a wonderful capitalistic society that makes the United States really inventive, but as with anything, you find some flaws in it," he told me. "The way our society has rolled out, the wealth that's created through that vehicle called capitalism ends up in too few hands. The entrepreneur who's fortunate enough to be there at the start ends up really receiving a disproportionate amount of the wealth. And all the working folks who enabled that success to take place share in little of that wealth. So we end up in a society with a wealth structure where the top of one percent owns 90 percent or something like that. It's so disproportionate that, in my heart, I'd say that kind of ownership structure is not sustainable. At some point, capitalism is going to burst because we haven't done right for the folks who have actually created that wealth."

Cabral discovered the alternative of self-ownership in 1990. The Chatsworth operation in the San Fernando Valley, where he was comptroller in division management, was discarded by the conglomerate that had acquired it only a few years before. The plants would be closed down, since the only interested buyers simply wanted to purchase the machinery and other hard assets for pennies on the dollar. Chatsworth was small and low-tech—it fabricates the metal frames for stacking computers in data-storage centers—while the Harris Corporation wished to be known as high-tech. The faddish practice of "rationalizing" product lines and balance sheets (better known to workers as downsizing) is popular with large corporations because it typically boosts the stock price and provides tax write-offs. It also destroys a vast, unmeasurable volume of viable production, not to mention jobs and careers. The destruction is what often motivates the preventive takeovers by employees. They know what is being lost.

5   "We valued ourselves higher than any outsiders would value us," Cabral said. "I must tell you, we had all the confidence this would work." After Harris stripped away some elements it wanted to retain, only one hundred or so employees remained but, led by eight top managers, they organized an employee stock ownership plan (ESOP). The ESOP's trust arrangement enables workers to borrow the money to buy all or a portion of their firm, then pay off the debt from the company's future earnings. The ESOP

device was invented nearly half a century ago by Louis Kelso, a San Francisco investment banker who elaborated his own seminal critique of capitalism's maldistribution between capital and labor. His idea did not really take off until the 1970s, when Senator Russell Long of Louisiana, chairman of the Senate Finance Committee, pushed through a series of tax breaks to sweeten the deal for owners and bankers. Long was a conservative Democrat with a deep understanding of how the American system really works. His father was Huey Long, the inflammatory 1930s populist whose "Share the Wealth" crusade deeply frightened the American establishment during the Great Depression. Russell Long used to say: "Remember, it was my father who was the revolutionary—I'm a reformer."

"When I read about ESOPs in *CFO* magazine, I thought, yeah, this really makes sense," Joe Cabral says. "Everybody is sharing in the wealth that they're creating. There's a fundamental philosophy of, We're all in this together. We're not just doing this for some outside shareholder, we're doing it because *we* are the shareholders. In most companies you want to do well in order to have a job or career advancement, but you're basically in it for the paycheck. In CPI we created this wonderful foundation of ownership and people were totally aligned with the success of the company."

The bonding of interests between Chatworth's managers and assembly-line workers was tested up front. Under the two-year purchase option Harris agreed to reduce the $2.5 million sale price if Chatsworth employees could cut operating costs and boost profits in the meantime (in effect, sharing the income gains with the workers). "We did some amazing things, making old equipment work for us and learning to operate with a lot less inventory," Cabral says. "It was kind of a neat period in that way, seeing how creative people can be when they're put in a situation, how they work their way through it." The employees managed in one year to knock $1 million off the purchase price. They raised some money from personal savings, borrowed the rest, and bought total control.

Through the nineties, Chatsworth Products flourished spectacularly, riding the Internet boom because its equipment supplied the celebrated Silicon Valley firms building the huge data-storage centers. CPI's employment grew more than sixfold. All six hundred became owners (a majority of the workforce is composed of minorities, Hispanic and Asian). Their privately held stock rose in value from $4 a share to $121. When the Internet bubble burst at the end of the decade, CPI hung on for a year and a half, treading water and furiously cutting costs, before it too was compelled to shrink its workforce. "We lost 150 owners," Cabral says. "It was traumatic, painful, but nobody was surprised or shocked. They knew how hard we tried to avoid this, that we pulled out all the stops. They created the wealth and, when they leave the company, their wealth goes with them. That's what it's all about."

People who started with Chatsworth in 1991 (and most who came in afterward) departed with six-figure checks or considerably more. Some of those who invested personal savings ten years before have accrued balances of more than a million dollars. "These folks could never have accumulated that kind of wealth in any other way," Cabral says. "Nobody ever got rich on a paycheck."

10　　Chatsworth's success is not typical, of course, since most employee-owned companies have less glamorous stories and less spectacular wealth accumulations: Nor is Joe Cabral a typical ESOP manager. Many of them are flinty, old-fashioned bottom-line guys, bemused or even irritated by his lofty talk about the just distribution of wealth. Cabral represents a hybrid type not widely recognized in the American business culture but that would have fascinated Veblen. "Humanist-populist-capitalists," ESOP consultant Christopher Mackin of Ownership Associates has dubbed them. His oxymoron mixes hard-nosed and idealistic, savvy accounting and human-scale vision.

Among the ones I've met, the social values seem fused with their practical business instincts, so comfortably integrated it is difficult to know which came first. Did they engineer the sale of a family-owned company to faithful, long-term employees because it seemed the "right thing" to do? Or to save the enterprise from failure and corporate predators? Or was the ESOP simply a "smart money" move to harvest the tax breaks? The deal, they would say, "made sense" for lots of reasons. Perhaps these "humanists" are an unintended by-product of American abundance, business people who know how to make lots of money but look around and ask: Is this all there is to life? In any case, their presence is strong enough among ESOP managers that Joe Cabral was elected board chair of the ESOP Association and speaks for thousands of them.

Louis Kelso's vision for achieving broadened, even universal ownership of the nation's capital assets is sometimes compared to the homesteading movement in the nineteenth century, when the federal government have away millions of western acres to the families who settled the land if they made it productive. In the modern industrial economy stock shares are roughly equivalent to land as the principal income-producing asset. The ESOP process is not "free," however. The new owners must "work off" the loan by producing profitably. The transaction may also dilute share value for other stockholders, though they will be well rewarded if the new worker-owners make the firm successful and more profitable. A better comparison may be with the New Deal credit reforms in the 1930s that enabled ordinary families to buy their own homes through liberalized mortgage terms. Two generations of broadening home ownership brought stability and a long-term time horizon to people's lives. Ownership anchors the "American dream" of middle-class prosperity that now feels threatened for so many families.

In the best of circumstances, an economy functioning with broadly shared ownership of enterprises would not eliminate the stark inequalities that already exist. But, over several generations, spreading wealth laterally through the society would generate profound social consequences, including greater family security, time, and satisfaction, as well as more deeply rooted connections with others. In time, the dominating political influence of concentrated wealth, both corporate and individual, on democracy would be greatly diluted, if not entirely extinguished. In time, if families accumulate substantial nest eggs, Kelso envisioned the financial assets generating a second stream of income that would make people less dependent on the "wage slavery" that early labor leaders decried and still exists for many Americans.

Essentially, there are three main arguments on behalf of a system of self-ownership that would replace employment as we know it. The first is David Ellerman's argument that the natural rights of people are inescapably violated by the enduring master-servant relationship, illegitimately separating them from self, from the personal accountability one never escapes in human existence. As a result, lives are stunted, confined, commanded, and dominated. People need democratic governance in the system of production in order to realize their full capacities as human beings.

The second argument, grounded in the economic theories of Louis Kelso, holds that universal ownership—and thus broad distribution of capitalism's returns—is not only more just, but is necessary to prevent an eventual economic and political crisis for the present system. As technology increasingly displaces labor in production processes, Kelso argued, the depressing pressures on wage incomes intensify while the wealthy minority accumulates a still greater imbalance of power. The economic danger, he suggested, is an eventual failure of available demand when workers lack the incomes to purchase what the economic system can produce. . . . When these conditions develop, Kelso warned, the government will face unbearable pressures to enlarge the welfare state and to intervene more profoundly in the free-running economy. As a libertarian conservative he dreaded that outcome, yet he saw it as inevitable unless workers accumulate the income-producing assets—that is, shares of ownership—that can complement their wage incomes.

The third argument, which draws on both of the others, simply observes that businesses perform better when the employees share a stake in the ownership. That is, the companies are more efficient because workers contribute more readily to the processes and signal managers when something is amiss. The emerging academic research on employee-owned companies supports this claim. ESOP companies, compared with similar firms where employees have no ownership, generate greater annual sales and faster employment growth. They are also more likely to survive profitably, pay higher wages, and provide benefits like diversified pensions.

Chris Mackin, whose Ownership Associates counsels both labor and management on employee ownership initiatives, summarized the research results from Joseph Blasi and Douglas Kruse of Rutgers University, as well as other scholars: "The combination of a substantial employee ownership stake and an effective program to communicate it and thereby realize the previously untapped imagination and enthusiasm of employees leads to competitive advantages of between 8–11 percent over the conventionally structured competition."

Questions for Discussion

1. Who is Joseph Cabral and what does he think about the future of capitalism? Do you agree with his statement that if it remains unchecked "at some point, capitalism is going to burst"? Explain why you agree or disagree with Cabral.

2. How does Cabral's company, Chatsworth Products, Inc. (CPI), provide a solution to the problems that result from our current form of unrestricted free enterprise? What are some of the problems that do result from a traditionally run business? What type of corporation is CPI? Who owns it?

3. Why is CPI's success atypical? What is unique about Cabral's management style? Why is the combination of "social values" and "practical business instincts" crucial to the business model that CPI is based on?

4. What are the three arguments for employee-owned companies discussed in this article? Do you believe these points of view are realistic? Do you think that these types of businesses can compete against conventional corporations?

Ideas for Writing

1. Write an essay arguing for or against employee-owned companies like the one described in this reading. What are the advantages or disadvantages of this type of business model? How can these types of companies better the economy and the working conditions of employees?

2. Write an essay in which you discuss why you would or would not want to work at an employee-owned company. Do some research to learn more about employee-run companies. In developing your discussion, compare and contrast the benefits and drawbacks of working for each type of company. After doing your research, you will need to develop issues or criteria for your comparisons and contrasts.

Extending the Theme

1. What have you learned about philanthropy, fundraising, and activism from reading this chapter and various other articles in the text? Write an essay that presents your opinion on the importance of philanthropy, fundraising, and activism. Refer to writers in this text, and your own experiences. Also research an organization that was built by fundraisers and developed by activists. Evaluate this organization and then conclude your essay with suggestions for ways that philanthropy, fundraising, and activism can become more important practices and values in your own community.

2. Write an essay that integrates several of the perspectives in this chapter on the value and need for creativity and cooperation in finding solutions for developing new jobs and a sustainable economy. Consider how creativity would be an aspect of these new jobs.

3. Write an essay that employs some aspect of all the writers' solutions to show how you could improve the quality of life in your workplace.

4. Write an essay that integrates all the perspectives from this chapter and any of the relevant others in this text to show how workers in a particular type of workplace can be fulfilled by their work. How do they need to be treated, what benefits do they deserve, and what sense of belonging do they need to have? Write a proposal for the transformation of the workplace you are studying.

5. Write about a workplace situation that failed because it did not inspire its workers. How can its failure be explained in terms of the perspective of the readings in this chapter? How could the workplace situation have been turned into a success?

CREDITS